STOICISM

How to Use Stoic Philosophy to Find Inner Peace and Happiness

BY JASON HEMLOCK

STOICISM: How to Use Stoic Philosophy
to Find Inner Peace and Happiness
by Jason Hemlock

ISBN: 978-1-7771849-4-0

CONTENTS

FOREWORD

If you are looking to build on some of the concepts shared in this book, I encourage you to check out my journaling book, *Practicing Stoicism: A Daily Journal with Meditation Practices, Self-Reflections and Ancient Wisdom from Marcus Aurelius.* There you will find daily inspirational quotes by Marcus Aurelius to start your day, morning journaling prompts to support you in developing a Stoic attitude, daily exercises to bring Stoic practices to life and evening journaling prompts to track the differences Stoicism is making in your life. All of the daily exercises presented in the journal will be based off of concepts from this book, so reading it after and/or at the same time will help you get even more out of this one.

Also, as a way of saying thank you for purchasing this book, I'm offering a three-page Stoicism cheat sheet for FREE. All you have to do is sign up for my email list, where you will also receive updates and future content from me. The cheat sheet includes quotes from some of my favorite Stoics and a short summary of the principles that were discussed in this book, which you can use for future reference.

You can sign up here: bouchardpublishing.com/stoicism

INTRODUCTION

"It's time you realized that you have something in you more powerful and miraculous than the things that affect you and make you dance like a puppet."
—Marcus Aurelius

In an uncertain world, many of us are searching for something that will help us, if not make sense of it all, then at least be able to cope with the fast pace of change. Although our very modern lifestyle would be unfathomable to our ancestors, it's widely recognized that the ancient Greeks and Romans had figured out the answers to many universal issues we still deal with today. After all, although they might not be able to comprehend a world of iPhones and electric cars, problems such as relationship breakups, job loss, financial difficulties, etc. were just as prevalent then as they are now.

If you're looking to realise your potential and make the most of your experiences, there's a lot to be learned from ancient philosophers, who dedicated themselves to the question of what constitutes a good life and how you can make the most of your opportunities. There's a good reason why the ancient philosophies have stood the test of time and persist to exert an influence over us thousands of years later.

Stoicism is a type of Hellenistic philosophy that enjoyed a resurgence twenty or so years ago. It offers up a code of conduct and ethics, which empowers its adherents to live a good life. While Stoicism places an emphasis on self-discipline and improvement, an inevitable side effect of that process is that it empowers you to achieve your potential, enabling you to live your best life.

It is for that reason that Stoicism has proven popular among countless leaders, successful businesspeople and entrepreneurs, as well as famous musicians, artists and actors. It offers not just a roadmap to happiness, but guidance on how to achieve your goals, stay calm in challenging times and be your best possible, most authentic self.

You can sum up Stoicism with one simple idea: you need to accept full control of and take total responsibility for your thoughts and actions. When you do this, you step onto the path of personal fulfilment. Regardless of your social status, health or abilities, Stoicism will support you to become more than you ever dreamed possible, which is why it's proven to be so popular with successful entrepreneurs and leaders in their field.

However, as you'll discover when you follow a Stoic philosophy, Stoicism has a far greater potential than just self-help, as if that wasn't motivation enough to practice it.

When you take on a Stoic approach, you'll discover it has the potential to change the world around you permanently and for the good of all.

A brief overview of Stoicism

Stoicism was founded by Zeno of Citium sometime in the early 3rd century BC. He taught philosophy at the 'Stoa Poikile,' which is what gave the movement its name. Meaning 'Painted Porch,' the Stoa Poilike was a colonnade by the Agora in Athens, and in choosing the site, Zeno already demonstrated that what he was teaching was different to existing schools of thought, as most philosophers refused to teach in public places.

Taking a logical approach to personal ethics, Stoicism teaches that happiness comes from accepting each moment as it comes, an attitude somewhat akin to modern mindfulness, which is currently very popular. Stoicism states that an individual shouldn't allow themselves to be driven by either fear or a thirst for pleasure, but instead should seek to understand the world in which we live, find and fulfil your place in nature, and work in harmony with others, dealing with them in a fair and just manner.

Stoics held that external goals, such as health or wealth, are neither inherently good nor bad, but instead are there to act as a facilitation for virtue. This pursuit of virtue sometimes involved intentionally depriving yourself of the finer things in life, which is how this ancient philosophy came to give us the term 'stoic.' A stoic in the dictionary sense of the word is someone who is able to endure difficulties without complaint, and this is just one of the many benefits of following this philosophy.

As Epictetus says, "Don't seek for everything to happen as you wish it would, but rather wish that everything happens as it actually will—then your life will flow well." This attitude means that Stoics are especially well suited to cope with hardships and tough times, and are equipped with the mental fortitude to survive situations that might break another person.

However, it would be a mistake to believe that a Stoic doesn't feel emotion or care about pain. The Stoics sought freedom from being ruled by their passions by using logic and reason. They weren't looking to eliminate their emotions so much as transcend them by developing clarity of thought and inner peace. They looked to achieve a high degree of self-control, self-awareness and self-discipline.

Stoicism was – and is – an imminently practical philosophy. It is not enough to say the right things. To the Stoics, the best demonstration of one's beliefs came from their behaviour. If you follow the natural order of things, this includes bad as well as good times, and the ability to move with the flow of the tides is key to living a good life. If you are able to free your mind to think clearly and without bias, you will be able to understand the *logos* or divine reason flowing through the cosmos. In addition, you'll be able to rise above negative, petty emotions like anger or jealousy, giving you a healthier outlook on and experience of life.

Stoicism was highly popular across the Roman and Greek empires until the 3rd century AD. The Emperor Marcus Aurelius was one of its most quoted proponents. His *Meditations* is still considered to be an important philosophical text even today, and is a book you should read if you're serious about your Stoic studies. A prolific writer, he wrote many other Stoic letters and works during his lifetime, but sadly these have been lost in the mists of time.

As Christianity grew to become the state religion of Rome in the 4th century AD, Stoicism's popularity waned, but it has seen many resurgences over the centuries, particularly during the Renaissance and, of course, in modern times.

Famous Stoics

Following a Stoic approach to life has proven popular with highly successful people throughout the centuries. Many of the most famous names in history have turned to Stoicism to help them through their challenges, giving us very clear examples of how important Stoicism has been over the ages.

If you are wondering what Stoicism could do for you, here's a small selection of some of the most famous stoics throughout history to give you some inspiration:

Epictetus started his life as a slave. With the permission of his owner, he studied philosophy under the Stoic Musonius Rufus, and after he was freed, set up his own school. While none of his writings have survived, one of his pupils, the famous philosopher Arrian, transcribed Epictetus' Discourses and Enchiridion.

"If evil be spoken of you and it be true, correct yourself, if it be a lie, laugh at it."
—Epictetus

Seneca was a philosopher, dramatist and close adviser to Emperor Nero. Following a failed assassination plot, Nero ordered Seneca to commit suicide. Although Seneca was probably innocent, he was more concerned about comforting his loved ones than his own death.

"We should every night call ourselves to an account:
what infirmity have I mastered today?
what passions opposed? what temptation resisted?
what virtue acquired? Our vices will abate of themselves
if they be brought every day to the shrift."
—Seneca

Marcus Aurelius was the last of the Five Good Emperors and ruled over the Roman Empire from 161-180. His Meditations is a series of personal notes and letters, written to help him reflect on compassion, restraint, and self-humility. While it isn't likely they were ever meant to be published, Meditations has become one of the most influential Stoic texts.

"Time is a sort of river of passing events, and strong is its current; no sooner is a thing brought to sight than it is swept by and another takes its place, and this too will be swept away."
—Marcus Aurelius

Why you should be a stoic

So now you've had a brief overview of Stoicism and seen just how many high achievers follow a stoic philosophy, it should be obvious that Stoicism delivers results, not just in terms of unlocking your potential but in helping you achieve that all-so-elusive state of contentment.

But if you still needed a little more convincing to get involved yourself, here are a few more good reasons:

Stoicism gives you resilience in difficult times

Stoicism arose during a period when the world was in chaos. Just a few brief decades before, Alexander the Great had conquered the world then died in his early thirties.

His passing had a devastating effect on his Empire, plunging it into uncertainty.

Stoicism had a natural appeal during these troubled years because it gave followers a sense of security and offered a solid foundation during a time of conflict. Unlike religion, it didn't make any promises of a tranquil life after death, but instead focused on giving people a sense of calm during this one.

Because you never know what might happen, Stoicism contains an important lesson on not relying on anything that is subject to change. Your bank balance will fluctuate. Friendships come and go. Even the healthiest of relationships can end. Throughout all this change, the only thing with the potential to remain unaffected is ourselves. Every moment of every day, we make a choice as to how we react and respond to things. It is the only real power we have.

Although we have an innate instinct to react to something that hurts us, the Stoic approach is to strive to remain indifferent to external forces and maintain happiness, regardless of life's ups and downs. While it can be a challenge to keep calm in the face of adversity, once you've mastered this skill, you experience a release from being ruled by emotion and conversely enjoy a greater control over your life.

This isn't to say a Stoic doesn't feel anything. It is natural to be upset when something bad happens, but rather, a Stoic appreciates that negative emotions have their place and only become a problem if we let them be.

Right now, we seem to be going through a particularly turbulent time in history with a great deal of political uncertainty, so it would make sense to turn to Stoicism to help us weather the storm.

As Seneca wrote, "We suffer more in imagination than in reality."

Stoicism teaches tolerance and acceptance of others

Ancient Graeco-Roman society was divided by nationality, religion and status. Stoicism was revolutionary in being possibly the first Western philosophy to teach that slave and emperor are alike when Epictetus wrote that we are all "a member of the great city of gods and men."

Given that happiness is to be found within, rather than through, external events, when we take this a step further, social divides appear arbitrary and unnecessary. While the Ancient Greeks and Romans kept slaves, the Stoics held that we should remember that we all live under the same sky and come from the same place. Everyone deserves respect, regardless of who or what they are.

Given how far-reaching the Roman Empire was, bringing together countless religions, races and societies, Stoicism was an ideal philosophy for a world society needing to live together in harmony. Given modern globalisation, Stoicism helps us appreciate and embrace all the different ways of being without attaching superiority or inferiority to any of them.

Stoicism is compatible with religion

If you have a religious background, you might wonder whether you can be Stoic and stay true to your religion. If this is the case, you'll be reassured to learn that many of the beliefs we associate with the main religions originated with Stoicism.

Don't believe me?

The concept of multiple facets of a single, unifying God? Stoic.

The importance of following your conscience? Stoic.

The idea of controlling our negative impulses rather than allowing them to rule us? Stoic.

There's so much we owe to the Stoics, yet despite the fact that they gave us many enduring, powerful principles, nowadays we're more likely to associate those ideas with religion rather than philosophy.

It's unsurprising that there's a big overlap between Stoicism and Christianity. After all, Stoicism was a major guiding force on Roman society for centuries during the time when Christianity was first established and was finding its way. In fact, many early Christian leaders followed Stoicism before they came to the Church, bringing its influence with them.

In the early days of the Church, religious thought *was* Stoic thought.

As Christianity grew and became a guiding principle in its own right, church leaders broke away from Stoicism to promote their own unique religion. But just as Christianity owes a great debt to pagan practices for many of its festivals, it also has Stoic philosophy to thank for some of its fundamental concepts.

Stoicism is built for leaders

If you aspire to be a leader of any stripe, whether in business, politics or any other field, Stoicism is the philosophy for you. It teaches you to pick yourself up after failure and guards against arrogance when things are going well.

If you aim to influence the world around you, which is part of the responsibility of a leader, Stoicism teaches you to control yourself first. After all, you are the only thing which you can ever have complete control over. If you attempt to dictate how things should be, you risk disappointment when you fail. But if you are able to control yourself and know the best course of action in any eventuality, everything else is a bonus.

While we all have to deal with change in our lives, leaders are in a particularly vulnerable position in terms of the amount of risk and uncertainty they face. A Stoic attitude can help you remain calm in the face of uncertainty and help you prioritise what needs your attention and what you can delegate or put off until later.

For example, Barack Obama has been quoted as saying that while he was President, he tried to cut down the number of decisions he had to make in a day, so he left it to others to choose his meals or his clothes. With so many important choices riding on his discernment, he wisely said, "You can't be going through the day distracted by trivia."

While Obama may not specifically describe himself as a Stoic, the notion that it is important to focus only on what's essential is Stoicism in its purest form.

The Stoics knew that you're more likely to fail than to succeed, and this is okay. They were fully aware that the human condition means we'll feel angry, nervous, jealous, and all manner of negative emotions when things don't go our way.

But they gave us an easy-to-follow way of coping with these inevitabilities – a roadmap, if you will – to help us traverse life's ups and downs.

It's easy to be philosophical when things are going well. It's when times get tough that we face a challenge in continuing to practise what we've been taught. Stoicism offers a very simple way of establishing healthy mental habits and attitudes, which will sustain you through whatever life throws your way.

In this book, you will learn about all of Stoicism's most important guiding principles, including why you should actively experience tough times, how you can transform obstacles into opportunities, how you can harness the power of journaling to improve your outlook, how to prepare for the worst, how the Stoics approached mindfulness and why your lack of control is a good thing.

Each chapter includes practical exercises you can get started with immediately, so you can quickly see the positive impact Stoicism can have on your life.

To quote Epictetus, how long are you going to wait before you demand the best for yourself?

CHAPTER ONE

SEEK OUT MISFORTUNE

"You don't develop courage by being happy in your relationships every day. You develop it by surviving difficult times and challenging adversity."
—Epicurus

One of the reasons why Stoicism is enjoying a resurgence is because it offers a simple approach to combating the stresses and complexities of modern life. We live in what is arguably the most stressful time in history. We are expected to do more than our ancestors ever did, while at the same time feeling disconnected from the people around us. For many, community is a thing of the past.

All the modern technologies we have access to were invented with the aim of making our lives easier. In many cases, that's exactly what they do, but just as they can help us, they also risk causing us harm. Are you glued to your mobile? Addicted to social media? Easily distracted by the latest Netflix series?

The problem with these technologies is that our culture of celebrity worship and emphasis on living the perfect life on social media means that many of us fall into the trap of believing self-promotion is more important than self-improvement. Instead of looking inside to think about how we can improve ourselves, we create a false front to show the world that we're not just meeting society's expectations – we're smashing through them.

With TV reality shows promising overnight fame and fortune to those lucky enough to appear on them, it's easy to think it's more important to be someone who is paid for being an over-the-top version of themselves rather than becoming the best possible version of themselves. When instant gratification takes too long, it's no wonder so many are opting for the allegedly easy route.

But is this really making us happy? After all, you wouldn't be reading this book if you were satisfied with your life the way it is.

Believe it or not, this isn't a new problem. The ancient Stoics realised that one of the biggest issues we have to deal with arises from our urge to want more than we already have. It doesn't seem to matter how many things we accumulate or how much money we earn; we're pushed to want more and more.

But what is the real driving force behind that urge? The desire for a better life. So why are we getting it so wrong?

In a highly consumerist, materialistic culture, it can be very hard to ignore the pressure to conform and buy the latest designer outfit or most up-to-date phone, but that pressure is one of the biggest reasons why we're so miserable. In contrast, the Stoics pursued a simpler life, one ruled by self-discipline, which meant resisting going along with what everyone else was doing.

One of the most fundamental abilities of a Stoic is resilience in the face of adversity. Many Stoic philosophers considered the question of why bad things happen to good people and came to the conclusion that difficult times were inevitable, so it was important to be able to develop coping mechanisms for when they came. Our biggest lessons come through overcoming life's challenges and, as Seneca says, "I judge you unfortunate because you have never lived through misfortune. You have passed through life without an opponent— no one can ever know what you are capable of, not even you."

Our challenges enable us to understand ourselves better and learn our limits, as well as our potential. Seneca discusses this in great depth in his work, *On Providence.* He states that it is "not what you endure, but how you endure [which] is important."

It is an interesting book with many fascinating philosophical arguments. He felt that, for a decent man, his "good fortune is not to need good fortune" because when you have achieved the inner harmony espoused by Stoicism, it does not matter what happens to you; you have the strength of spirit to withstand anything life can throw at you.

This being the case, it is important to become a 'good' man long before anything negative happens so you already have the moral fortitude to be able to cope with it. Not only will you be able to weather the storm, those tough times will strengthen you. To use Seneca's words to illustrate this point, "No tree becomes rooted and sturdy unless many a wind assails it… the fragile trees are those that have grown in a sunny valley."

Another Stoic philosopher, Musionius Rufus, asked, "Could we acquire courage by realising that things which seem terrible to most people are not to be feared but without practicing being fearless towards them?" After all, things are only labelled positive or negative because of our perception. When we shift our perception, we recognize the positive and negative in *all* things, and can cope with whatever comes our way.

Misfortune is therefore essential to a Stoic way of being. It is an important tool to build our virtue and helps us become better people. In fact, according to Seneca, "God hardens, reviews, and disciplines those whom he approves, whom he loves." In other words, bad things happen to good people because it helps them become even better.

Taking this concept to its logical conclusion, Seneca recommends spending a certain amount of time on a regular basis actively putting yourself through hardship. As one of Nero's advisers, Seneca was a wealthy man, so he felt it useful to experience poverty to give himself perspective and build character. He suggested cutting back on the food you eat and restricting yourself to a very basic diet; wearing worn, old clothing; leaving your comfortable home with its warm bed and spending time on the streets. Now while we might not go to such extremes, when you put yourself in a position where you have very little, you remove its ability to frighten you. You experience the worst so it no longer holds any power over you.

So even if you don't deprive yourself of a place to sleep, it is important to actively seek out misfortune. This is not a philosophical exercise where you sit for a while and meditate on all the bad things that might happen. You need to actively live a misfortunate life so you do not fear it. We can become trapped in jobs that make us unhappy, stress about losing our beautiful home, or fail to appreciate what we have because we're too worried about what might happen if we didn't have it.

Stoicism tells us to be practical about this. Rather than anticipating what if, actively embrace misfortune. Create it for yourself, so if the worst ever happens, it's nothing new and doesn't destroy your life. After all, when we feel anxious or worried, this is usually more to do with a fear of the unknown than any actual experience. Yet we can become consumed by these negative states to the point where we are incapable of doing anything to assuage them.

So when you literally confront your fears, not only do you release their hold over you, you can also come up with ways to deal with them. Even if you've hit rock bottom, life is unlikely to stay there for the rest of your life. Almost everything we experience will pass.

For many of us, the thought of being without our phones or social media is terrifying, which is why it's so important to drop out temporarily. Switch off your mobile for a few days. Deactivate your Facebook account for a couple of weeks. What happens?

Life goes on.

It's a very easy way of introducing yourself to living a Stoic life and experiencing a taste of what might happen if your phone were stolen or you lost access to the internet. You may be old enough to remember life before social media took over, or you may never have known a world without your mobile. Either way, stepping back for a while gives you an important reminder that there is more to life than maintaining a front for the benefit of the outside world.

One of the more insidious effects of being in constant contact with the world at large is that we have very little time that is ours alone. I'll touch upon this in more depth in a later chapter, but think about how easily we give away our time because of our need to be 'social.' Even when you've gone on holiday, you're usually still reachable by text or instant message. There's very little opportunity to simply sit with yourself and reflect on who you are and who you want to be. By switching off for a certain amount of time, you can get a taste of who you might like to be when you're not attempting to meet other people's expectations.

Disconnecting from modern technology also gives you the chance to appreciate how lucky you are to have the technology you do. Not everyone has access to the internet or a mobile phone. You are incredibly privileged to be able to connect with your loved ones at the touch of a button, so I'm not saying you should permanently dispense with your phone and social media; just put it into context.

That's the whole point of actively courting hardship and becoming more self-disciplined. It helps you understand how wealthy you truly are and question your priorities. Why do you even have a phone? Is it to stay connected with your loved ones or is it to send out a signal about your status?

The true misfortune lies in the erroneous belief that superficial things are important. When we fool ourselves into thinking that our money and property are the things that make us happy, we set ourselves up for a lifetime of disappointment because there's always something better, always someone wealthier.

When we step back and experience a more basic, simpler life, we can get a sense of who we truly are when we aren't living in accordance with others' expectations.

Practical Exercise

There are a number of different ways you can welcome misfortune into your life on a temporary basis. Whatever you decide to do, it should be something that truly scares you, makes you feel uncomfortable and pushes you out of your comfort zone. You need to experience something you would ordinarily never willingly do for this exercise to work.

Aim to practice misfortune on a monthly, weekly, or even daily basis, as appropriate. Here are a few simple suggestions for you to use as inspiration for how you'll court hardship and tough times.

- *Take cold showers.* Sometimes it's the simple things in life that matter the most, and there's nothing more luxuriating than a long, hot shower. If you love your showers, try switching off the hot water. It's a stark reminder that you should never take anything for granted, and you never know - you may well discover you find cold showers invigorating.
- *Keep your home at an uncomfortable temperature.* Modern air conditioning and heating means we never have to feel discomfort in our own home. You can use this to your (dis)advantage by adjusting the temperature. Turn it off in the winter, so you have to put on extra layers to keep warm or wrap yourself up in blankets. Make your house hotter in the summer so you can't cool down. Eliminating

modern conveniences make it easier for you to cope should you suddenly find yourself in a situation where you don't have the luxuries many of us consider necessities.

- *Eat a highly restricted, bland diet.* Decide you're going to eat nothing but rice and beans or bread and cheese or noodles for a set amount of time (e.g., a week or a fortnight). While you don't want to eat so unhealthily for a prolonged period, depriving yourself of everything but the bare minimum will show you that it is possible survive on very little in dire straits.
- *Fast on a regular basis.* Taking the restricted diet a step further, try abstaining from food completely for 24 hours every month or so. As long as you drink plenty of water, a day without food will not do you any harm (but check with your doctor if you have any medical concerns).
- *Step outside of your comfort zone.* We all have things that fill us with dread. Perhaps you don't have children and the idea of spending time surrounded by toddlers makes you shudder; maybe you don't like public speaking and do everything you can to avoid giving presentations at work. Whatever makes you feel uncomfortable, you should push yourself to do it. Offer to babysit a friend's colicky baby. Go to Speaker's Corner and give a speech about Stoicism. Go to a theme park and ride the biggest roller-

coaster. Sing at a karaoke event. Actively participate in whatever activity you can think of that would be your idea of hell. When you face your fears in this way, you discover there are no limits beyond those you place on yourself, and you're capable of anything you put your mind to. You may even discover you enjoy something you thought you'd hate.

- *Volunteer to help others less fortunate.* So many charities are short-handed, and volunteering gives you the opportunity to do something good in the world as well as put yourself in someone else's shoes. Try volunteering at a soup kitchen or food bank; work at an animal shelter and clean out the dirty bedding; go litter picking, etc. Whatever you choose, aim to make it something you will find uncomfortable rather than looking for something that matches your strengths. If it's something you would happily do anyway, it defeats the purpose of the exercise.
- *Do your own DIY or gardening.* You may not be particularly handy with power tools or enjoying weeding, but there may come a time when you are not in a position to hire someone to do these jobs for you. Making yourself do those tasks you'd normally outsource to someone else offers so many benefits. It forces you to do something you don't want to do, but it also makes you slow down and pay attention to the moment. Chances are you won't be as

good at the job as a professional, so you'll need to take care to do the best possible job. However, at the end of it, the feeling of accomplishment from doing something you wouldn't normally do and the knowledge you're learning a new skill is such a positive experience – and it reinforces your understanding of just how much you can do when you push yourself.

- *Buy your clothes from charity shops.* There are a number of reasons why this a good thing. Unwanted clothing is responsible for a lot of landfill and much of it ends up there purely because the owner decided they didn't want to wear it anymore. Buying second-hand clothes is an environmentally conscious way of shopping. However, this also serves the stoic purpose of courting misfortune because charity shops aren't necessarily up to date with the latest fashion. The choice is a lot more limited and restricted than in standard high street shops, although it should also be kept in mind that it's perfectly possible to find unworn or designer items in a charity shop, so in trying to be unfortunate, you may actually be fortunate!
- *Limit the amount of money you have to spend.* If you go out regularly, you may not be thinking about how much you spend on a night out. Try taking only a small amount of cash with you and once it's gone, don't get any more out. Take this a step

further, and limit how much you spend in a given period, say, a month. Live as though you earned a lot less than you do and adjust your lifestyle accordingly.

These are just some suggestions. Feel free to think of ways that would be the most effective for you. Some of these may well be your normal way of living or things that aren't that big of a deal for you, so be creative and start living your worst life on a regular basis.

Summary

Actively seeking out misfortune will help you prepare for when things get tough.

- Take cold showers.
- Keep your home at an uncomfortable temperature
- Eat a restricted diet.
- Fast regularly.
- Step outside your comfort zone.
- Do volunteer work.
- Do your own DIY or gardening.
- Limit your cash spending.

CHAPTER TWO

TURN THE OBSTACLE UPSIDE DOWN

"We are more often frightened than hurt; and we suffer more in imagination than in reality."
—Seneca

One of the Stoic's approaches to dealing with challenges was to use a technique called Turning the Obstacle Upside Down. This is the concept that inspired Ryan Holiday's book, *The Obstacle Is the Way: The Timeless Art of Turning Trials into Triumph.* Just as with other Stoic ideas, it's a very practical approach that requires you to implement it and not just think about it.

As the name would suggest, the point of this attitude is to invert a problem to look for the silver lining in every cloud. If you look at it from the right perspective, every negative experience provides you with an opportunity for growth, or a teachable moment. As such, it should be welcomed and appreciated for the lessons it contains rather than feared.

Marcus Aurelius states, "The impediment to action advances action. What stands in the way becomes the way." So, if you lose your job, this gives you an opportunity to find a better job, change your career path completely or even take a break and spend time with your family. If you're dealing with a difficult colleague at work, this is not the universe trying to make your life hard. Instead, you're being given the chance to learn how to work with different personality types, develop patience or try doing things in a new way. If your relationship is going through a rough patch, this is your chance to take stock, reflect on how things are and see if there's anything you can do to improve things. This is your chance to consider how much you value your partner and whether they are the right person for you.

Ultimately, it doesn't matter what happens. The only thing you can control is your reaction to situations. The more you can free yourself from the erroneous belief that situations are inherently negative or positive, and instead view them as simply obstacles for you to navigate in the most effective way, the more you can grow as a person, develop resilience and move in harmony with the ebbs and flows of life.

If you examine the lives of successful leaders and entrepreneurs, there is a very clear common theme: they all grasp every single opportunity that comes to them with both hands, but more than that, they *create* their own opportunities. Examine the life of any leading light and you'll see that there were plenty of failures along the way. An overnight success only happens after years of preparation and setbacks.

When you follow a Stoic philosophy, whatever happens, there is always opportunity. So, while bad or unexpected things are bound to happen, you have the power to transform these into opportunity.

In fact, you will find it useful to move away from a mindset of 'good' and 'bad.' These terms are meaningless to a Stoic. Everything comes down to your perception, which is the one thing you have the ability to change.

So, for example, if you lose your job, you can decide to view it as the end of the world and sink into deep despondency, or you can see it as just another event in your life and look for the opportunities now open to you. Which of these is more likely to lead to employment?

There are three main processes involved in turning the obstacle upside down. These are perception, action and will. Each of these feed into the other and helps you shift your reality to where you want it to be.

Perception

Perception is how you interpret and react to what happens around and to you. Never underestimate the power of perception, because this is what shapes your life experience. Your perception is what makes you happy or sad. If you choose to focus your perception only on what makes you miserable, allow yourself to become emotional, or fail to take a long-term view before shaping your perception, you make your problems worse.

If you want to make the most of everything life has to offer, you need to learn how to limit the hold your emotions have over you. This can be a challenge, especially if you have fallen into the habit of expecting and looking for the worst, but if you can filter out your prejudices and expectations and view any given situation dispassionately and objectively, you'll see it as it truly is. This is a very powerful tool when dealing with an obstacle.

Practical Exercise

Make a list of the worst experiences of your life. Think about job losses, relationship breakups, financial difficulties, etc.

How did you deal with those situations at the time? What other possibilities were open to you? Were you aware of these at the time or did they only come to light later?

What happened as a result of your chosen reaction? How might that have been different if you'd taken an alternative action?

Where was the opportunity within that obstacle? Were you able to identify it?

Write down your answers to all of these questions and then take a moment to look at any recurrent themes. Where are your personal weaknesses? What do you need to work on?

For many people, they find that when something bad happens to them, they ultimately end up in a better place as a consequence. Is that true for you? If not, how can you make it true?

Now that you know you can turn any difficult situation into an opportunity, do you still view obstacles as negative? Or are they simply an event, neither good nor bad?

Action

Whatever happens to you, you take action by default. Even if you do nothing, this is still a form of action, so it is important you make the right choice moving forward.

While you have always taken action in your life, the real question is whether you have always taken the *right* action. In order to follow a Stoic path, it is important you take consciously directed action, which is driven by purpose in order to get you to where you need to be.

Having decided on the appropriate action, you can slowly begin to tackle your obstacles, moving forward step by step until they are eliminated. The right action involves having the bravery to act in your best interests from a long-term perspective, so, for example, if you are in a relationship that is not fulfilling you, you should have the courage to walk away and find the right person for you instead of staying where you are and remaining miserable for the sake of being in a relationship.

Taking Stoic action means you are no longer a passive slave to the world around you. Action is the only possible solution to whatever is troubling you.

Practical Exercise

Think about a current obstacle in your life. Make a list of all the possible actions available to you, no matter how silly, outrageous or seemingly impossible. Let your imagination run wild and don't allow yourself to be limited by excuses for why something might not work out.

For each of those actions, make a list of possible outcomes. Be as honest with these as you can and again, don't let emotion or negative thinking make you discount an option.

Now look at all these outcomes and decide which one best fits your ideal.

This is your way.

Will

When you 'will' something to happen, you are following your true path and going with the natural flow of things.

If you are genuinely following your will, nothing can stand in your way.

Your will is frequently confused with your 'want.' Often, people will believe that because they badly want something, it is therefore their purpose or destiny, but that is a misunderstanding of this particular principle. What's more, if you're pursuing something just because you want it, you open yourself up to disappointment when things don't go your way. You have fallen into the trap of being driven by desire rather than virtue.

Sometimes, all the action in the world still can't get you to where you need to be because of the surrounding circumstances. This is where your will comes into play; if the only available outcomes are all 'negative,' your will allows you to learn and grow from the experience, gain some humility and support others who subsequently go through what you're going through.

Your will helps you comprehend where you need to be rather than where you want to be.

In order to gain the resilience for tough times, we need to be able to accept whatever comes our way and seek out the lessons contained within.

Practical Exercise

Think about a time in your life when you wanted to do something, but obstacles were constantly thrown in your way.

What were the lessons you were meant to learn? Did you find a way to turn those obstacles upside down or did you take a different path? Did that different path lead to somewhere better? Or was it simply easier to give up? Did you feel like you were stuck in a particular place because the universe constantly slapped you back when you tried to break free? Do you really think the universe was stopping you or was there something else at play? Were you sabotaging your own efforts without realising?

If there is something you would like to do but haven't been able to for whatever reason, make a list of everything that is stopping you or might stop you.

Are those obstacles insurmountable?

There is very little in life that is truly impossible. As the saying goes, where there's a will, there's a way.

Decide on something you would like to achieve. List out all the obstacles you might face and then all the actions you can take to use them to your advantage. Recognise that the unexpected is always possible, but know that if it occurs, you have the will to navigate troubled waters.

Now make a commitment to yourself that you'll take the first step towards that goal, knowing that with each action, you progress a little closer until eventually you're where you want to be. In addition, you have the reassurance of knowing you have a Plan B because you've already prepared for the worst and are ready to deal with it.

Ultimately, life is a long series of challenges and problems. The real test is whether you are willing to let obstacles stop you or inspire you. Taking a Stoic approach means that not only will you have the confidence that comes from knowing you have the ability to deal with every problem; you *thrive* on them.

Summary

View obstacles as opportunities rather than road blocks. Use them to inspire you to action.

- Change your perception. Reflect on challenges you've dealt with in the past and what they taught you.
- Learn how to choose the right action. Think about a current problem you're dealing with and brainstorm potential solutions to help you pick the right path.
- Follow your will and go with the flow. Set yourself a goal to do something you've always wanted to do. Plan out how you'll get it done and take into account potential obstacles. Then put this plan into practice.

CHAPTER THREE

THIS TOO WILL PASS

"Life is very short and anxious for those who forget the past, neglect the present, and fear the future."
—Seneca

Take a moment to think about all the billions of people who've walked this earth over the entirety of humanity's existence. How much do we remember of them now? Within a couple of generations, almost all of us will be completely forgotten.

And even if we look at the tiny handful of people who've attained immortality through fame or infamy, how much do we really know about them? How much can we understand the complexity of their individual existence? We know about the important events in their lives, but do we know what their favourite food was? How they felt about their parents? Whether they were truly happy?

The point is, while some things matter, a lot of things don't, and by the time you leave this mortal coil, very little of your life will be left behind.

This could be incredibly depressing if viewed from a certain perspective, but, as we examined in the last chapter, as Stoics, we're working on shifting our perspective. The important point here is that in the grand scheme of things, no matter who you are, we're *all* very small and trivial.

Back in Roman times, they would celebrate every big military victory with a 'triumph.' This would involve a grand procession of generals so everyone could cheer their efforts. Festivities would last all day and possibly into the next as everyone gave thanks for their win.

But behind the generals would stand a slave, whose job it was to whisper, "Remember you are mortal." Victory is fleeting and no matter how high you rise, you can come crashing back down to earth at any time.

So, if nothing lasts forever, what's really important? This moment right now. The *only* thing that matters is being the best person you can be at all times.

For example, Alexander the Great had the biggest empire the world has ever known. His influence was so great, cities still bear his name to this day. Yet all his achievements paled into insignificance when he got drunk and fought with his close friend, Cleitus, accidentally killing him. Alexander fell into a deep depression and wouldn't eat or drink for days. What did all his achievements matter after the loss of a friend? Is it really a good thing to have cities named after you if you're hurting the ones you love?

If you are your best, most authentic self in every moment, it doesn't matter what else happens. Nothing can take that away from you. As Marcus Aurelius puts it, "Be like the rocky headland on which the waves constantly break. It stands firm, and round it the seething waters are laid to rest." The world can go crazy around you, but if you have an inward focus and strive to do the right thing, you will navigate the storm.

We experience life in the present, but most of the time we're living in the future or the past, letting the present slip away without conscious thought. We're counting down the days until we next go on holiday, but while we're on vacation, we're worried about how quickly our break will be over. We fret about past mistakes and things we've done wrong or stress about what might happen in the future. We flit from thought to thought, but fail to stop and appreciate what's happening right now.

As a Stoic, you should aspire to live in the moment as much as possible. In modern times, this is what many people call 'mindfulness.' Living in the moment involves maintaining an active focus on the present, sitting with your thoughts as they arise, letting them be as they will rather than inviting or repelling them. When you are able to do this, you are able to fully live your life instead of letting it pass you by.

Living in the present moment has a number of documented benefits. Studies have shown it lowers stress, boosts your immune system and lowers your blood pressure. It can even help people cope with chronic pain and cancer. What's more, it leads to greater self-awareness and is another tool to help you cope with negative situations and people.

By now, you should be convinced of the positive impact of being mindful of the present moment. However, while in theory this is easy, in practise it's very difficult. The problem is that as soon as you start trying to live in the now because you want to enjoy the benefits, you make it impossible to embrace the present because knowing you'll receive something good from it puts your focus on the future, which undermines everything you want to do.

It's quite a Catch 22!

Switching your focus so you're genuinely living in the now takes determination, intention and active practice. You need to let go of the outcome and simply enjoy the process.

Practical Exercises

There are a number of different ways you can bring yourself into the present and stay there. Start with one or two from these suggestions and build upon them. You might find some work better for you than others, which is fine – this is an individual journey with many different routes to success.

- *Forget yourself.* Have you ever danced like no one's watching? Let your body move without caring what it looks like? Did you notice that it was much easier to perform a particular movement when you weren't actively thinking about it?

  As soon as you start thinking about being mindful, you lose the magic of the moment. You need to forget about what you're trying to do and just do it. The more you concentrate on why you can't be mindful and strive to achieve that state, the more impossible it becomes. Instead, forget about your thoughts or fear of failure, and see more of what's going on around you.

  See yourself as part of the current moment rather than separate from it. Immerse yourself in your current experience.

  At random moments during the day, pause and examine what's going on around you. What can you see? What can you smell? What can you hear?

  Take it a step further. Close your eyes and notice the little sounds you normally filter out. Maybe it's the background buzz of traffic. Perhaps you can hear birdsong if you concentrate.

  Open your eyes and look around you. See your surroundings with new eyes. And then breathe.

Inhale deeply three times and savour this unique moment in time, knowing it will never be exactly like this again.

- *Don't let the future or past spoil your enjoyment of the present.* Frequently, we get so caught up in thinking about what has happened or what might have happened, we can't fully appreciate what's happening in the present. Maybe you've been on holiday and thought 'this is the kind of lifestyle to which I want to become accustomed' without recognising this is *already* your lifestyle. Or you go to a restaurant and think the food wasn't as good as the last time you came.

  Choose a mundane activity, something you do every day, and slow it right down. It might be your morning cup of coffee or your walk to get lunch. Whatever you choose, take the time to actively consider every single second. *Feel* it with every single sense and appreciate the beauty of the fact you're here to have that experience.

  When your attention is solely on what is happening right now, it's impossible to worry about the past or future. This is how you can transform the mundane into a meditative experience.

- *Forget about time.* Can you think of a time when you were so caught up in what you were doing, you lost track of time? This is a state known as being in the flow.

On the surface of it, this concept contains a paradox. If you aren't aware of the current moment, how can you be living in it? But the point about flow is that you're so deeply focused on what's currently happening, it's impossible to notice anything else, including time. This is why time flies when you're having fun.

When you're in the flow, it's impossible to maintain it as soon as you become aware of it. And it's difficult to achieve intentionally because that runs counter to the nature of flow. All you can do is put yourself in a position where you're likely to enter that state and let it happen as it will.

How can you create the right conditions? First, give yourself a goal that will challenge you but is achievable. It needs to be easy enough you won't get frustrated, but not so easy you'll get bored. Then break it down into tiny little steps, so you know exactly where you're going. It might be doing another length in the pool, colouring another section of a picture or turning the page to read what happens next in your novel. You're anticipating what's coming while at the same time appreciating what's happening right now.

When you get into the flow, you lose all awareness of your surroundings and your world becomes nothing but yourself and your activity. You feel a continual sense of control over your current situation and you're getting a positive feeling from your activity, so you're working without feeling like you're making any real effort.

- *Stay in the zone.* We've all had those times of suddenly 'waking up' to realise we have absolutely no idea what's been happening over the past few minutes and have been working on autopilot. This is the very opposite of mindfulness – instead, you're being mind*less* because you're so caught up in your thoughts, you don't notice anything around you.

  This happens because you cease paying attention to things you think you know inside out. This is why you frequently zone out during your commute – you've done the journey so many times before, you think you know every aspect of it so it has nothing new to offer. Yet if you examine the world around you as if you've never seen it before, you'll quickly discover that everything changes all the time. As the saying goes, you can never step in the same river twice because it's never the same river and you're never the same person. The way the light falls, the expression on someone's face, how you're feeling that morning – all of these things change and make each experience brand new.

  Notice six new things about your environment every day. Actively seek out things you haven't noticed or look for how things have subtly changed since yesterday. Not only will this help you be more mindful, it also demonstrates very obviously how nothing ever stays the same.

- ❖ *Breathe.* This is one of the simplest ways to be mindful. If you feel yourself losing grasp on the present, simply become aware of your breath. When you do this, you automatically bring yourself into the present. It's always with you and always happening *now.*

  So if all else fails, just breathe.

Summary

All we truly possess is the current moment, so make every moment count.

- Stay in the magic of the moment.
- Don't let the future or the past ruin your experience of the present.
- Forget about time.
- Stay in the zone.
- Breathe.

CHAPTER FOUR

VIEW THE WORLD FROM ABOVE

"If anyone can refute me – show me I'm making a mistake or looking at things from the wrong perspective – I'll gladly change. It's the truth I'm after, and the truth never harmed anyone."
—Marcus Aurelius

Marcus Aurelius was very fond of following a practise called 'taking the view from above.' Also dubbed 'Plato's view,' this exercise involves stepping away from our lives and viewing it from a broader perspective. This goes beyond simply looking objectively at your problems, but seeing yourself as just one of billions of people, everyone all around the globe living their lives and dealing with their own issues.

Taking this approach reminds you of just how small you are in the grand scheme of things. Recognising that very few things are worth worrying about helps you put your current issues into perspective and see that stressing about them is a waste of energy.

However, this is just the first step in achieving Plato's view. If you want to get the most out of this technique, you need to go deeper and access what the Stoics termed 'sympatheia.' This is where you see yourself as having a mutual co-dependence with all of humanity. If you were able to go out in space and enjoy a literal view from above, you'd be able to see that we're all the same, no matter what our station in life, and that there is a lot we can all do to make the world a better place.

When you achieve Plato's view, you transcend your own concerns and remember your duty to those around you, both friends and strangers. Shifting your focus from your individual needs to that of the whole of humanity has the potential to make you massively change the way you see the world around you. The Stoics believed this would give you inner peace, as it would eliminate anger or pain, filling you instead with love and compassion, even for those who hurt us.

Looking at things from this angle, all people are equal, with no one life having more value than another, regardless of status. As Aurelius puts it, "Think of substance in its entirety, of which you have the smallest of shares; and of time in its entirety, of which a brief and momentary span has been assigned to you; and of the works of destiny, and how very small is your part in them."

Aurelius goes on to discuss that even for those who have achieved great fame, the second they die, they are no longer relevant. He goes on to say that even for those who are remembered for their deeds, this is "sheer vanity and nothing more."

Harsh words, but when you look into the underlying philosophy, what remains when you strip all your achievements away? The importance of living a good life, striving to always do what is right for the common good, and accepting whatever comes your way because every experience is a lesson. Further, while it may be that nothing of us survives after we're gone, when you see everything from an eternal viewpoint, there is beauty all around us, even at the moment of decay. That beauty comes from the fact that nothing lasts forever, so our own mortality is a beautiful thing. Aurelius argued that our lack of personal significance is irrelevant because we are all part of the cosmos, which is in itself inherently beautiful.

When you see yourself as a tiny speck in the eternity of the cosmos, everything is trivial. Nothing is important. Yet at the same time, everything we do matters, because we are all contributing to something far greater than ourselves.

Life is a gift all on its own. Anything else is a bonus.

Practical Exercise

We all know that meditation is good for us, but many people struggle to develop this practice. Regular meditation can combat stress, help you develop mental clarity and support your Stoic work.

Guided meditations are a great way to get into meditation if you've been struggling to meditate regularly. They don't require regular practice, so you can just do them as and when you feel the need.

This meditation is designed to give you Plato's view. You can try to memorise it and replay it in your mind, but you might find it more effective to record it in advance and play it so you can simply relax and enjoy the meditation.

Do not meditate lying down – you're likely to fall asleep! Instead, either sit cross-legged on a cushion against the wall, or on a chair that supports your back so you stay upright, alert and comfortable during your meditation.

Have some food ready to eat after the meditation is done so you can ground yourself.

Meditation to give you Plato's view

Sit comfortably and just take a moment to focus on your breath. Notice as you inhale and exhale… inhale and exhale…

Now as you inhale, imagine you are breathing in a beautiful, calming white light. And as you exhale, release any negativity or stress you may have been holding on to.

Continue to breathe in that beautiful white light. Feel it filling your body with peaceful energy, making you feel lighter… and lighter… and lighter…

And as your body continues to get lighter and lighter, feel yourself starting to float out of your body. You are completely safe as you hover above your body and look down on yourself.

Passively observe yourself sitting there. Notice how you look relaxed and calm and know your body is perfectly safe as you start to float higher and higher.

Now you are outside, hovering above the building your body is in. Look down upon it and see what it looks like from above. Examine the surrounding area – are there gardens? Streets? Cars? Are there people walking around?

Look carefully at the area. Notice all the little details. Think about the people in any buildings you can see going about their business, each of them having their own concerns and worries.

Now rise higher and higher until you are at cloud level. Look down beneath you. See the land stretching out as far as you can see. Notice the curve of the horizon off in the distance.

Feel yourself at peace, knowing you are safe so high in the sky. The world below you seems so small and insignificant, but your journey is not yet done.

You feel yourself going higher again, up, up and out of the atmosphere and into space. You are perfectly safe as you float out towards the moon. Looking back at the earth, it looks like a small ball below you. From this distance, all you can see are the clouds swirling around, the green of the land, the blue of the ocean.

Billions of souls are going about their lives but from this distance, they may as well be dust.

You feel yourself travelling farther and farther away from the earth until you find yourself deep in the heart of the cosmos. All around you are stars, twinkling in a stunning display of natural beauty.

Take a moment to breathe in the wonder around you. Appreciate that everything is as it should be, your life unfolding exactly how it needs to. See the countless stars and know that there are countless more out of sight.

Appreciate that the cosmos is infinite and you are infinitesimal.

When you are ready, take one last deep breath, inhaling the essence of the cosmos, then tell yourself it is time to return to your body.

You find yourself immediately back in your body, sitting where you started. Take a moment to focus on your breath, inhaling and exhaling as you ground yourself fully into yourself.

When you are ready, open your eyes and see the world around you anew.

Summary

Step back to take Plato's view to give yourself perspective.

- Do the Plato's view meditation.

CHAPTER FIVE

MEMENTO MORI

"Think of the life you have lived until now as over and, as a dead man, see what's left as a bonus and live it according to Nature. Love the hand that fate deals you and play it as your own, for what could be more fitting?"
—Marcus Aurelius

The concept of *Memento Mori* involves reflecting on your own mortality. This ancient practice actually predates Stoicism – it was Socrates who first stated that the purpose of philosophy was to consider "dying and being dead." The Stoics took this very important lesson and used it as inspiration. After all, you could die at any moment, so you should use that to inform everything you do, say and think. You shouldn't wait to live a life of virtue – there is no time like the present to follow a virtuous life because you may not have a future.

While you might think that considering your death might be depressing, that's only the case if you miss the point. To a Stoic, the thought of death is inspirational as well as humbling. Seneca advised to think 'you may not wake up tomorrow' when you go to bed and then 'you may not sleep again' when you wake up the next day.

Constantly reminding yourself that life is short so you should make the most of whatever time you have left should be a motivation to be your very best self all the time. This can be difficult to maintain, as death is one of the few taboos remaining in Western culture. Many of us are afraid to even consider it, let alone regularly meditate on it. From a Stoic perspective, however, if you have striven to live a meaningful life, there is nothing to be afraid of. Death comes to us all. It's a part of the natural cycle of life, so you cannot escape it. Doesn't it make sense to prepare for it by giving your life purpose?

Now it is easy to get caught up in fantasies when you start thinking about what you would do if this were your last day alive. If you knew you only had 24 hours to live, the chances are high you'd do all sorts of outrageous things, like stay off work, do something fun with your family and friends, and maybe even break a few laws because there's no chance of punishment.

This isn't exactly a sustainable way of leaving, and it's certainly not what the Stoics intended when they taught the practice of *Memento Mori.* Instead, you should be thinking about how you would feel if you died unexpectedly. Had you practised kindness? Had you worked as hard as you could? Did you attempt to be your best self at all times? In short, if you left this earth now, would you be happy with your legacy?

When you consider death from this perspective, it shouldn't be depressing or fearful. Instead, it should drive you towards making the most of every single day. Did you spend enough time with your children or did you play silly games on your phone instead? Did you binge watch Netflix instead of phoning your parents? In short, was this the best possible day you could have had, even if it was completely ordinary?

Practical Exercises

- ✓ *Read biographies and autobiographies about death and dying.* One of the best ways to demystify and remove the stigma around death is to immerse yourself in it. Reading memoirs on the subject can help you see how others have approached it and what they have learned through their experiences. Look at the biography section of bookshops, libraries or Amazon for any that appeal to you, or if you need a few suggestions to get you started, you could try *Nothing to be Frightened of* by Julian Barnes, *When Breath Becomes Air* by Paul Kalanithi, *The Year of Magical Thinking* by Joan Didion, *The Bright Hour: A Memoir of Living and Dying* by

Nina Riggs, *The End of your Life Book Club* by Will Schwalbe, or *Dying: A Memoir* by Cory Taylor.

✓ *Plan your funeral and write your own eulogy.* Planning your own funeral is a good idea, regardless of whether you're a Stoic or not. Not only is it surprisingly good fun, there's a lot to be said for making it easy for your loved ones to know what to do when the time comes to say goodbye. While funerals are for the living, knowing that it reflects exactly what you wanted gives a lot of reassurance to those you leave behind and gives them one final reminder of who you were.

When it comes to writing your eulogy, be honest about yourself. While those you leave behind will feel obligated to talk about the positive, you are under no such obligation. Will your children say you made time for them? Will your partner say you were thoughtful and loving? Will those who knew you say you always did your best to live a good life?

Or will they wish you had done more to be a better person?

It is okay if you realize you could have tried harder. It's never too late to change. So revisit your eulogy on a regular basis and reflect on what kind of legacy you're currently leaving behind and how you can change things so your eulogy reflects what you would want it to say.

- ✓ *At the end of every day, take a moment to look back and reflect.* Journaling is becoming increasingly popular because it helps us take stock of where we are and where we would like to be. Take ten minutes each evening to answer these simple questions:
    - If you don't wake up in the morning, would you be happy that this was your last day?
    - What would you do differently if you could go back in time?
    - Would you change how you interacted with people?
    - How will you use this reflection to have a better day tomorrow?
    - Did you meet your goals?

  Set a small number of actionable goals for tomorrow that will help you have a better day and help you work towards a more virtuous life, whatever virtuous means to you. Remember – Stoicism is a practical philosophy, so this will help you bring it into your daily life.
- ✓ *Meditate on your mortality. Literally.* We've already discussed the benefits of meditation. You can use this ancient practice to help you accept the inevitability of death, and support you in living your best life. Again, you may want to record this script and play it back to help you focus while you meditate. If you do that, leave some time where appropriate for you to reflect on the questions.

Meditation on death

Sit down and make yourself comfortable, ensuring your back is supported.

Take a moment to focus on your breath. Observe it as you inhale and exhale... Inhale and exhale...

And as you inhale, feel that breath filling you with warming energy, helping you relax.

And as you exhale, breathe out any negativity, any stress, any worry.

Continue to inhale that warming energy and exhale any negativity.

Now, as you inhale, feel yourself sinking down... down... down... Going deep into the earth.

You feel perfectly safe. Nothing can harm you here.

You find yourself standing on the edge of a river. Ahead of you is a small boat, a tall, silent figure dressed in black waiting patiently in the boat for you.

He holds out a hand and beckons you to join him on board.

You realise this is the River Styx and this is the ferryman, come to take you to the afterlife.

Once you cross this river, you will never be able to return. This is the end of your journey. Once you cross this river, you will be at peace, free from fear and pain.

But once you cross this river, you will never be able to see those you love again.

You imagine how everyone you know will feel when they learn about your passing. What will they say about you? Will they say you lived a good life? Will they say you always tried to do your best?

You think about the decisions you made that you regret. How did you learn from those experiences? How did you use them to do better in the future?

Now think about the moments when you were at your happiest and felt content. What were you doing? How could you have brought more happiness into your life?

The ferryman beckons to you again, but you shake your head. Now is not your time to travel with him.

He nods, knowing you will return to this place again.

You feel yourself travelling back to your body. Take a moment to appreciate the simple fact you are alive at this time, with a future of possibility ahead of you.

Notice your breath again, feeling gratitude for your life as you inhale and exhale.

And when you are ready, open your eyes.

Summary

Reflect on your own mortality on a regular basis. This will help you appreciate what you have all the more.

- Read biographies and autobiographies about death and dying.
- Plan your funeral and write your own eulogy.
- At the end of every day, take a moment to look back and reflect.
- Meditate on your mortality.

CHAPTER SIX

EMBRACE YOUR LACK OF CONTROL

"Sickness is a hindrance to the body, but not to your ability to choose, unless that is your choice. Lameness is a hindrance to the leg, but not to your ability to choose. Say this to yourself with regard to everything that happens, then you will see such obstacles as hindrances to something else, but not to yourself."
—Epictetus

How do you react when you find yourself stuck in traffic? Do you get impatient or angry? Do you yell at the cars in front of you, hoping they'll move?

Or what about when an activity you were looking forward to is cancelled because of the weather? Do you shake your fist at the sky, cursing the rain? Do you hurl abuse at the person who made the judgement call to cancel the event?

Does any of that change anything?

One of the most important aspects of living a Stoic life is recognising what you can and cannot change. Wasting energy on getting angry or upset with things that are outside of your control is futile when that energy could be better spent on the things you *can* control.

Whenever you face a difficult situation and your automatic response is to get angry or upset, ask yourself whether an emotional response will help you. Will it change the situation? Is the situation something you have any control over or is the only control you have your reaction?

When someone says or does something to you, it is your choice to decide that they are being insulting, offensive or audacious. As Epictetus noted, it isn't any particular event which upsets us, but our judgement about that event. Someone saying something you find hurtful has just uttered a few words. It is your choice to be hurt by them. When you get offended by someone, you have made yourself their accomplice. You have chosen to go along with their narrative and allowed yourself to be hurt.

It is incredibly liberating to realise that you have the power over whether you're upset or not. You have the freedom to ignore what someone is saying, go along with what they want you to do or politely respond. You do not have to buy in to what they're selling.

You have the power to move on. It is entirely up to you whether you use it or not.

The more intentional you can be with your reactions, the more Stoic you become. You should aim for an objective passivity in any trying situation before you decide what to do with it. The more you recognise which aspects of your life are outside of your control, the more you can let them go and focus on what you can change. Not only will this make you a happier person, it will give you a step up over others who are still caught up in this pointless struggle.

Practical Exercises

- *Start your day with a mantra.* Every morning, look at yourself in the mirror and recite this quote from Epictetus: "Some things are in our control and others not. Things in our control are opinion, pursuit, desire, aversion, and, in a word, whatever are our own actions. Things not in our control are body, property, reputation, command, and, in one word, whatever are not our own actions."
- *Don't ask yourself what would Jesus do; ask, what would my best self do?* We all have a vision of ourselves as we would like to be, that perfect person we could be if we weren't always tired or grumpy or overworked. Our best self eats properly, gets plenty of fresh air and exercise, doesn't procrastinate, is supportive and understanding of our loved ones and is a thoroughly good egg.

You do not have to wait for things to change to become that best self. You can be the best possible you right now. All you have to do is ask yourself, *what would my best self do?* in any given situation.

This is a useful practice in all situations, not just when you're facing a major issue. When you are honest about what your best self would do, you can consciously make the decision to *be* that best self – or recognise that you still have some work to do.

A few examples:

- Would my best self skip breakfast?
- Would my best self have hummus or a burger for lunch?
- Would my best self call my parents regularly?
- Would my best self actively reach out to friends beyond liking a few social media posts?
- Would my best self make the time to read a bedtime story to my children every night?
- Would my best self read a book or binge watch a Netflix series?
- Would my best self surf the internet during work?
- Would my best self hurl insults at the driver who cut me off on my way to work?
- Would my best self organise a babysitter so I can go out on a date with my partner?

- Would my best self drink wine every night?
- Would my best self go to the gym on a Saturday morning or stay in bed?

When you start asking yourself this question, it soon becomes clear what you need to do to be your best self. And it's okay if you can't be your best self all the time. We're only human and it takes persistent effort to be your best at every opportunity. But when you know what you should be doing, it becomes easier to move towards consciously making the best choice more often so you can start embodying your best self.

Summary

Strive to make good choices about the things that are under your control. Let go of any emotional attachment or response to the things you can't control.

- Start every day with a mantra.
- When faced with a choice, no matter how trivial or important, ask yourself, *what would my best self do?*

CHAPTER SEVEN

WORK WITHOUT LUST FOR RESULT

"Curb your desire—don't set your heart on so many things and you will get what you need."
—Epictetus

We've already discussed why it's important to differentiate between those things we can control and those we can't, and focusing our attention on the latter. However, while this is easy in theory, in practise it can be difficult to let go of our attachment to things we believe we can control, such as our career, our relationships, our environment, etc.

Yet our control over events around us is far less powerful than you suppose. Let's assume you've decided to join a five-a-side football club and you set yourself the target of scoring a goal at your first match. You might be an amazing footballer, but there are a number of factors that influence whether you'll succeed or fail, none of which is in your control.

The weather might be bad, which affects the quality of the pitch and how easy it is for you to play. Your shoelace might come undone so you trip at an inopportune moment. The opposing team might have trained harder than you or simply be the better team. You might fall badly and injure yourself so you have to leave the game.

None of these things is within your control, but can all mean you fail to achieve your goal. And having set yourself up to succeed, you're going to be disappointed when you don't.

This is why it's so important to *only* focus on what you can control – yourself.

So when you set goals, move away from thinking about results, which can be affected by external circumstances you cannot predict or affect. Instead, confine yourself solely to goals that are linked to your own efforts and ability. So, instead of having a target of scoring a goal, make it linked to training as much as possible, preparing yourself physically and mentally as much as possible, and promise yourself you'll do your very best during the match. You can do all of those things and still not score or win the match, but you've done everything possible to maximise your chances, so it's pointless wasting your energy on worrying about the result.

The effort is what's important.

You can apply this to every aspect of your life. So if, for example, you're job hunting, rather than making it a goal to get a specific job, which may or may not be the right job for you, make it your goal to research the company you're interviewing with, prepare answers to questions you're likely to be asked, etc. to give yourself the best possible chance of getting the job. You may well not get the job despite all of that effort, but if you've prepared as well as you can, the Stoic belief is that it wasn't meant to be.

Or let's assume you're single and want to be in a relationship. Instead of focusing on finding someone and risking your desperation scaring people away, focus on making yourself someone people would like to be in a relationship with. Dress well, get a good haircut, go out to places where you might meet someone you're interested in being with – but if you don't, you'll still have a good time.

When I wrote this book, I didn't set a goal around how many copies I wanted to sell. I can't control that figure. But I made my goal to research this book, put together material people would find truly valuable and write something people enjoy reading that gives the reader useful exercises to help them take a Stoic approach to life. Then I had a goal of organising my marketing and advertising campaigns so I could tell as many people as possible about my book. So while I might not know how many books I'll sell, I'll give myself a good chance of healthy sales.

Whether you've set yourself goals or not in the past, now is a good time to get into the habit. When you set goals in your personal life, you support yourself in creating your dream life. If you connect your goals to your effort and mindset (the things you can control), you have a much greater chance of getting to where you need to be – but you don't attach any emotion to that destination, recognising that it's the journey that matters, and the journey is where you learn and grow.

Practical Exercises

- *Examine your Wheel of Life.* Draw a circle and divide it up into segments. Now label each segment according to a different area of your life, e.g. family, friends, relationship, career, social life, spiritual life, etc. In each segment, write out where you would like to be and where you currently are.
    - What do you notice? Which areas of your life need attention? Which parts are you happy with and don't want to change?
    - When you take a moment to examine your life dispassionately, it helps you see where you should be focusing your attention and what needs work.
- *Set yourself goals and hold yourself accountable to them.* When you've created your Wheel of Life, it's very easy to see what kind of goals you should be setting. However, the key thing here is to keep your focus on your own effort rather than results. So,

for example, let's say you want to set up a business and make a certain amount of money from it. You can't guarantee how much money you'll make, but you can certainly break down the steps you need to work through to set up a business and then plan out what you need to do to make money from that business. So, if you're selling a product, you can have an advertising plan, or if you're selling a service, you can have a goal of reaching out to a certain number of potential clients with an offer.

Once you've set your goals, you need to keep yourself on track. You do this by checking in with yourself on a daily, weekly and quarterly basis. At the beginning of every day, briefly summarise the past 24 hours and write out what you're going to do that day to move closer to your goals. You might not work towards every single goal every day, but you should be making effort towards at least one of them. Once a week, go over all your goals and note your progress. This will help you see where you're falling behind so you can adjust what you're doing moving forward. Then, every quarter, review how far you've come and adjust your goals and plans where necessary to continue to move forward.

At the end of a twelve-month cycle, redo your goals. It may well be that you haven't achieved everything you set out to do, and this is okay. You will have learned a lot about yourself and your priorities in the process, and you will have discovered what works for you and what doesn't.

And the best part? When you set a goal attached to effort rather than outcome, progress is inevitable. While you might not end up where you intend to be, you'll find your life changes in so many positive ways, it really doesn't matter whether you get to where you wanted to go.

Summary

While goal setting is important, you need to make sure your goals are focused on effort rather than targets. You cannot fully control whether you meet your goals, but you have total control over your own attitude and whether you work hard or not.

- Examine your Wheel of Life.
- Set goals and hold yourself accountable to them.

CHAPTER EIGHT

THE POWER OF JOURNALING

"There is indeed a limit fixed for us, just where the remorseless law of Fate has fixed it; but none of us knows how near he is to this limit. Therefore, let us so order our minds as if we had come to the very end... Let us balance life's account every day... One who daily puts the finishing touches to his life is never in want of time."

—Seneca

Many of the Stoics whose writing inspire us today were avid diarists. Epictetus, Marcus Aurelius and Seneca all journaled regularly, Epictetus telling his students that they should "write down day by day" their thoughts on philosophy to "exercise themselves." Seneca would write in his journal every night after his wife had gone to bed. He said he would "examine my entire day and go back over what I've done and said, hiding nothing from myself, passing nothing by." He also remarked that after he'd carried out this serious self-reflection, he slept particularly soundly.

And it is most noteworthy to recognise that Aurelius entitled his journals as "to himself." A prolific journaler, Aurelius considered this process absolutely essential in his life.

In order for journaling to fulfil the purpose you need it to, it needs to go beyond simply noting down the events of the day. After all, this is a philosophical practice, so it is not enough to only list what happened.

As a Stoic, when you journal, you should consider what happened that day and what lessons you learned. You should also be thinking about the next day and how you can prepare for it. Consider your studies of Stoicism – are you reading any books written by the Classic scholars? Researching the philosophy further? Record your observations and personal experiences of applying their lessons.

Living a Stoic life is an ongoing process. It is not enough to read a few books and consider yourself a master. You need to put them into practice and then consistently reflect on how you're doing and make a conscious effort to improve your attitude and outlook to become the best possible person you can be.

Journaling allows you to reflect on how successful you are in applying everything you've learned and how you can continue to apply those lessons.

As if that wasn't enough, there are many other reasons why journaling is a positive habit for you to develop.

- *Journaling reduces stress.* Modern living is incredibly stressful and anything you can do to reduce that stress must be a good thing. There have been many studies that have shown that journaling is a great way to help you manage stress. Indeed, if you journal just a couple of times a week for 15-20 minutes, you can bring down your blood pressure and improve your liver function. (If you don't believe me, just check out https://www.mic.com/articles/110662/science-shows-something-surprising-about-people-who-still-journal for all the references and other proven health benefits!) Choose a time of day that is best for you. This could be first thing in the morning or last thing at night. Journaling at the same time every day will help you establish it as a habit and help you focus your mind where it needs to be.
- *Journaling improves your memory.* On the one hand, it seems like a no-brainer that journaling will help you remember things. After all, you've got a written record of your experiences, so even if you can't recall exactly what happened, you can look back over your notes to remind yourself. But it would seem that the act of recording your life on a daily basis helps you get better at remembering things in

general, improving your memory and potentially even helping your brain's cognitive processes.

- *Journaling puts you in a better mood.* One of the many benefits of journaling is that it can help you retain a more positive outlook on life and improve your emotional wellbeing.
- *Journaling makes you more self-aware.* It should be unsurprising that when you regularly reflect on life's events and how they make you feel, you develop a stronger understanding of who you are. The more you journal, the more you connect with your inner needs and drives while retaining perspective. It also helps you cope during difficult times and transitions, supporting you in identifying pivotal times and going with the flow. Even if you're not a creative type, journaling helps develop your creativity, bringing out more of your brainpower.

Realistically, there's no reason not to journal and countless reasons to get started.

Practical exercises

Just get started. Journaling will come more easily to some people than others. The very thought of writing anything might fill you with dread. But I'd refer you to the first chapter where you were told to push yourself out of your comfort zone – if journaling makes you feel uncomfortable, good!

Buy yourself a nice notebook, something that you find attractive and makes you want to fill it with your thoughts. Journaling by hand is a much more immersive experience. When you physically write your words, it stimulates your brain in a way that typing on a computer just cannot.

Then write something. Anything. Even if you only write one sentence a day, promise yourself you'll do that much/little. That sentence could sum up the past 24 hours; it could detail what you had for dinner. It doesn't matter what you say as long as you say *something*. Once you've established the habit, you can then develop it further to be more reflective.

And most importantly, switch off your inner critic. No one is going to be reading your journal other than you. It doesn't matter whether your spelling is correct or your grammar is perfect. All that matters is that you've journaled.

Write every day. There is no excuse. You can find time to write a single sentence every day. If that is all you write, that is more than enough to get started and you'll find that sentence organically grows into more.

If you need a prompt to get you started, here are a few questions for you:

- What was the most significant event of the past 24 hours? How did it make you feel?

- What are you currently reading? Are there any important lessons you've learned from the book?
- What are you grateful for? Can you list at least three things?
- If you've followed the earlier exercises in the book, you should have some goals you're working towards. What did/can you do to move closer to those goals?

Summarise your week. Once a week, do a more in-depth journaling session to review the previous week and examine your progress towards a more Stoic life. If you have goals, chart what you've done towards them and see what needs prioritising for the coming week.

Make a note of the biggest lesson you've learned that week and how you're applying your Stoic studies to your life, as well as how things are changing for the better as a result of a Stoic attitude.

Summary

Journaling has many valuable health benefits, as well as being an important part of a Stoic lifestyle. You should keep a journal to help you deepen your understandings and Stoic practices.

- Just get started. It is more important to document your thoughts than to worry about crafting beautiful prose.

- Write every day.
- Take things a step further and summarise your week in detail.

CHAPTER NINE

PREPARE FOR THE WORST

"Nothing happens to the wise man against his expectation… nor do all things turn out for him as he wished but as he reckoned—and above all he reckoned that something could block his plans."
—Seneca

There is a Stoic practice known as 'premeditatio malorum.' Literally translated this means 'the pre-meditation of evils' and involves visualising everything that could go wrong or losing everything that is important to you. After all, as they say, life is what happens when you're busy making plans. You can have everything worked out to the finest detail only to have the rug pulled out from under you by a nasty accident, job loss or relationship breakup. It doesn't matter how hard we work; we don't always get what we deserve, no matter how much we've earned it.

Premeditatio malorum, or what we might call now 'negative visualisation,' means you can mentally prepare for the worst because, at some point in our lives, bad things will happen. For a Stoic, this is not a negative thing because you've anticipated this and have the resilience and fortitude to withstand all the slings and arrows life can throw at you. Not only do you develop mental strength, you also develop a renewed appreciation of all the blessings in your life, which you may not currently recognise.

It is important to walk a fine line between anticipating trouble and becoming consumed by stress and worry. When you practice negative visualisation, this shouldn't be done with a mindset of 'this is what's definitely going to happen.' It's more a case that you simply can't know what's going to happen, so you're open to all possibilities.

Look at it another way. Is a glass filled to half its capacity half empty or half full? To a Stoic, neither would be the case. The Stoic interpretation is that there is water to drink, so be grateful for it. And the fact that the water is contained within a glass? Bonus!

So, when you visualise losing your family, you're not doing this because you genuinely believe they're going to die. But the knowledge that they might not always be there will help you be grateful for their presence in your life and have more patience on those days when things aren't going well and there's friction among all of you. Done properly, negative visualisation will help you feel true gratitude for the blessings your life enjoys, whether that be financial success, a happy marriage, or simply the feel of the sun on your face as you walk outside.

When we anticipate tough times and use that visualisation as a spur to squeeze every benefit from every second life gives us, we remove most, if not all, of the power negative events have to devastate us. Change is inevitable and not always for the good; but when we lose something or someone important to us, that loss isn't as overwhelming when we are armed with the knowledge that we really did embrace every possible ounce of happiness while we could.

Practical exercises

❖ *Journal it out.* Writing out a list of everything that could go wrong and the potential consequences is a good way of getting things clear in your head. It can also help you come up with contingency plans and even make preparations to mitigate the impact of the worst things.

Pick an event you have coming up and list everything that could possibly go wrong or even stop it from happening altogether. For example, if you have a holiday booked, your list might include:

- Losing your passport.
- Your flights being cancelled.
- Your luggage being lost.
- Extreme weather, e.g. hurricanes, storms.

- Natural disasters.
- Being robbed.
- Getting food poisoning.
- Getting severely sunburnt.
- Having an accident during an exciting activity.

I'm sure you can think of many more things that could go wrong, so make your list as long as you possibly can. Don't worry about including items that are highly unlikely – they're still possible and the point of this exercise is to prepare yourself for *every* eventuality.

Once you've completed your list, go back and document how it would make you feel if that happened. Really immerse yourself in that feeling, as if you're experiencing it right now, so should that event actually occur, you already know how you'd deal with it.

Finally, for each item, note what you could do to either minimise the likelihood of it occurring or, if it's outside of your control (as most things are), what you can do to minimise its disruption to your trip. By doing this, you've prepared yourself for the worst – but also allowed for the possibility of the best, because if nothing on your list happens, you'll feel grateful for a stress-free break. You'll enjoy your holiday all the more because you'll have a full understanding of how bad it could have been, so you'll be motivated to have as much fun as you can throughout your entire trip.

❖ *Meditate on the worst.* While brainstorming every negative possibility is a valuable exercise, you'll also find it helpful to practise actual visualisation to experience the event as if it were happening right now. Done properly, this is a very emotional experience, so make sure you choose a time and place for this exercise where you won't be disturbed and can immerse yourself in the moment without feeling like you have to self-censor for the sake of those around you.

Choose one of the worst things you could experience. It might be losing a loved one; it could be experiencing a life-changing accident. Perhaps you want to think about becoming homeless following a redundancy. Pick something which is your absolute worst nightmare, the one thing you really *don't* want to see come true.

Sit yourself comfortably, making sure your back is supported, so you can meditate without being distracted by your body needing to fidget. Close your eyes and imagine someone telling you the news you didn't want to hear. Picture their face, the sadness in their eyes as they tell you what happened and how sorry they are for you. Allow yourself to be flooded with emotion as you feel denial it could be possible, anger that it's happened, sadness that things will never be the same again. If you need to cry, cry.

Don't think about what to do next. This is not the time to come up with contingency plans. Instead, immerse yourself completely in the feelings of the moment. Know that there was absolutely nothing you could have done to change this outcome, so all you can do is accept that this is how it is and adjust your reality accordingly.

This too will pass. No matter how badly you feel in the moment, this moment is not forever.

Summary

Regularly visualise worst-case scenarios to help plan and prepare, as well as develop the mental resilience to cope with it.

- Journal what could happen and how you'll deal with it.
- Meditate on your worst nightmare and fully immerse yourself in the emotions arising from that.

CHAPTER TEN

AMOR FATI

"All that is in accord with you is in accord with me, O World! Nothing which occurs at the right time for you comes too soon or too late for me. All that your seasons produce, O Nature, is fruit for me. It is from you that all things come: all things are within you, and all things move toward you."
—Marcus Aurelius

The term '*amor fati*' is most commonly associated with Friedrich Nietzsche, who used it to denote a love of fate we should all aspire to. In his book, *Ecce Homo: How One Becomes What Is,* he wrote, "My formula for greatness in a human being is *amor fati*: that one wants nothing to be different, not forward, not backward, not in all eternity. Not merely bear what is necessary, still less conceal it—all idealism is mendacity in the face of what is necessary—but love it."

However, while he may have popularised this attitude, it was one very popular with the Stoics a couple of thousand years ago. Marcus Aurelius wrote, "A blazing fire makes flame and brightness out of everything that is thrown into it," meaning that it doesn't matter what happens – if you have the right state of being, whatever comes your way will be transformed and assimilated into your life experiences.

Essentially, *amor fati* is the attitude that regardless of what comes your way, every experience is to be welcomed and accepted, regardless of whether it appears to be positive or negative. When it comes to challenges, *amor fati* goes beyond simple acceptance. You should love whatever difficulties you face because they are what forge you into a better person. So just like fuel for a fire, those tough times are fuel for your personal growth.

We discussed earlier how little is within your control and that principle is the foundation to *amor fati.* Because the only things you have true control over are your thoughts and deeds, the faster you can fully assimilate that into your philosophy of life, the faster you can move past anger, frustration or misery when the universe throws you a curveball. It is deeply empowering to know that you have the ability to make the most of the events in your life, no matter what. The very notion of fate, which is tied up in the concept of *amor fati,* means that we have no control over our destinies. All we can do is love the life we're given.

Most of us are pessimists. We feel that things are going to go wrong sooner or later while the good things in life have to be worked for and can be taken away at any moment. Yet we fight against that, trying to control the uncontrollable. This is why so many of us are unhappy with our lot. We're trying to swim upstream against the flow.

When you accept that difficulties are going to come, you have a choice. Resent that and continue to be unhappy, or love the challenges they give you and the chances they provide for you to grow, adapt and evolve. While everything may be fated on some level, *amor fati* means that everything happens for a reason, but it's entirely up to you to decide on what that reason will be. Is it to make you miserable or is it to give you opportunities you could never have imagined?

Practical Exercises

✓ *Journal your thought process.* Again, your journal is an important part of developing the right mindset.

Look back on everything you've documented so far. Highlight those times when you were able to utilise a Stoic acceptance of what was going on around you and the difference this made to your reactions. Think about how you would have reacted to that situation before you started following a Stoic path.

Choose a Stoic quote that sums up *amor fati* for you and write your thoughts on what it means and how you can incorporate it into your practises. Do you think this will be easy or difficult for you? What challenges can you anticipate and how can you overcome them?

✓ *Keep your mind on the right track.* Training your mind is one of the hardest things you can do. You can promise yourself as much as you like that you're going to accept the present as it comes, but you'll soon find yourself slipping into hoping the future will be the way you want, or wishing the past had been different.

So every morning, when you wake up, say to yourself, "I accept today as it is, not as I would like it to be." Whenever you notice yourself sliding into thinking about the future or the past, repeat this mantra to bring your attention back to the present.

One way you can support this process is by wearing an elastic band around your wrist. Every time your thoughts stray away from the present, ping the band against your wrist so that you experience a mild discomfort. This will help you keep your attention where it needs to be.

✓ *Stop complaining.* Do you know someone who does nothing but complain about how much they hate their job but when you suggest they find another one, they come up with a million reasons why they can't? How frustrating is it? The solution to their problem is right there, but they'd rather complain than take actual steps to improve their situation.

It's a natural human reaction to complain, and airing our grievances is healthy. However, when we get stuck in a cycle of complaining, we waste energy we could be putting towards improving our lot. What's more, complaining doesn't actually make you feel better. It just reminds you about how bad things are. And the reality is, there's not a lot that happens we can't do something about.

Accepting what comes without complaint doesn't mean you passively lie back and let people walk all over you. Instead, it means you dispassionately observe whatever situation you find yourself in and look for the opportunity in the obstacle.

So if you break your arm, you don't complain it's hurting but do nothing to fix it. You get yourself to A&E and get it set. You accept you won't be typing much for the next few weeks. You think about installing dictation software to help you with your workload. (You may even find you like it so much that you continue using it after your arm is healed!) You take it as a sign to slow down and maybe read a few books on Stoicism while you heal.

See if you can go a whole week without complaining once. And if that's too much, start with a day and build on that. Journal the process and note how many times you complain so you can work on reducing that number.

✓ *Talk to your future self.* When the printer jams or someone cuts in front of you on the motorway, it can make your blood boil. But if you took a moment to think about how that's going to affect your future, the reality is it really isn't that big of a deal. You can unclog the printer and get on with your work. The chances are high you'll overtake the person who raced past you as you get further down the motorway – and even if you don't, you'll still arrive at your destination when you need.

Very little will negatively impact your future if you take a moment to breathe and consider just how important your frustrations are. Even major events lose their impact over you given enough time. That nasty breakup probably won't be haunting you five years from now when you're happily married to the love of your life. That embarrassing foot-in-mouth moment when you said something stupid in an interview for your dream job won't be important when you're running your own company a few years down the line.

It doesn't matter what it is. When something negative happens, ask yourself, "How will I be feeling about this event in ten years' time?" The reality is that in almost every single instance, the answer will be "I won't feel this bad." That doesn't mean you won't always mourn the loss of a parent, for example, but you won't feel their loss so intensely.

You shouldn't punish your future self because of things you are experiencing now. Eventually, you'll be able to put it into perspective and accept it as another one of life's myriad lessons. Whatever happens, it could always be worse.

Another way of looking at it is to think about what advice you'd give to a friend who was going through what you're going through. Realistically, you're likely to be telling them not to worry, that everything's going to be all right, it'll all work out in the end.

✓ *Life is a game, so play it with all your heart.* Whether you're a Candy Crush fan or a hard-core gamer, the one thing you want from a game is that it challenges you. There's a buzz that comes from winning that difficult level or beating that tough opponent you simply don't get when the game is easy.

It's the same with life. Sure, you may not understand all the rules, and there are parts that may not make sense to you, but that's the playing field you're on. The Stoic approach is to accept that the rules are random, but play the game as hard as you can. Win or lose, it's all about the experience. While setbacks can be frustrating, if you see it as part of the game you need to beat in order to level up, you're a long way towards being Stoic.

✓ *Be grateful for whatever happens.* It's easy to be grateful for the blessings we have. It can be much more difficult to be grateful for the hardships, but it's important you feel just as thankful for the bad things in life as the good.

One piece of advice I was given by my dad really resonated with me and is very relevant here. He said that when you first hold your child in your arms, you want to protect them from anything bad that can happen, but that's doing them a disservice. The times when you've grown the most have been when you've been challenged. Why would you deprive your child of that lesson?

When we're in the middle of a difficult time, we feel that our emotional response is the 'correct' one. We feel it's the only logical, natural reaction, yet if you ask your future self what good things came out of that moment, the bigger picture shows us that there was a lot of positive to love in that moment, even if it didn't feel like it.

Maybe your car won't start so you're going to be late for work. Frustrating, right? But what if there had been a major accident on your route and if you'd left on time, you'd have been involved in it and potentially suffered serious injuries? Your car not starting suddenly becomes a blessing.

While we can't know what would have happened if we had done something different, we can trust that the path we're on is the right one for us and the problems we have are meant to teach us something valuable. So be grateful for them, because if you really want to be your authentic, powerful self, you'll love whatever comes your way because every single event is an opportunity to make your life even better.

Summary

Love all aspects of your life, the ups and the downs, because everything is a lesson and helps you grow into a better person.

- Use your journal to help you appreciate your life.
- Keep your mind focused on the present moment.
- Stop complaining.
- Put things in perspective by talking to your future self.
- Treat life as a game and play it to the best of your ability.
- Be grateful for everything you have, good and bad.

CHAPTER ELEVEN

TIME IS ON YOUR SIDE

"Begin at once to live, and count each separate day as a separate life."
—Seneca

With all the exercises you've been give so far in this book, you may be feeling a little overwhelmed by this point, so now's a good time to remind you to breathe. At its essence, Stoicism is a very simple, practical philosophy.

Seneca's essay '*De Brevitate Vitae*' (On the Shortness of Life) discusses the fact that people waste a lot of their time engaging in meaningless pursuits. His argument is that we are all given enough time to do what is truly important, so it is up to us to make appropriate use of however long we have on this earth. He felt that the best use of our time was to live in the present moment with an intentional, purposeful attitude.

Most people waste their time, according to Seneca. We cannot afford to do anything other than live in the now because tomorrow could be too late. We never know when our time here is up, but for the Stoic, this is not a bad thing because they are always ready to take their last breath, as they have the reassurance of knowing they've always valued the gifts of life. In comparison, most people stress about how short life is because they're obsessing about the bad things that have happened in the past, worried about what the future will bring, failing to notice what's going on in front of them right now.

Seneca states that we waste time because we don't value it in the way we do our money or things. After all, it's difficult to pin down time. It slips through our fingers when we try to hold onto it and it doesn't have any tangible properties, so we're happy to give it away to others who want it from us because we don't see its worth.

To a Stoic, time is the most valuable thing you have, if not the *only* thing, so you need to live in the present with purpose and in harmony with Nature. Not only does this ground you in the current moment, it also gives you power over both the past and future, empowering you to be truly free and happy.

We've already touched on mindfulness and will be delving into it in greater depth in the next chapter, but it's worth mentioning again because this is key to making the most of your time. When you set your intention to be fully aware of everything you do and pay attention to your thoughts and actions, you open yourself up to unexpected possibilities. Not only that, you find yourself becoming more creative, more thoughtful and engaged in the world around you. When you are mindful of wanting to benefit from every waking moment, sleep becomes the last thing you want to do because there's so much more to experience.

If you've been sleepwalking through life, now's the time to wake up.

Although Stoicism encourages a detachment from material things and tough times, this does not mean you become indifferent to them. Instead, you reprioritise your expectations so you're focusing on being your best self rather than feeding your ego. When you are your best, success naturally follows without your putting effort or attachment into the result, which is one of the most empowering feelings you can experience.

Pursuing money, status and material possessions is not the Stoic way. The only thing worth chasing is virtue. Wisdom, justice, self-awareness, bravery – *these* are the goals you should be aiming for. After all, you could have all the money in the world and still be miserable. You could be highly educated with multiple doctorates yet be a deeply unpleasant person supporting an unjust system that favours the rich over the poor.

As Marcus Aurelius put it, "A branch cut from its neighbouring branch is necessarily cut away from the whole tree. In the same way a human being severed from just one other human has dropped from the whole community. Now the branch is cut off by someone else, but a man separates himself from his neighbour by his own hatred or rejection, not realising that he has thereby severed himself from the wider society of fellow citizens. Only there is this gift we have from Zeus who brought together the human community: we can grow back again to our neighbour and resume our place in the complement of the whole."

While it is only natural to feel a greater loyalty to our friends and family than the populace at large, Stoicism teaches that we're all part of a universal citizenship, so while we might think local, everything we do is a global act because when we focus on living a virtuous life and treating those around us with respect, this creates a ripple effect, building a society that is harmonious instead of selfish.

We looked at how you can turn obstacles into opportunities, but this isn't just something to do by yourself. Collectively, society as a whole can do this together. It's very easy to believe there's nothing you can do as an individual to improve the world at large, but little things add up. You can choose where you spend your money, the kind of food you buy, the type of car you drive (or if you even drive at all), what clothes you wear, etc. All of these choices are an expression of your beliefs and values, so now is the time to be more intentional in your consumerism.

As a Stoic, it is your responsibility to question whether you truly need to buy something and, if you do, where you should source it. Purchasing something you don't really need doesn't just undermine your personal path to virtue; it also undermines society's. If you don't choose ethical suppliers, you're supporting the use of sweatshops and slavery, the destruction of the rainforest and unethical behaviour by big corporations.

It would be a mistake to assume that Stoicism is anti-capitalism. Stoicism transcends politics and eschews a dogged adherence to any specific political ideology. Instead, it takes a more pragmatic approach. Reason does not have a political leaning, so it is for a Stoic to look at the facts of any given situation and follow where reason takes him. It is up to you to define what you view as reasonable and just and champion that. It is also your responsibility to combat inequality and immorality as best you can in whatever way makes most sense to you. This is still your personal path and it is up to you to define it in the manner that makes most sense according to your unique experience.

Or, to quote Marcus Aurelius again, "Do only what the reasons inherent in kingly and judicial powers prescribe for the benefit of mankind... change your ground, if in fact there is someone to correct and guide you away from some notion. But this transference must always spring from a conviction of justice or the common good:

and your preferred course must be likewise, not simply for apparent pleasure or popularity."

It takes courage to stand up when we see someone being racist or sexist. It takes wisdom to navigate the nuances of societal expectations and norms to see where true inequality exists, let alone come up with a way of combating it. But as a Stoic, it is your duty to do so, so that we can transform society to a more just and equitable one. It is, quite simply, the right thing to do.

Practical Exercises

- *Become an intentional consumer.* It is impossible to live in our modern time and not cause harm in one form or another. Unless you walk everywhere, your choice of transport contributes to pollution. Unless you grow your own food, everything you eat has a carbon footprint. You can drive yourself insane worrying about the damage your mere existence is doing with every breath.

  What's more, there are also budgetary concerns. It's great to want to only eat organic, but if you can't afford it, you shouldn't starve yourself.

  Stoicism is a journey that comes with the understanding that you can only do your best. If someone is a more ethical consumer than you, so what? Start small. Plan out your meals for the week so you can plan your purchases. Consider eating food that is in season, so you only buy items you can source locally. If you can afford to, shop at the local market or small, family-owned businesses rather than large supermarkets.

Or look at your toiletries. Are you buying from companies with an ethical attitude towards their products? Is your shampoo biodegradable? Does your soap contain palm oil? Educate yourself about the products you buy and look into alternatives if you discover you can do better.

➢ *Give time, not money, to charities.* It's easy to think that you've done your bit to be virtuous by donating to a worthy cause. But it's our time that is the most valuable thing we have. Spend it wisely by giving it to a local charity whose aims you support. Maybe you could clean up a local beauty spot or visit an old people's home. Look for something you will find rewarding and enjoyable, as well as genuinely improving your little corner of the world.

Many large charities do not spend their funds in the most ethical manner, and instead operate in a way that is more akin to big business than in keeping with their philanthropic aims. Small, local charities are far more likely to be in need of your help and will be all the more appreciative of it. What's more, you'll be able to see the results of your efforts and know you're genuinely making a difference. While you shouldn't be doing this to fuel your ego, having direct experience of helping others brings with it the feel-good factor and incentivises you to do even more.

Summary

Time is our most valuable possession. Spend it wisely and focus your efforts on living a virtuous life that contributes to a just, equitable society.

- Shop ethically and intentionally.
- Donate your time to charity instead of money.

CHAPTER TWELVE

TAKE A STOIC APPROACH TO MINDFULNESS

"Every hour focus your mind attentively...on the performance of the task in hand, with dignity, human sympathy, benevolence and freedom, and leave aside all other thoughts. You will achieve this, if you perform each action as if it were your last..."
—Marcus Aurelius

We've touched upon mindfulness in previous chapters. Now it's time to really dig deep into the topic.

Why is mindfulness so important? To quote Marcus Aurelius again, "Each man only lives in this present instant...all the rest either has been lived or remains in uncertainty." This ties in very much with the Stoic approach to life. If all we possess is this present moment, it makes sense to focus all our attention on it. While the ancient Stoics might not have dubbed their attitude mindfulness, in a modern context, it's a similar principle.

Epictetus talks about '*prosoche*' in his texts. Roughly translated as 'attention,' he argues that *prosoche* is essential for anyone wishing to live an ethical life and that it doesn't matter what you're doing; even singing along to the radio or reading a book can – and should – be done with *prosoche.* He felt that once you've let your mind go off in whatever direction it wants, you've lost power to keep it directed at what's right. Your mind needs to be geared towards moderation and self-awareness at all times.

On the surface, this seems like hard work. Needing to constantly keep your mind focused on the now without straying towards the past or future requires continual effort, and the very thought can be daunting, let alone starting the process.

But Stoicism is a journey. It's okay to stumble along the way. You don't have to be a master. You just have to do your best and know that the more you do, the better you become.

Remember, focus on what you can control and don't worry about what you can't. The more you do this, the easier it becomes to be mindful in your actions. As you make your way through your day, ask yourself, "How am I handling this situation? Am I focused on what I can control or am I letting what I cannot control overwhelm my thoughts?"

Let's look at a few examples. Let's say you are put in charge of putting together an important presentation at work. You know that if you do well, your manager will be happy with you and if you don't, she'll disapprove. You could even be demoted or promoted as a consequence of how the presentation goes.

A natural instinct would be to work with your manager's approval in mind. Your goal would be to make them happy, but as a Stoic, you should appreciate that their happiness is outside of your control. You cannot choose whether someone feels happy or not. All you can do is do your job to the best of your abilities without attaching any importance to winning the approval of your manager. Of course, if you do the presentation well, the chances are high that your manager will be happy with you, but that is a side effect. What is in your control is the amount of effort you put into the presentation, developing a good relationship with your manager so you know what they are looking for when reviewing your work, and focusing on working to the best of your abilities – or even seeking training to improve your skills. *These* are the things you can control. Your manager's feelings are not among them.

Epictetus gave another example of this principle in play when he discussed a singer suffering from stage fright. He wrote:

"When I see man in anxiety, I say to myself, 'What can it be that this fellow wants? For if he did not want something that was outside of his control, how could he still remain in anxiety? That is why when singing on his own he shows no anxiety, but does so what he enters the theatre, even though he has a beautiful voice. For he does not wish merely to sing well, but also to win applause, and that is no longer under his control… Why is this? Why, he simply does not know what a crowd is, or the applause of a crowd…hence he trembles and turn pale.'"

Epictetus argues that stage fright is all down to a fear of the audience not applauding the performance. So a vocalist with the wrong mindset will feel amazing if the crowd claps and cheers, but if they don't get the reaction they want, they'll feel depressed and likely suffer even greater stage fright next time.

In contrast, a Stoic singer doesn't place any importance on the audience's enjoyment of his performance. He just practises and prepares and sings to the best of his abilities, regardless of whether the audience likes his singing or not.

It doesn't matter what it is you're doing. If you worry about winning the approval of others, your focus is in the wrong place. And the beauty of paying attention to the things that are in your control, e.g. how hard you work, how easily you go with the flow, etc. is that all this effort is likely to mean you do a good job and make it far more likely you gain the support of others. Conversely, when you worry about what others think, you risk undermining your efforts because you're so worried about getting it 'right,' according to other's standards, that you can't do your best because you're too stressed.

When you are trying to change the way you think and reprogram your mind, it is important to maintain self-awareness so you don't fall into any of the potential pitfalls in your way. One possible issue with focusing on yourself is that you risk becoming selfish and not caring about what others think or feel. After all, their feelings are under their control and not your responsibility, right?

Yet if this is how you interpret this mindset, you've misunderstood what the Stoics were hoping to achieve. Remember, Stoicism isn't just about being your best self and living a virtuous life; this virtue is intended to build a better society, a community of people who are working together for the common good to create an environment which is positive for everyone involved.

It is your responsibility as a Stoic to remember that it is up to you how virtuous you are, that you have the choice to do the right thing that will benefit all concerned. When you do your best, this automatically helps everyone. You might not be aiming to make your manager happy, but if you've done your best and hit all your targets, by default your manager will be satisfied.

Under Stoicism, your relationships can only flourish when you actively choose to place your priorities where you can control what you do *and* combine it with an active aim to be a good person. In Epictetus' words, "For where one can say 'I' and 'mine,' to there will the human being incline. If 'I' and 'mine' are placed in the flesh, there will the human being's ruling power be; if they are in the moral purpose, there must it be; if they are in externals, there must it be. If, therefore, I am where my moral purpose is, then, and then only, will I be the friend and son and father that I should be. For then this will by interest – to keep my good faith, my self-respect, my forbearance, my co-cooperation, and to maintain my relationships with other human beings."

In other words, whatever you are giving attention to is what is going to manifest the most in your life. If you're stressing about external factors, they'll continue to rule you and you'll continue to be miserable and worried. If you're only concerned about your personal happiness, you'll miss the opportunity to grow into the valuable member of society you have the potential to be. But if you constantly strive to do your best by considering only those things you have control over, everyone benefits, not just you.

The ancient Stoics always looked to nature to inspire them and they believed that humans were designed by nature to live in harmony with each other. As the saying goes, it takes a village to raise a child, and the Stoics felt that if we are to live according to our nature, we should be caring and compassionate towards one another as a matter of course. Further, we should be doing the right thing because it is the right thing to do, not because we want to be applauded for it or have everyone see that we're 'good.' So, if you're volunteering with a local charity, the only reason you would have to tell others about it would be if you genuinely believed they may be able to help out at all. Otherwise, simply get on with the work and move from one good act to the next and the next.

Or, as Marcus Aurelius puts it, "Like the vine that produces its grapes, seeking nothing more once it has given forth its fruit…so the good man having done one deed well, does not shout it about, but turns to the next good deed, just like the vine turns to bear forth its fruit in due season."

So, while we can see modern mindfulness in the Stoic's approach, they take this further than simply living fully in the moment. You should be staying present *and* paying attention to what you can control and doing that to the best of your ability with a driving motivation of being kind towards your fellow man. Indeed, it was the Stoics who original coined the notion of a 'community of humankind.'

Practical Exercises

- *Check your focus.* Rather than waiting for an event to happen and take a reactive approach to maintaining your focus on what you can control, weave this attitude into your day until it becomes second nature. At regular intervals during the day, ask yourself, "Where is my focus?" You might find it useful to set an alarm to go off every hour to remind yourself to keep your attention in the right place. Remember, if something is outside of your control, it is not your business to give it any energy, freeing you up to give your all to the things you do have agency over.

- *Love everyone.* When someone undermines you at work or cuts in front of you when you're queuing, it's very difficult to remember that we should be acting with compassion towards everyone. This loving kindness meditation will help you practice love towards everyone, regardless of how they treat you. The more you recognise that everyone is worthy of love, the easier it becomes to act with kindness in accordance with your best self.

  Make yourself comfortable with your back supported and close your eyes. Turn your attention to your breath and observe as you inhale and exhale… inhale and exhale…

  And as you breathe, feel yourself filling with peace and perfect love. With every exhalation, breathe out your stress, fear and worry, and with every inhalation draw in more peace and love until you feel a deep, fulfilling calmness. Know that the universe loves you. You are worthy of love. You deserve peace and love at all times.

  As you feel this beautiful sensation of calm and peace, think of someone you love, your partner, your children, your parents, a close friend. Whoever you think about, send that beautiful peace in their direction. See them being filled with love and harmony until they are as calm and happy as you are in this moment.

Do this again for all your close loved ones.

Now move on to people you are not so close to. Perhaps your colleagues, your neighbours, the person who regularly serves you at your favourite restaurant. Send this love and peace towards them, filling them up with calm, peace and contentment.

Finally, think about those who have done you wrong, those you do not like, those who have made your life difficult. They, too, deserve love, so send them the same waves of love and peace, accepting them for who they are and knowing that they are worthy of love because they have taught you valuable lessons and helped you become the person you are today.

When you have finished sending love to everyone who needs it, sit a little longer, feeling this beautiful, peaceful energy.

When you are ready, open your eyes, knowing that this love and peace is always with you.

Summary

Being Stoic in your mindfulness means that not only do you live in the present moment, you combine this with solely focusing on what is under your control and acting with love, kindness and compassion at all times.

- Regularly check your focus throughout the day so you only care about what you can control.
- Do the loving kindness meditation whenever you feel in need of extra love or need to remind yourself that we are all worthy of love.

CHAPTER THIRTEEN

EVERYTHING IN MODERATION

"In your actions, don't procrastinate. In your conversations, don't confuse. In your thoughts, don't wander. In your soul, don't be passive or aggressive. In your life, don't be all about business."
—Marcus Aurelius

The ancient Greeks and Romans were notorious for their huge parties. So many movies depict decadent orgies, massive indulgences in the pleasures of the flesh, symbolic of a society that knew how to celebrate in style.

On the surface, such parties would seem counter to a Stoic way of life, so it may surprise you to learn that Seneca owned an incredible 300 tables, which he kept solely for the purpose of entertaining. These weren't just any old tables either. They were made of ivory, an expensive, luxurious item.

He wasn't the only ancient philosopher who enjoyed the finer things in life. Cato was fond of unwinding with a drink, as was Socrates. It's a pretty safe bet to assume Marcus Aurelius and Epictetus were the same.

So given that our view of Stoicism is one of a more ascetic lifestyle, how on earth can you square that with the fact that the Stoics loved their wine?

There's one little detail that explains it all. While we tend to drink our wine as it comes, the Greeks and Romans always diluted their wine with water. In fact, if you didn't, you would have been viewed as barbaric and someone with no self-discipline. The Roman poet Hesiod advised that the best way to savour your wine was to mix three parts water to one part of wine, something many of us would view as sacrilegious today, but to the Romans it was the other way round. Only an alcoholic would imbibe neat alcohol.

When we know the full picture, it fits perfectly with what a Stoic lifestyle should be. When you mix water with wine, you get a symbolic action representing one of the essential Stoic virtues: moderation. The Romans and Greeks made their wine strong, so it didn't take much for you to get drunk on it. So if you wanted to enjoy this simple pleasure to its fullest, it made sense to dilute it so the taste wasn't so strong and you could drink more of it without getting intoxicated.

It's an important metaphor for how you should be living a Stoic life. You can have whatever you want, but it's best taken in moderation. This way, you don't risk being seduced away from a virtuous path onto one that is solely about the pursuit of pleasure, diverting your focus away from what is under your control and instead placing it on chasing the next thrill, meaning you will never be satisfied.

Practical Exercises

- ✓ *Water down your vices.* Make a list of what vices, bad habits or indulgences you allow yourself to have. Think about the things you know your best self wouldn't do, but they're your weakness and possibly the only 'bad' thing you do, so you make allowances for that single thing.

  I am not going to tell you that you have to give that thing up or, even worse, go cold turkey. Yes, we've discussed how you should embrace difficulties and make yourself undergo hardship to prepare yourself for the worst, but that doesn't mean you should deny yourself everything that makes you happy. (Now, if your vices are making you miserable, then your Stoic philosophy means you'll want to do something about that, but this is not the purpose of this particular exercise.)

  Once you've written out your vice(s), think about a way in which you can water it down.

So, for example, if you like fizzy drinks, can you switch to diet or even flavoured fizzy water? If you like sugar in your tea or coffee, trying halving the amount you use and gradually cutting back. If you love to unwind in front of the television, alternate evenings watching with reading a good book. You could start by reading the works of the ancient Stoics to give you further inspiration. If you go out for a big night with your friends, alternate your alcoholic drinks with non-alcoholic ones. If you enjoy going to the movies with your partner, try going by yourself on occasion.

You can also apply this to the things you do that are good for you. If you spend every day at the gym, give yourself a rest day or try doing a gentler exercise like yoga or swimming on alternate days. If you work long hours, put some boundaries in place for yourself so that you will finish by a certain time and won't work any longer, or make sure you have a full day off at the weekend without getting caught up in chores and other types of work.

Summary

Moderation in everything is key. Dilute your vices and virtues for a more balanced life that enables you to appreciate everything for what it is.

- Recognise your vices and virtues and find ways to dilute them.

CHAPTER FOURTEEN

BE YOUR BEST SELF

"How easily dazzled and deceived we are by eloquence, job title, degrees, high honours, fancy possessions, expensive clothing, or a suave demeanour. Don't make the mistake of assuming celebrities, public figures, political leaders, the wealthy, or people with intellectual or artistic gifts are necessarily happy… Stop aspiring to be anyone but your own best self: for that does fall within your control."
—Epictetus

As if you haven't already seen just how advanced the Stoics were in their thinking, another aspect of their philosophy that deserves examination is their focus on what we would now term 'soft skills.' Unlike the skills we need to do our job, these are the traits that enable us to facilitate a supportive, productive working environment. As Marcus Aurelius puts it, "These are the characteristics of the rational soul: self-awareness, self-examination, and self-determination. It reaps its own harvest… It succeeds in its own purpose…"

If you have been following the exercises given in this book, you should already have a stronger understanding of how you interact with others. You should have been paying attention to your behaviour and how you react when things don't go your way, which will give you a sense of your strengths and weaknesses. While it can be hard to admit to our flaws and examine them for ways in which we can improve, to a Stoic, this is a source of joy. While others may try to keep up with the Joneses in a vain attempt to chase happiness, the Stoic looks at improving themselves rather than their material possessions, a pursuit that brings its own delight and reward.

Heraclitus was a philosopher who had a huge influence on the Stoics. He wrote that "self-deception [is] an awful disease and eyesight a lying sense." With the best will in the world, we can still be blind to our faults and fail to understand our contribution to our life experience. We tend to default to our comfort zone and learned behaviours, justifying our actions to ourselves that this is what's worked for us in the past so is clearly the best way forward.

But if what you've been doing in the past really was working for you, you wouldn't be reading this book, would you?

The Stoics had a very simple, two-step process for developing self-awareness. The first was to be suspicious about your perception and opinion about the people and events you encounter until you've tested them; the second was to take the opposite approach when it comes to evaluating other people's behaviour, by being sympathetic to their plight rather than automatically suspicious of their motives.

Epictetus advises us to take time out before reacting negatively, a little like counting to ten so you don't respond with the full force of your anger when something annoys you. He wrote, "First off, don't let the force of the impression carry you away. Say to it, 'hold up a bit and let me see who you are and where you are from – let me put you to the test.'"

Initially, it can seem difficult to always wait before reacting. In the real world, we don't always have time to breathe before we deal with a situation. But the more we do this, the easier it becomes.

Epictetus repeatedly used a word to reference this process: '*dokimazo.*' This means to test in the sense of someone checking to see whether a gold coin is pure gold or a gem is real. When we take a beat to test the situation and understand what is actually happening without peering through the fog of our preconception, we become better and better at it until we're able to instinctively understand the nuance of a situation and determine the best course to navigate through.

I'll say it again: *the only thing we can control is ourselves.* So it behoves you to act as compassionately and without judgement as possible while giving the other person the benefit of the doubt.

Marcus Aurelius advised, "Whenever you take offense at someone's wrongdoing, immediately turn to your own similar failings, such as seeing money as good, or pleasure, or a little fame – whatever form it takes. By thinking on this, you'll quickly forget your anger, considering also what compels them – for what else could they do? Or, if you are able, remove their compulsion."

If you are a leader in your field, or aspire to be, this is particularly important. People in positions of power are notorious for allowing that power to corrupt them. I'm sure you can think of a manager you've worked with who demotivated you and made it difficult for you to want to do your best. Yet Aurelius, one of the most powerful Roman emperors to have ever lived, was known for his compassion and humanity towards those around him.

As a Stoic, Aurelius believed we're all apprentices of life, constantly learning and never able to say we've conquered it because there are always more challenges to come. All we can do is our best, even when it seems that others have got it in for us.

He used wrestling as a metaphor to illustrate this point: "When your sparring partner scratches or headbutts you, you don't then make a show of it, or protest, or view him with suspicion or as plotting against you. And yet you keep an eye on him, not as an enemy or with suspicion, but with a healthy avoidance… You should act this way with all things in life. We should give a pass to many things with our fellow trainees. For, as I've said, it's possible to avoid without suspicion or hate."

If you can view life as a game and the people around you as your fellow competitors, with happiness as the prize, it becomes easier to make allowances for other people's weaknesses.

This ancient attitude has found its way into modern psychology. The notion of emotional intelligence arose from the methods of being suspicious of our own assumptions and judgments and having sympathy towards what someone else might be going through and trying to see things from their perspective instead of your own.

This is a lifelong practice and builds upon what we discussed in the chapter about taking the view from above. When you take Plato's view, you look at everything going on in the world – births, deaths, marriages, divorces, war, peace, crime, punishment, all possible combinations of the human experience balanced by their opposite and all containing a lesson and a striving towards balance.

This ebb and flow of polar opposites frequently causes us stress and friction, yet this is the natural way of the world and something we should welcome. All these events offer us the chance to engage with them to the fullest, learning more about ourselves and the world around us so we can be our most productive and happiest. They all give us the chance to be our very best self, no matter how challenging the current situation.

Seneca recommends that we should all "find our own Cato." This is someone you admire for the way they live their life and against whom we can measure up to become our best selves. Seneca said, "We can remove most sins if we have a witness standing by as we are about to go wrong. The soul should have someone it can respect, by whose example it can make its inner sanctum more inviolable."

Imagine your Cato is standing by your shoulder at all times. Would they approve of the way you're behaving or could they give you advice on how to improve?

This constant attention on how you can be your best self is at the heart of self-awareness and helps you develop your emotional intelligence. Over time, you'll find yourself become more even-tempered and self-controlled, able to work with others in a way that is just and harmonious and supports them to be the best they can be.

If you aspire to make the most of everything life has to offer by being your best self, you *need* your own Cato.

A common theme within Stoicism is to live according to nature, and this is something we've discussed a number of times throughout this book. This is particularly important as your Stoic practice develops and deepens, because we learn what is in our own nature and how we can nurture our desired traits and channel our more negative qualities in a positive direction.

As Seneca wrote, "Let us keep to the way which Nature has mapped out for us, and let us not swerve therefrom. If we follow Nature, all is easy and unobstructed; but if we combat Nature, our life differs not a whit from that of men who row against the current."

At first glance, this seems like a recipe for disaster. I mean, people are crude, selfish, mean, nasty... But while we may have learned behaviours and base impulses, the Nature the Stoics referred to was our gifts of logic and reason, our ability to rise above our instincts to act with care and deliberation.

This was best defined by Michel Dew, a modern Stoic scholar, who defined 'Human Nature' as "the condition of a human who is expressing the very best in his or her development, that is their ultimate 'best self'. They are growing and changing in an effort to reach the ultimate goal for a human being."

Thus, when you aspire to be yourself, you're not acting in a way that is unnatural for you. You are not trying to force yourself to be something you're not. You are, in fact, following the path that is your natural course and when you do what comes naturally, life becomes that much easier, regardless of the obstacles coming in your way. Indeed, to a Stoic, when you accept the limits and frustrations of your life and work with them rather than railing against them, that's when you are truly free.

As you continue on this journey towards self-awareness, you may well discover things about yourself you were previously unaware of. It may even be that you realise you're in the wrong career, for example, or there are things you should do that would bring you deep satisfaction but have not had the courage until now to pursue.

The more you learn about your innate inclinations and abilities, the more you can make the most of them to live a Stoically natural life. If you try to be something you're not, or attempt to do something for which you are not currently equipped, you'll make yourself miserable – and likely those around you too. But if you're living in harmony with your true self, you'll find you naturally gravitate towards where you're meant to be.

According to the Stoics, greed is not a natural desire, because it always drives us to want more and can never be satisfied. As such, if you allow yourself to be ruled by greed and continue to chase wealth, power and physical pleasures, you'll only be disappointed. You'll never be satisfied with what you have and can only ever be frustrated.

In any case, as Seneca puts it, wealth and poverty are all relative: "The man who restrains himself within the bounds set by nature will not notice poverty; the man who exceeds these bounds will be pursued by poverty, however rich he is."

In the first chapter of this book, you were advised to seek out misfortune. This is because you could lose everything at any given moment, so if you are prepared for it, you are more likely to have the fortitude to withstand the loss. When you stop constantly chasing an elusive definition of happiness and simply focus on yourself, you achieve a balance and contentment that are priceless.

As part of your quest to be your best self, you should approach your mundane, daily life with the same intensity and focus as if you were training for a marathon or concert performance. To a Stoic, no activity is more important than another – they all deserve the same care and attention in order for you to be your best. Being your best self is a habit you can develop through practice and determination and one anyone can acquire.

Like Epictetus said, "Desire and aversion, though powerful, are but habits. And we can train ourselves to have better habits. Restrain the habit of being repelled by all those things that aren't within your control, and focus instead on combating things within your power that are not good for you."

One way in which you can develop good habits is assessing your weaknesses and doing the opposite. Perhaps you love going out every night and getting drunk. Switch the alcohol for non-alcoholic drinks for a while and see the difference it makes. Maybe you have an irrational fear of spiders. Look into how you can overcome this so that while you may never love the creatures, you can tolerate them – you may even end up keeping one as a pet. They're surprisingly easy to care for!

Stoics placed a high emphasis on the truth and there's nothing more important than being honest with yourself. When you kid yourself about something, like staying in a relationship that is making you miserable or working in a job you hate, you become disconnected from your natural self and lose your way. A Stoic is brutally honest with themselves and others (although they are tactful in how they express that truth to those around them, being mindful of other people's circumstances.)

Epictetus advised you to "see things for what they really are, thereby sparing yourself the pain of false attachments and avoidable devastation." After all, it doesn't matter how we perceive something. Our perception doesn't change reality, so it is better for us to be honest with ourselves about the world about us and take Plato's view at all times. Instead of avoiding things that make us feel uncomfortable, actively examine those events causing us pain. When you face up to the reality of loss and disappointment, you break free from the chains of illusion and make it easier for yourself to be your best and stay alert at all times to ensure your motives and actions are in line with your nature.

It can be difficult to maintain this honesty with ourselves, particularly when we know tough times are on their way. But sticking your head in the sand and pretending everything will be fine will not help anyone and stunts your spiritual and emotional growth. Your best self knows how to weather the storm because it understands that this is temporary, as is everything else you experience in life.

Remember when we examined *amor fati* and how to turn obstacles into opportunities. Everything in life is an opportunity to be your best self. The onus is on you to rise to the challenge at all times. As Marcus Aurelius said,

"Loss is nothing else but change, and change is Nature's delight."

Death is the ultimate loss and the one thing many of struggle to deal with, even if we have a resilient attitude to everything else we've experienced. But Seneca told us we should not fear death, because "if you regard your last day not as a punishment but as a law of nature, the breast from which you have banished the dread of death no fear will dare to enter."

Death is the ultimate motivating force for us to be our best selves, because if we can truly say on our death bed that we always did our best, death holds no power over us.

The entire process of being our best arises from following our inner nature, and the cycle of life is part of that natural process. If you become in tune with your nature, it is easy to always choose the action or thought that is in accordance with your best self, whilst recognising that this is an ongoing process and a journey with no final destination beyond death.

You excel by knowing your personal limits and paying attention to only what's in your control. Following a Stoic philosophy in every waking moment of your life means you have a constant commitment to seeking the truth in reality and acting with kindness and respect as part of your responsibility to society at large. Accept death as a natural part of life and know that every new day is a gift you should be grateful for.

This is how you become your best self and fulfil your potential.

Practical Exercises

- *Change your perception.* Think about an argument or disagreement you've recently been involved in. In your journal, create a mind map of the situation. First, look at your own motives and actions. Try and be as objective as possible, as if you were discussing someone else. What did you do wrong? What could you have done differently? Why do you think you behaved in the way you did? What other explanations might there be for your behaviour? What would a Stoic approach have looked like?

  Next, look at the motives and actions of the other person. What are the possible explanations for why they did what they did? What might be a factor for them that you are unaware of? What might be going on in their life that impacted their reactions to you?

  When you are finished, choose the kindest explanation you can come with for the other party's behaviour and the harshest explanation for your own.

  How does this change your understanding of the situation?

What will you do differently when something similar occurs in the future?

- *Find your own Cato.* In your journal, write a description of someone you know whom you admire and hold in high esteem. Why do you feel that way about them? What do they do that makes them worthy of your respect? What is it about their behaviour you would like to emulate?

  Now detail what your best self looks like. Work with the person you are and don't include qualities you feel 'ought' to be there because other people will like them. Who are you now and what would the best version of that look like? Are you successful? What does that success look like? Are you wealthy or content with just having enough to pay the bills? How do you treat other people? What would your life be like if you were always this best version of yourself?

  Now think about a situation recently that you found difficult to handle. How would your best self have reacted? How might things have been different if your best self was in that situation?

  Every day for a week, write in your journal in the evening. First, detail what happened and then write it as if your best self had experienced that day. How would it have changed your day?

Repeat this exercise until you only have to write one version of the day because you have been at your best at all times.

- *Actively oppose your flaws.* Make a list of all your weaknesses, bad habits and undesirable traits. Choose one and come up with a way in which you can do the opposite to replace your negative tendencies with a more positive action. Maybe you love chocolate. Find an alternative healthy food you can snack on. Perhaps you're always late. Set your alarms ten minutes early and your clocks ten minutes fast to help you get ahead of yourself and arrive on time.

  Whatever you choose, think about what your best self would do and train yourself in that habit.

Summary

Aim to be your best self at all times and work on developing positive habits in accordance with your true nature.

- Change your perception by examining a recent situation from all angles.
- Find your own Cato to help you make choices in accordance with your best self.
- Plan out a strategy to help you actively correct bad habits and negative thinking.

CHAPTER FIFTEEN

FINAL THOUGHTS

"That's why the philosophers warn us not to be satisfied with mere learning, but to add practice and then training. For as time passes we forget what we learned and end up doing the opposite, and hold opinions the opposite of what we should."
—Epictetus

After reading this book, you might be wondering where to start because there's so much there to do to be truly Stoic, but it is important to remember that Stoicism is a practical philosophy. It is meant to be learned through living. If you pick just one exercise that resonates with you and start with that one, you are already on your way.

You do not have to do everything at once. Even if you only take tiny steps, you will eventually reach your destination. This isn't a race. The more you work towards a

Stoic way of being, the easier it becomes and you won't worry about whether you can get it all done. You'll simply do it.

Two words are important here: '*Summum Bonum.'* It's a phrase first coined by Cicero and it translates to 'the highest good.' Whatever exercises you choose to do, they should be done with the highest good in mind, which, to the Stoics, meant virtue. Everything that happens to you is an opportunity for you to practice virtue in your response. No matter how painful, frightening or difficult the situation, if you react with virtue, the Stoics believed that the inevitable outcome would be all those things that are so important to us – happiness, fulfilment, success, honour, love, reputation.

In Cicero's words, "The man who has virtue is in need of nothing whatever for the purpose of living well."

According to the Stoics, there were only four virtues that someone should be ruled by: wisdom, courage, justice and temperance. If you allow your thoughts and actions to be determined by these four principles, you cannot go wrong.

Let's examine each of these virtues in more depth, starting with wisdom. The Stoics defined wisdom as the ability to determine what is good, what is evil and what is neither, what things to avoid and what would make no difference to your life of virtue, as well as being able to choose the right course.

Some things matter; a lot of things don't. A Stoic has the wisdom to determine which is which.

Or, as Epictetus put it, "Where then do I look for good and evil? Not to uncontrollable externals, but within myself to the choices that are my own." Between action and your reaction, there is a moment and it is in that moment you have the ability to decide how to respond. That moment is your opportunity to take everything you have learned and put it into practice or forget it all and allow yourself to be ruled by your irrational impulse.

Ultimately, how wise you are comes down to one thing, according to Seneca: "Works not words."

The next Stoic virtue was courage. In Epictetus' *Discourses,* he describes life as being "like a military campaign." By this, he meant we should always be on our guard for symbolic enemies that could disrupt your life. "One must serve on watch, another in reconnaissance, another on the front line… So it is for us—each person's life is a kind of battle, and a long and varied one too."

We all have an important role to play in our own personal battlefield of life. It's a very Stoic way of viewing things. Ultimately, nobody wins at life. We all eventually fall. Yet, despite the fact that death is inevitable, a Stoic continues to fight bravely to be virtuous at all times and not be corrupted by the countless temptations that continually bombard us.

One of the last things Seneca said was that "Nero can kill me, but he cannot harm me." Following a failed plot to overthrow the tyrannical emperor, Nero ordered the deaths of many leading figures, including his adviser, Seneca. While it is unlikely Seneca had anything to do with the plot, Nero was insistent that Seneca should kill himself, so the philosopher did as his ruler commanded.

His death was not easy and he took a long time to carry out Nero's orders, but Seneca died according to the philosophy he'd followed through life, knowing that this was merely another experience to be embraced.

This is an important notion to bear in mind when you are faced with your worst nightmares. You have the ability to stand up and do what's right, even if it costs you your life, because if you do, you cannot be harmed. This requires a lot of courage, particularly if you're going against social norms or the expectations of your loved ones. It takes grit and determination to stand up for what you believe in, but that's the Stoic way.

Even if you do not face the extreme situation Seneca was forced into, do not underestimate the daily battles we all have to deal with. Indeed, if you cannot recognise the conflict around you, the chances are high you need to work more on your self-awareness. When you start to follow a Stoic philosophy, you'll be in conflict with your former self, which will resist change and fight against your desire to improve yourself. You'll have to battle yourself when you go to bed and realise you haven't journaled that day, so you'll need to get up again to write down your thoughts. You'll have to battle against your natural inclination to yell insults at someone who pulls out in front of you in traffic. You'll have to battle against your desire to see an unpleasant colleague get in trouble when they ask you for help that you would rather not give.

Stoic courage goes beyond the obvious. It is that courage that drives everything we do.

You demonstrated courage when you decided to follow a Stoic philosophy. Now you need to continue to be brave as you continue down this path.

The third Stoic virtue is justice, which Marcus Aurelius viewed as the most important and "source of all the other virtues," and Cicero described as "the crowning glory of the virtues." After all, you can be brave but use that bravery to do stupid, dangerous things. You can be try to be wise but fail to take in the big picture.

Just as with the other virtues, the Stoic interpretation of justice goes beyond the superficial. Cicero examined this principle in great depth in his work "*De Officiis.*" Translated as "*On Moral Duties,*" Cicero described justice in this text as the bond that holds society together and builds community.

He gave a number of points that were important to being just, which included never harming anyone and having respect for communal property because everyone needed to enjoy it while equally respecting private ownership. He said that none of us was born to be an individual alone; we are all here to treat each other well and follow our nature to act for the good of society as a whole.

Justice means always acting in good faith and being steadfast and true. Conversely, injustice is anything that injures or harms another. Cicero felt that the main reason people behaved in an unjust manner was because they were greedy and hurt others in order to get something they wanted. So, living in accordance with Stoic philosophy means that you should always strive to act with the good of the whole in mind, putting the needs of society before your own.

This doesn't mean you should martyr yourself for the sake of others' happiness. (Remember – focus only on that which you can control. You have no control over someone else's feelings.) However, a common thread throughout Stoic texts is the belief that everything is part of the whole, so as Marcus Aurelius puts it, "what injures the hive injures the bee."

Epictetus is even clearer. He wrote, "Seeking the very best in ourselves means actively caring for the welfare of other human beings." When you actively seek to do the right thing and avoid harming others, you become a just person.

Moving on to the notion of temperance, to a Stoic, this is all about finding that balance between overindulgence and asceticism, which will lead to a state of contented tranquillity. Finding that happy medium between chasing what you want and denying yourself pleasures will lead to misery. While it is important to experience times of deliberate hardship (as discussed in Chapter One), when you do this because you want to maintain an appearance of being a good person instead of simply experiencing it in the now, it's just as dangerous as giving in to temptation all the time.

Marcus Aurelius observed that "most of what we say and do is not essential. If you can eliminate it, you'll have more time, and more tranquillity. Ask yourself at every moment, 'Is this necessary?'"

If you have everything you need, you are truly rich, regardless of how much money you have in the bank. The only limit to wealth, according to Seneca, is "First, having what is essential, and second, having what is enough."

Stoics frequently referred to temperance as 'self-control' and they meant this on a holistic level. This self-control works on every level, from your ability to control your spending and consumerism, your ability to show compassion towards the people around you, even when they're behaving badly, and your ability to look for the opportunity in every obstacle and welcome it as a chance to learn and grow.

Strive for temperance and balance so you aren't relying on external things to make you happy or risk something bad happening, which can destroy your happiness.

That's it. Those four virtues are your key to a happy, fulfilling life. If it sounds simple, that's because it's meant to. The Stoics were all about breaking things down to their most basic form rather than dressing things up in complicated verbosity.

If you take only one thing away from this book, let it be the knowledge that you cannot control what happens around you, but you have full mastery of your response, and that response should be born out of courage, temperance, justice and wisdom. When you accept your lack of control, but know that your virtuous actions contribute to building a better world, it's a genuinely liberating feeling. It doesn't matter what happens; you *always* have the ability to do the right thing.

To finish, I'll leave you with this thought from Epictetus:

"Now is the time to get serious about living your ideals. How long can you afford to put off who you really want to be? Your nobler self cannot wait any longer. Put your principles into practice – now. Stop the excuses and the procrastination. This is your life! … Decide to be extraordinary and do what you need to do – now."

He was right. You cannot afford to wait. You've only got a limited amount of time left on this earth.

So make the most of it. Start living like a Stoic and make the most of the gifts you were born with.

THANKS FOR READING

I hope that you enjoyed reading this book and that the practical exercises have been valuable.

If you are looking for more daily practical exercises, as well as quotes, journaling prompts, self-reflections and more, I encourage you to check out my journaling book, *Practicing Stoicism: A Daily Journal with Meditation Practices, Self-Reflections and Ancient Wisdom from Marcus Aurelius.*

Also, be sure to check out my email list, where I am constantly adding tons of value. You will also receive my three-page cheat sheet that you can use for reference as you move forward on your Stoic path.

You can sign up here: bouchardpublishing.com/stoicism

Kindest regards,
Jason Hemlock

Printed in the USA
CPSIA information can be obtained
at www.ICGtesting.com
LVHW010726271223
767526LV00006B/172

9 781777 184940

The Economy and Business Environment of Vietnam

Roderick Macdonald
Editor

The Economy and Business Environment of Vietnam

palgrave
macmillan

Editor
Roderick Macdonald
University of Quebec at Montreal
Montréal, QC, Canada

ISBN 978-3-030-49973-0 ISBN 978-3-030-49974-7 (eBook)
https://doi.org/10.1007/978-3-030-49974-7

This Palgrave Macmillan imprint is published by the registered company Springer Nature Switzerland AG
The registered company address is: Gewerbestrasse 11, 6330 Cham, Switzerland

Preface

This book was completed in the midst of the 2020 pandemic.

In the current phase, we are spending more time at home with family than ever before, reminding us that wealth and the economy are not the most important things in life. However, when this situation reaches its end game, we will also be reminded that wealth and the economy, although not everything, do help us in the pursuit of happiness. Medicine and health services are founded on science, but also upon prosperity. Feeding, sheltering, and educating our families require the supply chains that bring food and other resources to our homes. The creation of beauty in music, visual arts, and the written word requires leisure, again dependent upon some degree of affluence. Power, whether exercised to subdue others, or channeled to the service of others, ultimately reposes upon wealth.

We will be less rich when the pandemic ends.

So far, the twenty-first century is a rerun of the twentieth century, although we have avoided a world war so far. Punctuated by a financial crisis, the first twenty years have been marked by rapid technological and business changes reaching deep into our daily lives as consumers. With the onset of the pandemic, Western countries appear to have repeated the same errors and blame games as in 1918–1919. In contrast, many East Asian countries, more severely tested by SARS, appear to have been more proficient in dealing with the situation.

Our world's economy may be quite different in the aftermath of the pandemic, or it may remain "the same, only more so." The aftermath of the 1918 pandemic was an economic boom in Europe and North America, followed by a worldwide bust that was reinforced and prolonged by an ideology of protectionism and autarky. Will this repeat? Today, as in 1930, there are leaders who argue that all of our problems are explained by our openness to the rest of humanity. Many people believe them. After the pandemic, as before, the greatest enemy of humanity will be ignorance.

What is certain is that the global linkage of trade will have been interrupted, and that there will be delays and difficulties in priming the pump of our problematic symbiosis with nature. Possibly China will find itself somewhat isolated, although currently it is exerting great efforts to overcome widespread reticence to shared trade and investment ventures. China is not the only game in East Asia. It would be a pity if all East Asia were to find itself isolated from the rest of the world, or if East Asia were to become a single trade bloc economically pitted against the rest of the planet. Hopefully, this book will help to open hearts and minds to the business opportunities of the East.

Ho Chi Minh City, Vietnam
April 2020

Roderick Macdonald

Contents

Notes on Contributors

Victor L. Kane is Associate Professor and Head of RMIT Asia Graduate Centre, Vietnam. He acquired ten years of business experience in analysis and sales, as well as an executive, before entering the academic world in the USA. He has published about 15 articles and conferences.

Roderick Macdonald is Retired Professor of Management and Technology at ESG-UQAM, Canada. He continues teaching international business and has published Eurocritical (2018) and Southeast Asia and the ASEAN Economic Community (2019) with Palgrave Macmillan since retiring.

Robert McClelland is Associate Professor and Head of the Department of Management at RMIT University, Vietnam. He has authored six books and well over a hundred refereed publications and has produced 15 articles and conferences in the past five years.

Trung Q. Nguyen is Discipline Lead of the International Business Program at RMIT, Vietnam. He is co-author of *Business Forecasting* (2016) as well as author or co-author of more than 20 academic articles and conferences since 2007.

Hiep Cong Pham is Lecturer in logistics and supply chain management at RMIT Vietnam. He has previous experience in management, consulting and lecturing in IT and operations optimization in Australia and Vietnam. He has published 15 articles since 2013.

Nghĩa Huỳnh Phước is Associate Dean for Marketing, School of International Business, University of Economics Ho Chi Minh City, Vietnam. He has published six articles in the past three years and acquired ten years' experience in sales and event management before entering academia. He remains active in the business world as a consultant and as Vice President & General Secretary of the Vietnam Marketing Association.

Burkhard N. Schrage is Discipline Lead for Management at RMIT, Vietnam. Previously at the Wharton School and at Singapore Management University, he has extensive experience in the finance industry in Australia, Brazil, and France. With multiple awards for research and teaching excellence, he has published particularly on finance in emerging markets and privatization.

Pham Van Thuy is Lecturer and Vice Chair of the Department of World History at Vietnam National University, Vietnam. He is the author of *Beyond Political Skin: Colonial to National Economies in Indonesia and Vietnam 1910s–1960s* (2019) as well as of 30 academic articles and conferences since 2005.

Van-Hong Vu is Lecturer and Researcher at Yncréa Hauts-de-France. She completed her Ph.D. in 2018. She is co-author of three papers on Vietnam's Banking industry in the SSRN e-library pending publication.

List of Figures

List of Tables

CHAPTER 1

Vietnam, Land of Opportunity

Roderick Macdonald

Abstract Vietnam has overcome internal and external difficulties in the twentieth century to create a very inviting business environment as testified both by GDP per capita growth and by foreign direct investment in the twenty-first century. This chapter briefly touches on the different aspects of this environment that are detailed in subsequent chapters: economic policy and performance, participation in value chains, privatization, the market and financial services. It also provides an overview of the history and geography of the country.

Keywords GDP per capita · FDI · Economic freedom · Ease of doing business · Enterprise survey · Policy

1.1 Introduction

Vietnam experienced a very difficult twentieth century. It started the century as a French colony. After the French were repulsed in 1954, Vietnam experienced an internal struggle for power at the same time as

R. Macdonald (✉)
University of Quebec at Montreal, Montréal, QC, Canada
e-mail: macdonald.roderick@isb.edu.vn; macdonald.roderick@uqam.ca

R. Macdonald (ed.), *The Economy and Business Environment of Vietnam*, https://doi.org/10.1007/978-3-030-49974-7_1

one party in that struggle (mostly the North with some support located in Central and Southern Vietnam) fought against the American "helpers". Both the French and American opponents were militarily superior, and the Northern Vietnamese won by accepting an incredibly high number of casualties. This meant that any industrial base acquired under the French was decimated. Although the "American war" ended more than 40 years ago, the US-led embargo dragged on for another two decades. The first 94 years of the century were economically horrendous. Since then, the country has had barely 25 years of normality to build up an industry and skills base. The wars of the twentieth century have also left a legacy of (fading) tension between the hierarchy-oriented North and the market-oriented South. Also, as in many countries in Southeast Asia, locals of Chinese descent are prominent in the economy.

Vietnam's government used the years under embargo to test and discard several doctrinaire communist methods borrowed from Russia and China for dealing with economic policy, from communal farming to command economics. While it is still true that local and central governments can be heavy handed towards their citizens and there is also some evidence of state-related actors carrying out cyber warfare on behalf of well-connected private sector actors (Carr 2017; Lyngaas 2019; Mitre 2019), successive administrations have been realistic and pragmatically visionary in creating an environment that is business-friendly and allows entrepreneurs to flourish. Several chapters in this book detail this, especially Chapter 2 on the evolution of economic policy in Vietnam, Chapter 3 on the privatization process and Chapter 6 on financial services.

Vietnam now has become a land of business opportunity for locals and for foreigners. Vietnam is worthy of consideration by any business looking to expand internationally, particularly into Asia.

Southeast Asia is a fast-growing region and, of the larger economies in that region, Vietnam and the Philippines are the fastest growing. Cambodia, Laos and Myanmar are also growing as quickly, but have small economies that are far less developed. Of the more advanced economies in the region, only Malaysia exhibits a comparable growth rate. Between Vietnam and the Philippines, who are neck and neck in economic growth, Vietnam is clearly far friendlier towards foreign business investment than the Philippines. Since their devastating experience of free trade with the United States at the time of independence, the Philippine business elite has influenced government policy to limit foreign competition and ownership. The "People Power Revolution" did not change this. Since the early

1990s, Vietnam has gradually done the opposite, both opening up to foreign investment and increasing the portion of the economy that is market oriented. There is increasing opportunity in Vietnam.

Vietnam does indeed have a communist government. However, governments are run in practice and not in theory. The contrast with regimes in other countries is that the politicking is done within the Communist Party. Although the quest for power involves instances of sponsor–patron relationships, it is far less damaging than the feudal-like patronage to be found in countries such as the Philippines. Politics in Vietnam also appears to be less dumbed down than it appears to be in countries like Canada and the United States. Finally, the fading memories of the poverty of the previous century perhaps mean that more politicians are patriotic than in other countries. Whatever the reasons, the track record of Vietnam's government is one of enlightened economic policies and respect for the property of foreign firms. Government management of the COVID-19 pandemic illustrates its competence and willingness to act as necessary, although no one foresees what the state of the pandemic will be when these words are read. Bereft of the resources that allowed Singapore, Korea and Taiwan to do extensive testing, the government of Vietnam was the first to act outside of mainland China and Taiwan. A few local lockdowns were imposed in early January 2020. There was effectively no classroom instruction after mid-January because the government interdicted it after Tet, the Lunar New Year holiday. Most schools moved quickly online, and the government informed citizens how to slow the transmission of the virus from hand washing to separation and masks, including a catchy video clip that went viral in several countries.

Tourists arriving by air from abroad who apply for visa on arrival are surprised to see uniformed men and women processing their documents. They may think they have landed in a police state. However, the clerks handling the documents are employees of the airport, not police or military. Many occupations in Vietnam have uniforms. There is no police state atmosphere noticeable even during increasingly severe restrictions with the coronavirus epidemic as of early April 2020. Although the state is officially atheist, it does not impose atheism. Some small municipalities interdict places of worship, and there are reports of mistreatment of Hmong Christians, but this is not representative of the experience of most people across the country. Most Vietnamese are Buddhists, and the world's major religions (in historical order: Hinduism, Judaism, Catholicism, Islam, Protestantism) and Caodaism have places of worship and individuals enjoy freedom to practise their religion in Vietnam.

Although the skills base of Vietnam is limited, that is the nature of a less developed nation. Far more relevant is the "can do" attitude of Vietnamese. This can be seen in all walks of life, from restaurants to the university classroom, from large businesses to small sidewalk businesses with no employees. Vietnamese get things done without worrying about shortage of resources or the accepted methodology. Vietnamese in the diaspora are famous for their success in their new home countries. This could perhaps be ascribed to the selection process of escape from Vietnam in the twentieth century. Surprisingly, however, the same drive and initiative can be found today in Ho Chi Minh City. Vietnamese are intelligent, resourceful and diligent. Rural and low-income urban families see study and knowledge as the path out of poverty. The government spends nearly 6% of GDP and 20% of its budget on education, and Vietnam placed 7th in the world (behind Canada and ahead of Hong Kong) in the 2015 PISA ranking.[1] The United States placed 25th. These rankings are of course imperfect—in particular, about half of Vietnam's students leave school by 15, before the PISA tests are applied, thus biasing the result—but do suggest the strength of basic education in Vietnam, basis for any industrial training.[2]

1.2 The Country of Vietnam

Part of the ASEAN economic community, Vietnam shares a border with China and is a short plane or boat ride away from the East Asia powerhouses of Singapore, Hong Kong, South Korea, Taiwan and Japan.

1.2.1 Geography and Climate

Vietnam is an S-shaped sliver of land stretching south from China along the South China Sea. Laos and Cambodia on its western borders separate Vietnam from Thailand. Much of the western border is mountainous. The country is less than a hundred kilometres wide from Hue to Vinh, but expands in the north and—to a lesser degree—in the south. The largest cities are Ha Noi (the capital city, located in the north) and Ho Chi Minh City (formerly Saigon) in the south, each with about 8 million population. These are the official figures. In the case of Ho Chi Minh City, the real population may be as high as 12 million. Hai Phong (a seaport at about the same latitude as Ha Noi), Can Tho (in the Mekong Delta), Bien Hoa (about 30 kilometres north-west of downtown Ho Chi Minh City) and Da Nang (roughly halfway up the coast) are the next largest cities, in order from 2 million to one million.

The area south of Ho Chi Minh City is dominated by the Mekong Delta with its economy based on farming and fishing. The population of 21.5 million in this region grows slowly as young people seek their fortune in the big cities. The region also faces a double threat. First, new dams along the Mekong to the north, particularly in Laos, affect water levels (DW.com 2019) and thus fishing and rice production, two great economic dynamos of this region. Second, ground subsidence and the spectre of a rising sea level are threats that could obliterate the entire region (Minderhoud et al. 2019).

The Food and Agriculture Organization of the United Nations divides Vietnam into seven different climate zones (FAO 2011); however, this is commonly simplified. North, Central and South Vietnam each has its own weather patterns, although the entire country is tropical. This is complicated by the threefold topology of mountains, jungle and coast. November to April are dry and cold months in the North. Hanoi and much of the North enjoy four seasons. The coldest months in Hanoi are December, January and February with lows around 15 degrees centigrade and highs around 21. From May through October, the weather becomes hot, wet and humid. The rainy season is longer in Ho Chi Minh City, also starting in May but lasting to November. Typhoons reinforce the end of the rainy season during the months of August, September and October, although they usually only affect the North and Central Vietnam. Climate researchers and local people alike say these patterns have become less regular. It will be interesting to see if the changes in the level of economic activity brought about by the COVID-19 impact these variations, or if they are independent of economic activity.

1.2.2 History and Society

Like much of Southeast Asia, Vietnam is characterized by heavily populated plains and coasts and more sparsely populated mountainous regions with distinct ethnic groups. The Kinh represent 85% of the population, while the next most populous ethnic group, the Tay, account for about 2%. The mainstream history of Vietnam revolves around the Kinh, but it is also true that a sixth of the population have different mother tongues and traditions.

Vietnam has a venerable history that stretches far back in time. Various precursors of contemporary China occupied Vietnam and were repulsed many[3] times over the last two thousand years. The French colonization of Indochina, including Vietnam, and the subsequent attempt of the United States to counteract the supposed domino effect of communism spreading from China, should be seen against this historic background. While Ho Chi Minh did acquire a communist ideology from French intelligentsia of the early twentieth century, and the current regime is an administration by the Communist Party of Vietnam, this ideology was an instrument of patriotic efforts to oust foreign occupiers from the country. The years immediately following the withdrawal of US forces were difficult. The Maoist Pol Pot regime in Cambodia had exterminated a quarter of that country's population and was seen as a threat to the Vietnamese, whose troops entered Cambodia on Christmas day 1978, and overwhelmed the Pol Pot army in a couple of weeks. Then, China invaded Vietnam on February 17, 1979, withdrawing by March 18 of that same year. About a half million Chinese troops were stationed along the border throughout the 1980s, harassing with minor actions combined with clandestine sabotage activities and a psychological campaign. In addition to these real and costly military security issues, Vietnam had to deal with economic sanctions (by China 1975-1978 and those led by the United States from 1975 to 1994).

1.3 More Recent Economic Policy and Performance

After reunification in 1975, the government began with the same errors committed by the communist regimes of Russia and China—multi-year plans for a command economy, but by the end of 1978 began to allow some private initiative in farming, with further liberalization through to the mid-1980s. The sixth national congress of Vietnam's Communist Party explicitly acknowledged the role of a "mixed" economy and is considered pivotal for the renovation (đổi mới) of the economy. Implementation was spotty, however, and the country was soon on the road to severe macroeconomic imbalance. Inflation had varied from 25 to 100% in the first half of the 1980s, but skyrocketed to 453% in 1986 and 375% in 1988. Nonetheless, annual production began to increase for several indicator industries such as steel (8%), cement (11%), electricity (11%) and zinc (10%), and Vietnam became a major exporter of rice (Nguyen et al. 2016). In 1989, the government began to push true reform, liberalizing prices and exchange rates as well as curbing state subsidies to state-owned enterprises (Tran 2002; Vu 2014). It also improved macroeconomic management, raising interest rates. These reforms and liberalization of the economy were not seen as a contradiction of socialism. The official party position was that greater economic progress was required before socialism would be possible. Chapter 2 examines the evolution of economic policy in greater detail. Personal experience and convictions have evolved since that time, and while a large part of economic activity (as measured by GDP) remains under the control of the state, efforts to change this are ongoing since 1990 (see Chapter 3).

The economy of Vietnam did not achieve stable growth until 1992. It then surged and has continued through to the present. The US-led trade embargo ended on February 3, 1994. Vietnam became a full member of ASEAN in 1995 and joined the World Trade Organization in 2007. As of March 2020, the country has entered into negotiations for 26 free trade agreements (see ARIC 2020 for a list), the latest of which are the Comprehensive and Progressive Agreement for Trans-Pacific Partnership and the agreement with the European Union ratified by the European government on February 12, 2020. Many domestic firms have adjusted to this change, improving their productivity to compete in both foreign and domestic markets.

Vietnam began presiding the United Nations Security Council in January 2020, in its second term as non-permanent member.

Wealth is imperfectly measured by GDP, which grew at a rate of nearly 10% before slowing to "only" 5% with the Asian financial crisis and has mostly bettered 6% in the current century (see Fig. 1.1). Although agriculture, forestry and fishing continued to grow, their relative importance for the economy has shrunk to around 15% because of the more rapid growth of industry and services typical of development (see Fig. 1.2). However, over 35% of the population still are employed in that sector. The largest categories of goods exported are "machines" (including electronic as well as mechanical machines and parts) at 46%, textiles and clothing including foot and head wear at 24% (AOC 2019). Exports began to surpass GDP in 2016. This is possible because Vietnam imports abundant intermediate goods which it processes, adding some value, and then re-exports (see Fig. 1.3). Samsung alone accounts for over 25% of exports (Nguyen 2019), suggesting there is room for more large foreign

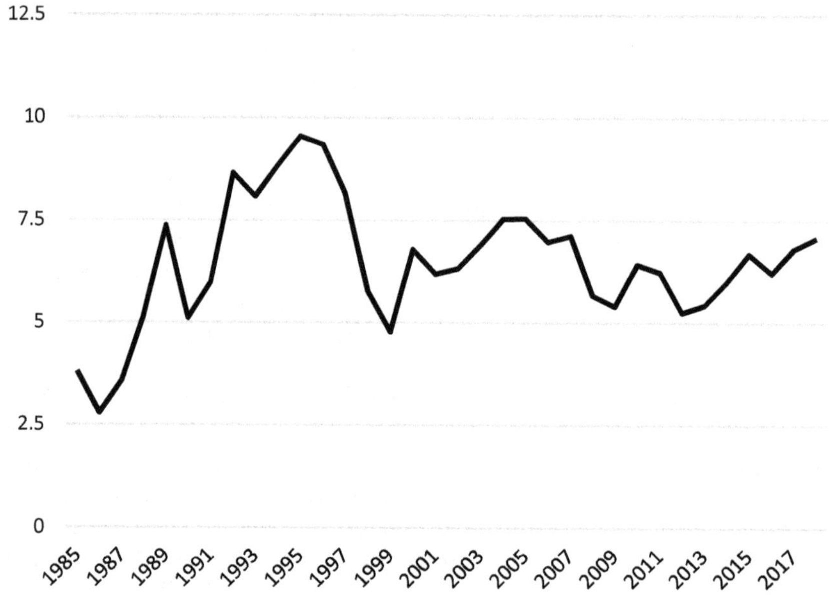

Fig. 1.1 Per cent GDP growth of Vietnam 1985–2018 (*Source* World Bank national accounts data, and OECD National Accounts data files)

investors and certainly a need for Vietnam to diversify its portfolio of foreign investment. Because nearly 46% of exports are "machinery", it might be concluded that the skill level of the country is relatively high, but this would be a misunderstanding of Vietnam's current place in global value chains (see Chapter 4). The domestic value added in information industries has been decreasing in Vietnam while increasing slightly in Singapore and notably in Thailand, as Fig. 1.4 shows. This is a crude indicator[4] of the evolving level of sophistication of Vietnam's economy, and the government is attempting to address this (FDI Vietnam 2020; see also VietnamNet 2018; Vietnam Law and Legal Forum Magazine 2018).

Vietnam is decentralized not only as regards administrative power but also as regards the redistribution of funds without which executive power is mostly theoretical. This helps explain why the Gini coefficient of Vietnam is relatively low. Although there is not the multigenerational accumulation of fortune to be found in Europe, there are rich and extremely rich persons and families. The greater equality in the distribution of wealth is rather at the bottom end. Poor people in a lower-income

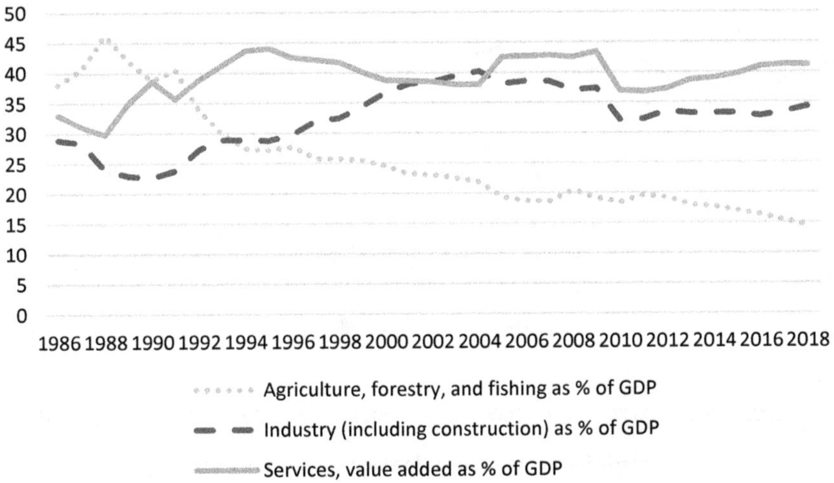

Fig. 1.2 Economic contribution by sector (*Source* World Bank national accounts data, and OECD National Accounts data files)

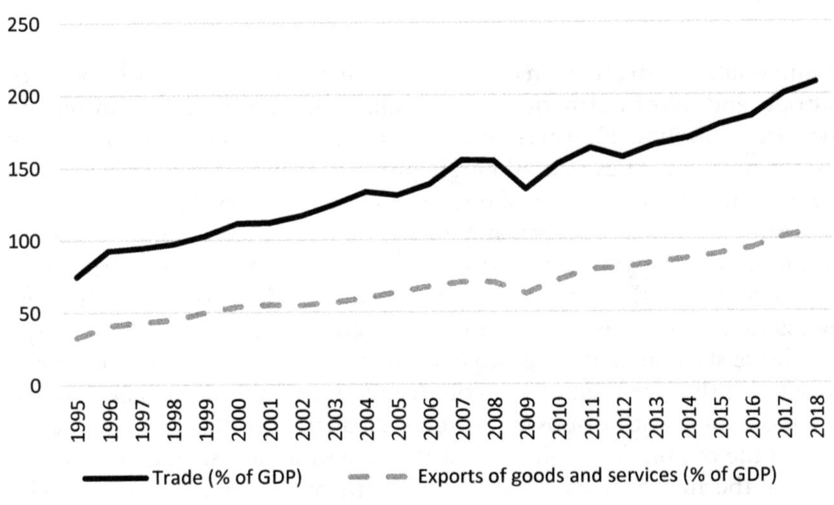

Fig. 1.3 Total trade and total exports as % GDP (*Source* World Bank national accounts data, and OECD National Accounts data files)

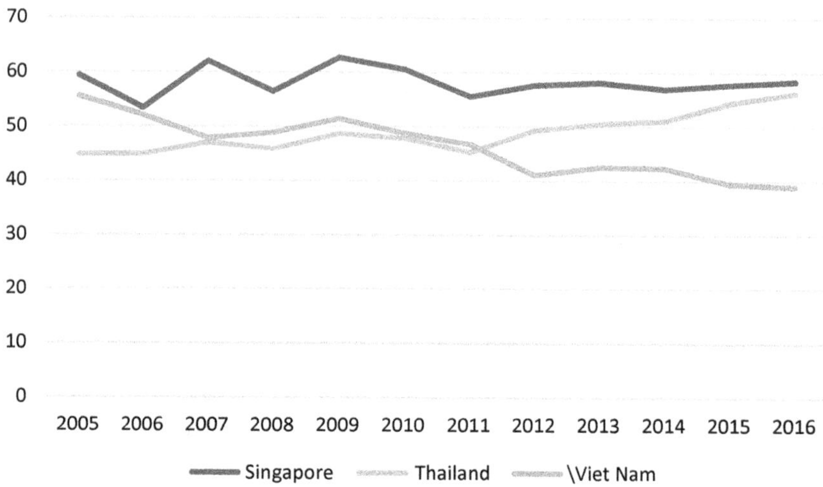

Fig. 1.4 Domestic value added share of gross exports in information industries (*Source* OECD.stat 2020, TIVA principle indicators, https://stats.oecd.org/Index.aspx?DataSetCode=TIVA_2018_C1# [Accessed on February 16, 2020])

country like Vietnam do have lower living standards than the poor of Europe and North America, where some beggars listen to music on their smartphones. However, there is no squalor in Vietnam. There are poorer areas in cities, but they are not drug and crime-infested areas breeding future generations of poverty. On the contrary, because increases of wealth have been recent and rapid, opulent new developments are incentives for the young to work to better their capacity to earn rather than a reminder that they are doomed to an underclass where the only successful role models are exceptional athletes, entertainers lucky enough to achieve stardom and drug dealers. The trend is towards greater income equality in the city than in the countryside (see Table 1.1). The result is a demographic with disposable income distinct from that of other countries in the region: large numbers with some modest discretionary means, few for the luxury market. Also, the Vietnamese consumer seems relatively sophisticated when it comes to sifting information from hype in advertising. The Vietnamese consumer and other aspects of marketing in Vietnam are described in Chapter 5.

Table 1.1 Index of income inequality distribution (Gini index) by region and year

	2002	*2004*	*2006*	*2008*	*2010*	*2012*	*2014*	*2016*	*Prel. 2018*
WHOLE COUNTRY	0.42	0.42	0.424	0.434	0.433	0.424	0.43	0.431	0.424
Urban	0.41	0.41	0.393	0.404	0.402	0.385	0.397	0.391	0.372
Rural	0.36	0.37	0.378	0.385	0.395	0.399	0.398	0.408	0.407
Red River Delta				0.411	0.408	0.393	0.407	0.401	0.392
Northern midlands and mountain areas				0.401	0.406	0.411	0.416	0.433	0.443
North Central area and Central coastal area				0.381	0.385	0.384	0.385	0.393	0.383
Central highlands				0.405	0.408	0.397	0.408	0.439	0.44
Southeast				0.41	0.414	0.391	0.397	0.387	0.373
Mekong River Delta				0.395	0.398	0.403	0.395	0.405	0.399

Source GSO

Vietnam channelled massive funds into capital investment in the past, nearing 40% before the global financial crisis. Recently, the ratio of capital formation to GDP has approximated that of neighbouring countries (see Fig. 1.5). ICOR, a sometimes misleading measure of return on investment, was quite high (meaning poorer returns), although it has dropped somewhat in recent years to 5.97 in 2018 (GSO 2019). An effort to extend more credit private enterprise as opposed to state-owned enterprises probably has helped. Figure 1.6 shows how domestic credit to the private sector has increased rapidly from 1998 to levels comparable with neighbouring countries (in contrast to the Philippines). However, one legacy of overly generous credit to state-owned enterprise in the past is a high ratio of non-performing loans on the books of Vietnam's banks (Katagiri 2019). Vietnam lags its neighbours in financial freedom, a measure of government (as opposed to market) influence about upon finance, but its score has increased throughout this century (see Fig. 1.7). Chapter 6 provides an overview of financial services available in Vietnam. Foreign funding began to enter the country in 1988 and has continued to grow quickly, with the two interruptions of the Asian financial crisis in 1997 and the global financial crisis ten years later. Much of the funding that returned to Southeast Asia after 1997 targeted mergers and acquisitions. These were restricted in Vietnam, and as a result, FDI into Vietnam remained flat for nearly a decade after the Asian crisis. It then spiked before the global crisis, faltered and then continued to grow (see

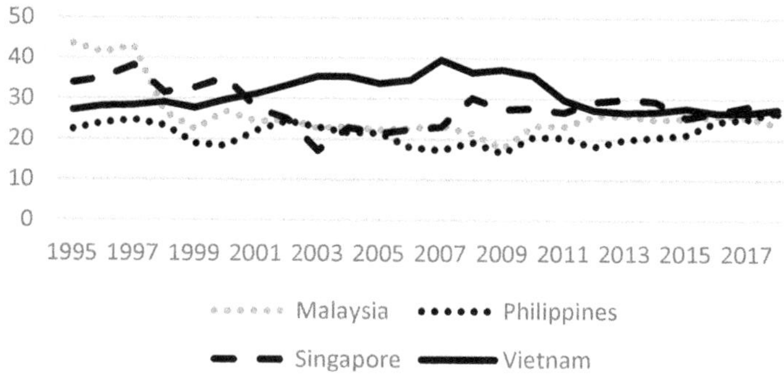

Fig. 1.5 Gross Capital Formation (*Source* World Bank national accounts data, and OECD National Accounts data files)

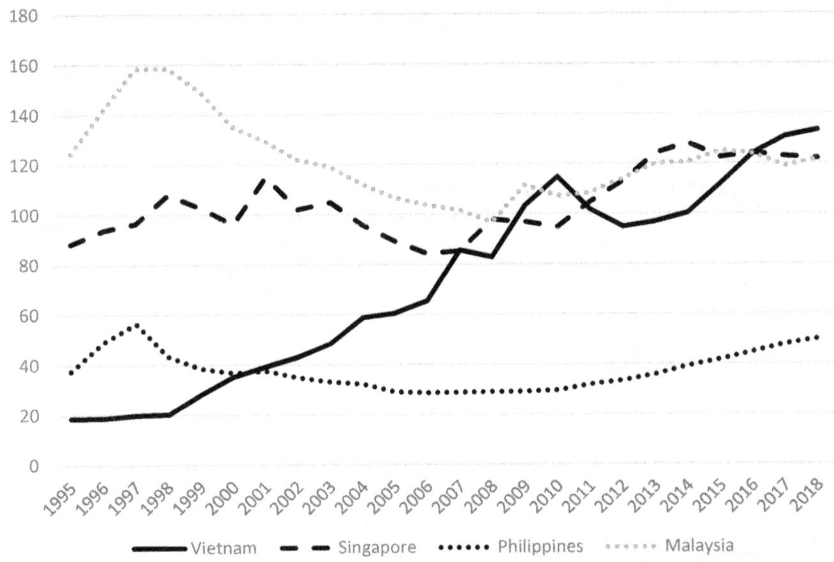

Fig. 1.6 Domestic credit to private sector as per cent of GDP (*Source* International Monetary Fund, International Financial Statistics and data files, and World Bank and OECD GDP estimates)

Fig. 1.8). Although greenfield investment dropped in 2019, clearly businesses have been bullish about Vietnam's potential in the recent past compared to most other countries in the region (see Fig. 1.9). This book argues that the proximate future is also bright, and provides some preliminary information for businesses and researchers interested in that economy.

1.4 Doing Business in Vietnam

How easy or difficult is it to run a business in Vietnam? Scoring 69.8 in the 2020 Ease of Doing Business Index, Vietnam trails Singapore, Malaysia and Thailand (ranking 2nd, 14th and 23rd worldwide, respectively) but does better than Indonesia (slightly) and the Philippines. The government is trying to improve the ease with which business is carried out by reducing paperwork, moving procedures online, simplifying taxes and tax procedures, and disseminating decisions of business court cases. There is much room for improvement in protecting minority investors,

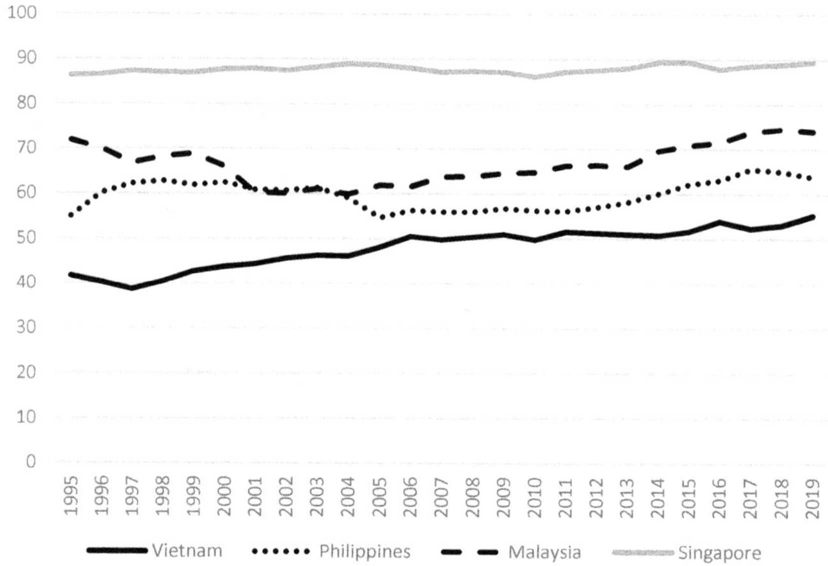

Fig. 1.7 Financial Freedom (*Source* Heritage Foundation and Wall Street Journal 2019)

resolving insolvencies, enforcing contracts and reducing the burden—time and money—of taxes. (See World Bank 2019. The index score for Vietnam is based on Ho Chi Minh City data.)

Vietnam has improving scores for economic freedom over the past 25 years, although the country marginally lags the Philippines and the World average (Fig. 1.10).[5] Table 1.2 shows that the weaknesses of Vietnam with respect to the Philippines lie in government spending and fiscal health, on the one hand, and financial and investment freedom, on the other.

Government spending is a factor in calculating the economic freedom index. The score for it diminishes quadratically as the ratio of government spending to GDP increases. Expenditure by the government of Vietnam reached 38% of GDP in 2009 and 2010, but has decreased since then, with 26% projected for 2020. The score is based on the values for the most recent three years available. Government spending has amounted to 28.3% of the country's output (GDP) over the past three years (in contrast to the Philippines' 20.1%) (Heritage Foundation and Wall Street Journal, 2020).

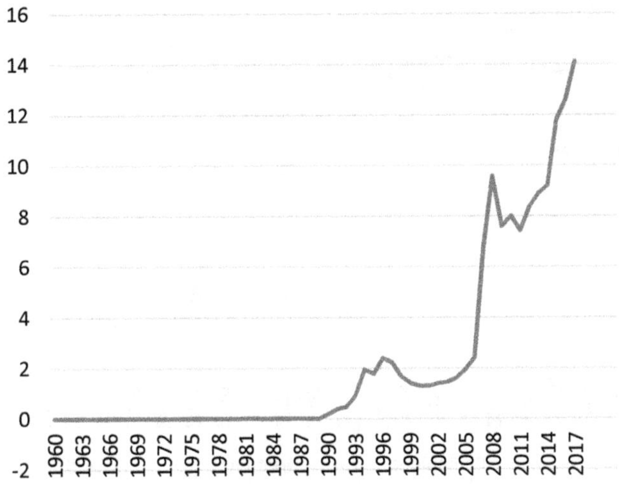

Fig. 1.8 Vietnam FDI 1960–2017 (*Source* International Monetary Fund, Balance of Payments database, supplemented by data from the United Nations Conference on Trade and Development and official national sources)

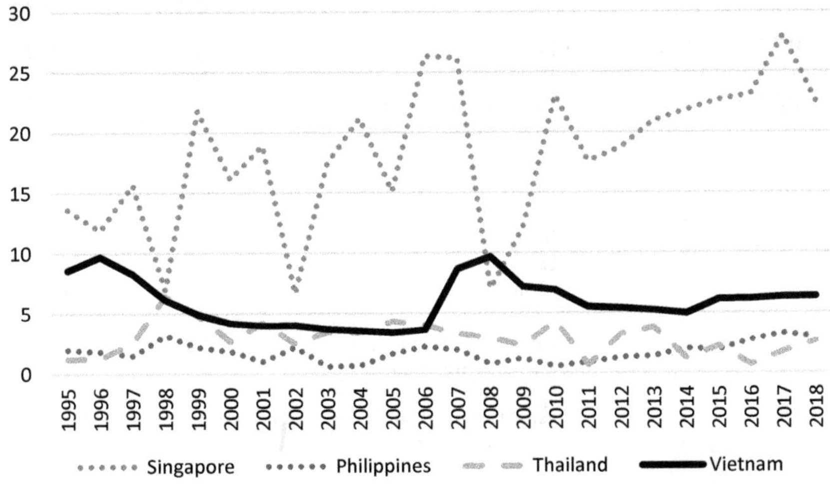

Fig. 1.9 Vietnam FDI/GDP compared (*Source* International Monetary Fund, International Financial Statistics and Balance of Payments databases, World Bank, International Debt Statistics, and World Bank and OECD GDP estimates)

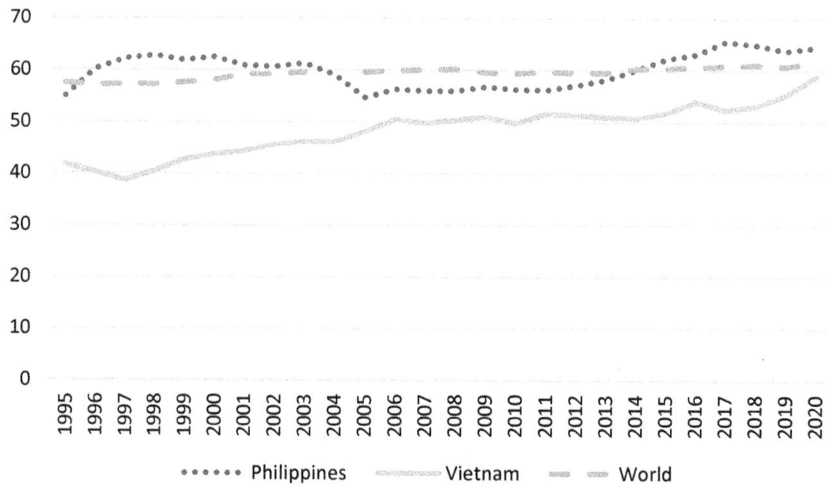

Fig. 1.10 Economic freedom score for Vietnam compared (*Source* Heritage Foundation and Wall Street Journal 2019; see also Gwartney et al. 2019)

Table 1.2 Elements of economic freedom compared across Vietnam and the Philippines

Country Name	*Philippines*	*Vietnam*
2020 score	64.5	58.8
Property rights	54.6	52.6
Judicial effectiveness	34.2	40.1
Government integrity	38.7	33.8
Tax burden	76.7	79.5
Government spending	87.9	75.9
Fiscal health	96.3	58.0
Business freedom	59.5	65.6
Labour freedom	57.4	62.5
Monetary freedom	66.9	68.2
Trade freedom	81.6	79.6
Investment freedom	60	40
Financial freedom	60	50

Source Heritage Foundation and Wall Street Journal (2020)

Budget deficits have averaged 4.7% of GDP with public debt at 57.5% of GDP. This contrasts with the case of the Philippines, where budget deficits averaged 0.6% of GDP and public debt reached 39.6% of GDP.

Although Vietnam clearly has "inferior" numbers for the scoring of government spending and fiscal health, it would be difficult to say the government has been less responsible than that of the Philippines. Much of the difference in deficits can be explained by education and health expenditures by the respective governments: 9.9% of GDP for Vietnam and 7.1% for the Philippines according to the latest data available from the World Health Organization Global Health Expenditure database and the UNESCO Institute for Statistics. Infrastructure has also been targeted in expenditures by the government of Vietnam. It is difficult to see how this decreases rather than increasing economic freedom. Government debt ratios for both countries are moderate compared to those of most wealthy nations, particularly as their rapid GDP growth would quickly bring down the ratios with a few years of balanced budgets. A recent report from the IMF lauds Vietnam's expenditures on health, education and infrastructure (Baum 2020).

Investment and financial freedom provide another story, particularly since Vietnam scores more poorly even than the Philippines, where foreign investors rarely can obtain controlling shares in a business no matter how much cash they invest. The score for financial freedom is partly a measure of the efficiency of the banking system—and Vietnam has only recently begun to develop credit access for private enterprise—and the degree of government control of financial markets, with much of the banking system in Vietnam remaining under government ownership (see Chapter 6). The movement of capital is restricted somewhat by the government, although these restrictions are gradually diminishing. The State Bank of Vietnam publishes sporadic circulars (e.g. SBV 2019) providing updated information and the large accounting firms regularly comment these (e.g. KPMG 2019; PwC 2019).

The latest Enterprise Survey for Vietnam suggests that Vietnam is on par or better than other countries in the region for most questions posed regarding regulations and taxes, crime, formalization of business and even innovation with the exception of product innovation. Finance, as we have seen already, and corruption are weak points (real estate and privatization have particularly been vulnerable to cronyism—see Lê 2008: 175–178). However, these results are from 2015 and the situation is rapidly evolving. Anecdotal evidence indicates that there is still too much corruption in

Vietnam. The 2015 data (measuring the opinions of business executives contacted) indicate that Vietnam performs poorly regarding extortion of funds by public officials "in order to get things done" and in order to secure a government contract (Enterprise Surveys, n.d.). A smaller but more recent study confirms the need for controlling corruption, but notes that mid-sized Vietnamese firms are more frequently victims than smaller or larger Vietnamese firms or foreign firms (Maruichi and Abe 2019).

Vietnam earned the greatest improvement in global competitiveness score worldwide in 2019 (Schwab 2019). This was in part possible because there was much to improve, and this remains the case. Vietnam does best for market size (thanks to the population of 100 million that, while poor, still has discretional spending power), adoption of ICT (information, computer and telecommunication technologies) and macroeconomic stability.

The weaker global competitiveness scores of Vietnam are for infrastructure, skill, labour market, business dynamism and innovativeness—although Vietnam does perform above expectations for this last dimension as compared to other lower-middle-income countries (Dutta et al. 2019). Innovativeness of Vietnam's small to mid-sized firms is examined in Chapter 4 under the heading "Innovation Capability".

The road system of Vietnam is poor, so the trucking industry is less efficient. Intercity roads are dangerous. The country scores well for airport connectivity and sea liner capacity, but there is a bottleneck in both air transport and seaport services. As for utility infrastructure, water supply is a weak area.

Vietnam's efforts to improve from its limited skills base are reflected in rising scores for nearly all measures contributing to the skills "pillar" of the global competitiveness score. However, there remains much ground to be covered as Vietnam ranks 93rd out of 141 countries. Businesses entering Vietnam hopefully will collaborate with government's industrial plan to upgrade the skills base.

1.5 Conclusion: Vietnam and Business Opportunity

Vietnam has a particularly remarkable record for the rate of greenfield investments attracted in this century (Barklie 2015) although this has dropped recently, particularly in the first half of 2019. FDI was flat globally and across most of Asia in 2019 (UNCTAD 2020), although

Singapore saw a 42% increase over 2018. Part of the reason is particular to Vietnam. While the government of Vietnam was happy to attract investment to increase the size of the economy, create jobs and increase tax income, it was particularly keen to harvest the real prizes of FDI: knowledge acquisition and local supply sourcing. This has not happened at the desired pace, with many foreign firms sourcing from suppliers outside Vietnam.

Singapore in fact saw a huge upsurge in FDI from the United States after the global financial crisis (SingStat 2020). Singapore seems the simplest choice for entry into Asia, with a sophisticated workforce, business-friendly bureaucracy and world-class environment.

Doing business in Vietnam is not the same as doing business in the rich democratic countries of Europe, North America and Oceania. Logistics and paperwork are more challenging, and the skill base is less extensive. However, there is a reason that Vietnam has already attracted a third of a trillion dollars of foreign investment. Vietnam's citizens and central and local governments are eager for the growth afforded by foreign business investment and offer good and fair deals to make that investment profitable. Although Vietnam is open to initiatives from Asian neighbours, it is also true that the Vietnamese have a great admiration for Western people and things.

For some time, businesses have been considering a "China plus one strategy" as a manner to deal with rising wages in China operations and China-based suppliers. The trend became accentuated with the pre-COVID-19 trade war between the Trump administration in the United States and Xi Jinping's China. This in turn led to a jump in new factories being built in Vietnam and appearance of logistic bottlenecks. Hopefully, the aftermath of the current pandemic will lead to a more gradual but steady increase of FDI inflows.

There are five ways a business can enter into Vietnam:

1. Greenfield investment
2. Acquisition
3. Merger
4. Joint venture with a local firm
5. Simple business arrangement with a local firm as a supplier or a customer.

All modes of entry, but particularly mode 5, may bring the Vietnamese firm into a value chain, hence the relevance of Chapter 4—Participating and upgrading in Global Value Chains: SMEs in Vietnam. Modes of entry 2, 3 and 4 may involve either local private firms, or firms that are state-owned enterprises either recently privatized or in the process of "equitization" (the Vietnamese equivalent of privatization). This is one of the motivations for including Chapter 3— State-Owned Enterprises in Vietnam: Challenges Facing the Privatization Process.

Given the current and probable future rate of growth once the COVID-19 crisis is overcome, Vietnam represents an opportunity for many businesses. More information is required. Much of that information is industry specific and region specific. This current book cannot provide such specific information, but does provide the reader with starting point for further research by both businesses and academics.

Notes

1. OECD did not report a 2018 ranking for Vietnam for technical reasons. See OECD (2019).
2. The primary challenge for doing business in Vietnam is language. Some businesses may be cowed because the Vietnamese language is difficult. Perhaps the language of money is universal, but the language of management is not. The use of the Latin alphabet in Vietnamese is misleading. Vietnamese has the same number of tones as Cantonese, tongue-twisting sequences of phonemes and frequent use of imaginative combinations of words. A motorcycle taxi, for example, is a *xe ôm*: vehicle embrace. This gives Google's AI great difficulty translating to and from Vietnamese. And the number of tones is not really the same as Cantonese, because Vietnamese varies from region to region. The number of tones varies both by region and by whom you ask. So does the rest of pronunciation, such as initial consonants. However, if Vietnamese is difficult, it can be learned. Far more important is the desire of virtually all young and middle-aged Vietnamese to learn English if they do not already speak it.
3. Perhaps as many as a dozen times: in 905, 931, 938, 981, 1077, three times of anti-Mongol-Yuan invasion (1258, 1285, 1288, 1427, 1789, 1946, 1979), not including several times during a thousand years of the Chinese occupation between 179 BCE and 905 (personal communication with Phạm Văn Thuỷ). Of course, the identity of the invaders/occupiers and of the "repulsers" varied over time as societies and cultures evolved.

4. DINFO or information industries include international standard industry classification codes D26, D58T60, D61, D62T63 but exclude pharmaceuticals, medical services and financial and business services. Also, non-electronic machinery can also be sophisticated (e.g. tunnel boring machines).
5. What neither the Heritage Index nor the Fraser Institute Index of Economic Freedom reveal, however, is that economic freedom in the Philippines is freedom for the exploitation of businesses controlled by family dynasties (Cruz 2019). Large family interests, not government, are the enemy of economic freedom in that country.

References

AOC. 2019. Atlas of Economic Complexity Profile for Vietnam. https://oec.world/en/profile/country/vnm/. Accessed December 2, 2019.

ARIC. 2020. Free Trade Agreements. Asia Regional Integration Center. https://aric.adb.org/fta-country. Accessed March 23, 2020.

Barklie, Glenn. 2015. Vietnam Leads Emerging Market Greenfield FDI Performance Index. FT.com. Accessed February 8, 2020.

Baum, Anja. 2020. Vietnam's Development Success Story and the Unfinished SDG Agenda. IMF Working Paper WP/20/31.

Carr, Nick. 2017. Cyber Espionage Is Alive and Well: APT32 and the Threat to Global Corporations. FireEye. https://www.fireeye.com/blog/threat-research/2017/05/cyber-espionage-apt32.html. Accessed December 8, 2019.

Cruz, Elfren S. 2019. Rise and Fall of Family Dynasties. *The Philippine Star*, May 16. https://www.philstar.com/opinion/2019/05/16/1918274/rise-and-fall-family-dynasties. Accessed March 20, 2020.

Dutta, Soumitra, Bruno Lanvin, and Sacha Wunsch-Vincent (eds.). 2019. *Global Innovation Index 2019: Creating Healthy Lives—The Future of Medical Innovation*. Ithaca: Cornell University; Fontainebleau: INSEAD; and Geneva: WIPO.

DW.com. 2019. A Dam-Building Race Threatens the Mekong River. https://www.dw.com/en/a-dam-building-race-threatens-the-mekong-river/a-50049206 Accessed November 30, 2019 and December 4, 2019.

Enterprise Surveys. n.d. www.enterprisesurveys.org. The World Bank. Accessed March 21, 2020.

FAO. 2011. Strengthening Capacities to Enhance Coordinated and Integrated Disaster Risk Reduction Actions and Adaptation to Climate Change in Agriculture in the Northern Mountain Regions of Viet Nam. Climate Change Impacts on Agriculture in Vietnam. FAO. UNJP/VIE/037/UNJ. Available at http://www.fao.org/climatechange/34068-0d42acdf5fb7c4d80f3013c038ab92ce6.pdf. Accessed June 26, 2020.

FDI Vietnam. 2020. Vietnam: Registration of Technology Transfer Now Mandatory. http://fdi-vietnam.com/fdi-news/vietnamregistration-of-technology-transfer-now-mandatory.html. Accessed February 14, 2020.

GSO. 2019. Social and Economic Situation in 2018. General Statistics Office of Vietnam. Available at https://www.gso.gov.vn/default_en.aspx?tabid=622&ItemID=1904. Accessed December 7, 2019.

Gwartney, James, Robert Lawson, Joshua Hall, and Ryan Murphy with Daniel L. Bennett, Rosemarie Fike, Fred McMahon, Boris Nikolaev. 2019. *2019 Annual Report*. Economic Freedom of the World. Fraser Institute.

Heritage Foundation and Wall Street Journal. 2019. Heritage Index of Economic Freedom. Heritage Foundation. https://www.heritage.org/index/visualize. Accessed December 6, 2019.

Heritage Foundation and Wall Street Journal. 2020. Heritage Index of Economic Freedom. Available at https://www.heritage.org/index/download. Accessed March 24, 2020.

Katagiri, Mitsuru. 2019. Credit Misallocation and Economic Growth in Vietnam. IMF Working Papers.

KPMG. 2019. Legal Update. New Rules on Foreign Exchange Control Applicable to Foreign Direct Investment Activities in Vietnam. https://home.kpmg/content/dam/kpmg/vn/pdf/Legal-Update/2019/Legal%20Update%20-%20August%202019%20(EN).pdf. Accessed March 21, 2020.

Lê, Đăng Doanh. 2008. Market Economy with Socialist Orientation in Vietnam and the Concept of the Social and Ecological Market Economy. In *The Social and Ecological Market Economy—A Model for Asian Development?* Eschborn: Deutsche Gesellschaft für Technische Zusammenarbeit.

Lyngaas, Sean. 2019. Vietnam's Premier Hacking Group Ramps Up Targeting of Global Car Companies. CyberScoop. https://www.cyberscoop.com/apt32-ocean-lotus-vietnam-car-companies-hacked/. Accessed December 8, 2019.

Maruichi, Daisuke, and Masato Abe. 2019. *Corruption and the Business Environment in Vietnam: Implications from an Empirical Study*. Asia and the Pacific Policy Studies. Wiley. Available at https://onlinelibrary.wiley.com/doi/pdf/10.1002/app5.275. Accessed March 21, 2020.

Minderhoud, P.S.J., L. Coumou, G. Erkens, et al. 2019. Mekong Delta Much Lower Than Previously Assumed in Sea-Level Rise Impact Assessments. *Nature Communications* 10: 3847.

Mitre Group. 2019. APT32. https://attack.mitre.org/groups/G0050/. Accessed December 8, 2019.

Nguyen, Dan. 2019. Samsung Vietnam Sees 2018 Profits Plummet. VnExpress International. https://e.vnexpress.net/news/business/companies/samsung-vietnam-sees-2018-profits-plummet-3893548.html. Accessed February 3, 2020.

Nguyen, Thi Tue Anh, Minh Duc Luu, and Duc Chieu Trinh. 2016. The Evolution of Vietnamese Industry. The Brookings Institution.

OECD. 2019. Results from Pisa 2018. Available at https://www.oecd.org/pisa/publications/PISA2018_CN_VNM.pdf. Accessed December 4, 2019.

PwC. 2019. New Foreign Exchange Control Regulations for Foreign Direct Investment in Vietnam. https://www.pwc.com/vn/en/publications/legal-news-brief/190823-circular-06.html. Accessed March 21, 2020.

SBV. 2019. Circular Providing Guidance on Foreign Exchange Control with Respect to Foreign Direct Investment in Vietnam. No. 06/2019/TT-NHNN.

SingStat. 2020. https://www.tablebuilder.singstat.gov.sg/publicfacing/partialDisplay.action. Accessed February 8, 2020.

Tran, Van Tho. 2002. Economic Development in Vietnam During the Second Half of the 20th Century: How to Avoid the Danger of Lagging Behind. In *The Vietnamese Economy: Awakening the Dormant Dragon*, ed. by Binh Tran Nam and Chi Do Pham, Chap. 2. London: Routledge.

UNCTAD. 2020, Global FDI Flows Flat in 2019. https://unctad.org/en/PublicationsLibrary/diaeiainf2020d1_en.pdf. Accessed February 8, 2020.

Vietnam Law and Legal Forum Magazine. 2018. Vietnam Seeks FDI in New Technology-Based Sectors. http://vietnamlawmagazine.vn/vietnam-seeks-fdi-in-new-technology-based-sectors-6447.html. Accessed February 16, 2020.

VietnamNet. 2018. FDI Technology Transfer remains Low. https://english.vietnamnet.vn/fms/business/205950/fdi-technology-transfer-remains-low.html. Accessed February 12, 2020.

Vu, Khuong M. 2014. The Institutional Root Causes of the Challenges to Vietnam's Long-Term Economic Growth. *Asian Economic Papers* 13: 159–189. See also the comments in subsequent pages.

Schwab, Klaus. 2019. *The Global Competitiveness Report 2019*. World Economic Forum.

World Bank. 2019. *Doing Business 2019: Training for Reform*. Washington, DC: World Bank.

CHAPTER 2

The Road to Doi Moi in Vietnam

Pham Van Thuy

Abstract While hard work under adverse conditions contributed to the turnaround of Vietnam's economy in the last 30 years, economic policy was crucial in channeling that work. This chapter documents the evolution of that policy in four sections. A first section describes early efforts beginning with the independence of the North from French colonization in 1945 and 1954 to the first decade after the war with the United States of America. The second section details the economic reforms (đổi mới) of the Sixth National Congress in 1986. The third section covers amendments and implementation up until recent years. The final section reports the results of these policies.

Keywords Vietnam economy · Doi Moi · Economic reform · Economic transformation · Economic history · Economic plan

P. Van Thuy (✉)
Faculty of History, University of Social Sciences and Humanities, Vietnam National University, Hanoi, Vietnam
e-mail: Thuypv@vnu.edu.vn

R. Macdonald (ed.), *The Economy and Business Environment of Vietnam*, https://doi.org/10.1007/978-3-030-49974-7_2

At its Sixth National Congress taking place in Hanoi between 15th and 18th December 1986, the Communist Party of Vietnam (CPV) initiated a radical reform called Doi Moi. This event signified a milestone in the development of Vietnam, marking a fundamental change in economic ideology and management, a shift from the command economy to the socialist-oriented market one. The immediate cause of Doi Moi was attributed to the failure in economic leadership and management of the CPV and the State inducing critical social and economic crises in the late 1970s and the early 1980s (Ngo Dang Tri 2016; Dean Forbes et al. 1991; Vincent Edwards and Anh Phan 2013). In a broad sense, Doi Moi can also be seen as the ultimate result of a long process of policy experiments and gradual reforms in Vietnam, starting immediately after independence of 1945. Likewise, over the past thirty years, the Doi Moi policy has been regularly amended and supplemented by the CPV and the State of Vietnam in accordance with new circumstances.

This chapter discusses the reform policy in Vietnam during the long transition from the initial reforms carried out by the Vietnam Workers' Party in the early years after independence to the radical and far-reaching reform conducted by the CPV since 1986. Attention is given to the main economic policies of Doi Moi, particularly those related to the markets. The author argues that the CPV's adoption of Doi Moi in 1986 was a result of many experimental policies and reforms conducted by different regimes in Vietnam. The Doi Moi was not a complete disruption of the former economic model; rather it is a hybrid third way between a planning system and capitalism, in which the economy is operated on the market mechanism, under the State governance and the Party's leadership (Dang Cong san Viet Nam 2013). The chapter also analyzes the amendments and supplements of the Doi Moi policy throughout the CPV's Congresses as well as the initial achievements of the Doi Moi over the past three decades.

2.1 Early Attempted Reforms

Vietnam obtained independence in 1945 as a direct result of the August Revolution following the capitulation of Japan at the end of World War II. After the War, the French returned in an attempt to re-establish their former colonial rule which they had surrendered to the Japanese. The nine-year armed resistance of the Vietnamese people culminating in the

Dien Bien Phu Battle eventually forced the French to recognize the independence of Vietnam in 1954. Following the provisions of the Geneva Accord, however, Vietnam was divided into two parts along the 17th parallel: North Vietnam under the Communist-led Democratic Republic of Vietnam (DRV) and South Vietnam under the US-backed Republic of Vietnam. The Vietnamese struggle for national unification and independence, often called the Vietnam War, lasted until 1975 with the collapse of the Saigon regime.

Under such wartime conditions, the successive governments in North and South Vietnam understandably could only carry out sporadic reforms. Although Ho Chi Minh's newly independent government had introduced several new economic policies in the late 1940s (Pham Van Thuy 2019), a far-reaching reform was only implemented in the early 1950s when the Vietnam Workers' Party organized the drastic land reform in the northern provinces. The reform concentrated on the confiscation of the land belonging to French colonialists, Vietnamese landlords and rich peasants and distributed it to poor and landless peasants (Moise 1976: 234–236). This land reform was concluded in 1956, but a process of collectivization began in North Vietnam. Peasants were reorganized into agricultural production cooperatives. French factories, mines, and public utilities which had once operated in the areas north of the 17th parallel were rapidly taken over by the DRV government and subsequently developed into State enterprises. Privately owned Vietnamese firms were reorganized into either industrial cooperatives or joint State-private enterprises. By 1960, the tendency toward socialism in economic transformation had become established in North Vietnam (Dang Phong 2005; Pham Thanh Vinh 1966).

In September 1960, at the third National Congress, the Vietnam Workers' Party passed a Resolution fostering the transition to socialism in Vietnam. The Resolution emphasized the socialist industrialization along with the agricultural development in Vietnam. The socialist industrialization was anticipated to be accomplished through three five-year plans. The first five-year plan (1961–1965) launched at the end of 1960 focused on the development of heavy industries, particularly electricity, chemicals, fertilizers, coal mining, iron, and steel. The investment was mainly allocated to State enterprises, whereas local artisans were reorganized into handcrafts cooperatives (Dang Phong 2005). While the plan was being implemented, in late 1964 the United States bombed North Vietnam

(Moise 1996). North Vietnam shifted to a wartime economy. In addition, the escalated hostilities in the South prompted the government of North Vietnam to send reinforcements for the southern liberation forces. Economic efforts of North Vietnam now had a twofold objective of building socialism in the North and supplying the liberation army in the South for the ultimate goal of national unification.

In South Vietnam, the Republic government of Ngo Dinh Diem also carried out land reforms and deployed various measures to strengthen control of the economy. Diem's government concentrated the limited financial resources accrued from foreign aid and the export of agricultural products on developing State enterprises and the purchase of foreign companies. The major French rice plantations were purchased by Diem's government and resold to Vietnamese peasants, who were encouraged to participate in cooperatives. Diem's efforts to achieve economic nationalism conflicted with the aid policy of the United States, whose goal was to turn South Vietnam into an anti-communist outpost in Southeast Asia (Pham Thi Hong Ha 2017). Diem's economic policy, in addition to the increasing military pressures from North Vietnam which threatened the viability of an anti-communist State in Vietnam, prompted the US government to intervene more directly in South Vietnamese politics. The anticipated consequence was a *coup d'état* led by the army under American auspices in November 1963, which ended the Ngo family's rule of South Vietnam.[1]

After Diem's assassination, the government of South Vietnam changed hands at least five times before General Nguyen Cao Ky took the premiership in June 1965. In 1967, Nguyen Cao Ky was in turn replaced by General Nguyen Van Thieu as the top leader of South Vietnam until the end of the war in 1975. This unstable political environment in addition to the escalation of war since 1965 harmed any economic reform efforts in South Vietnam. Although the economy of South Vietnam continued to grow thanks to massive aid from the United States, the investment was mainly allocated to the service sector, light industry, and agriculture. Consequently, South Vietnam became stagnant when the US aid was slashed drastically following the withdrawal of the US army in the early 1970s. By the end of the war in 1975, South Vietnam had become self-sufficient in rice, and that was one of the major economic achievements of the governments of the Republic of Vietnam (Doulas C. Dacy 1986: 9–18).

Since peace was restored and the nation was reunified, the Vietnam Workers' Party (renamed as the Communist Party of Vietnam in 1976) lost no time in resuming its long-term plan for socialist economic transformation in Vietnam, which was interrupted by the war since 1964. Between 1976 and 1986, two five-year plans—the second five-year plan (1976–1980) and the third five-year plan (1981–1985)—were implemented. Both plans pursued socialist industrialization with major focuses on heavy industry and rapid agricultural growth, although the former placed heavy industry at the forefront and the later gave the first priority to agricultural development. Economic rehabilitation and the socialist transformation of private sectors in South Vietnam were also promoted (Ngo Dang Tri 2016).

Nevertheless, the second and third five-year plans did not produce satisfactory results. Between 1976 and 1980, the economy grew by only 0.5% in comparison with the targeted 13–14%. By 1980, the second five-year plan achieved only 50% of the planned targets (Dang Phong and Tran Dinh Thien 2012). No significant progresses were made in the period of 1981–1985, and planned targets of the third five-year plan were only partially met: 95.8% in food production, 67.1% in cement production, and 94.5% in electricity output. The government budget deficit increased from 18.1% in 1981 to 36.6% in 1985 (Kim Tran Hoang 1996). The most critical problem was inflation soaring from 164.6% in 1984 to 774% in 1986 (Dang Phong 2009: 27–42, 2016: 258). After unification and a decade of multiple efforts, Vietnam was on the verge of economic collapse.

2.2 The Economic Reform Policy of the Sixth Congress of 1986

The second and third five-year plans were carried out in the difficult context of the US embargo and the concurrent wars on the northern and southwestern borders. Nevertheless, the economic failures were primarily attributed to the mistakes and shortcomings in economic leadership and management of the Party and the State. The command economy based on centrally planned, subsidy, and autarkic principles leaving out the incentives of market mechanisms, had been essential during the wartime but proved to be inappropriate in the peaceful development stage (Truong Chinh 1988; Dang Cong san Viet Nam 2002). Realizing these shortcomings, at its Sixth National Congress, which took place in Hanoi from 15th to 18th December 1986, the CPV adopted the Doi Moi, embarking upon a new course of profound transformation in modern Vietnam. It is important to note that with the Doi Moi, the CPV by no means intended to change its ultimate goal of building socialism; rather it provided new and feasible guidelines and policies to achieve this goal.

The Doi Moi is a comprehensive reform program with the primary focus on the economic field. The main economic reforms of the CPV's Sixth National Congress were presented in the following points:

2.2.1 Reorganizing the Structure of Production and Investment

For a long time, Vietnam had mistakenly focused on promoting industrialization while the country did not have necessary conditions. This created a situation that, despite an agrarian country with the peasants accounting for more than 90% of population, Vietnam often suffered food shortages. The Sixth Congress considered this situation as caused by mistakes in leadership and implementation. Following the experimental policies made in the third five-year plan (1981–1985), the Congress determined a reorganization of the structure of the national economy in which *agriculture would take the leading role*. The Congress emphasized the need for mass production in agriculture in order to quickly increase the volume and the value of agricultural commodities. The Congress also stressed the necessary amendment and supplement of land policies to increase the efficient management and use of land. The development of forestry and fishery must be associated with agricultural development, environment preservation, and processing industry in order to meet the domestic demands and increase exports.

Light, small-scale and craft industries should meet the population's demand for basic goods, ensuring the requirements of processing agricultural, forestry, and sea products and quickly increasing the volume of processed goods for exports.

Heavy industry and infrastructure construction must be directed to economic goals and defense in the first stage, and based on practical capability, preparing the basis for economic development in later stages. Priority should be given to the energy industry (coal, oil, and gas); mechanical industry and mining and minerals industry would be reorganized and specialized in support of light industry and agriculture. The products that the country was unable to produce or produced insufficiently should be imported. The development of transportation and communication systems was encouraged to facilitate the production and circulation of goods and travel of the people.

Particularly, the Congress emphasized the importance of expanding and improving the efficiency of foreign economic relations. The country should develop a comprehensive relationship with the Soviet Union, Laos, Cambodia, and other socialist countries, while fostering economic, scientific, and technical cooperation with other countries, international and private foreign organizations on the principle of equality and mutual benefit. Upon the implementation of these guidelines, the Sixth Congress set out three target programs: foodstuff, consumer goods, and exports, considering them as the spearheads of the fourth five-year plan (1986–1990).

2.2.2 Conducting the Socialist Transformation

The Sixth Congress stressed that, in order to be able to reorganize the structure of production and investment, it was important to clearly define the sectoral structure of the economy and provide policies to appropriately utilize and transform the economic sectors. The socialist economy consisted of three main sectors: State, cooperative, and household. Other sectors included small-scale manufacturing sector (craftmen, individual farmers, individual traders, and service providers), private capitalist sector, and State capitalist sector. The Congress laid down that while the State and collective sectors would play the leading role, other sectors should also be utilized in appropriate scale and technical level according to each stage of production and circulation. The State would have the preferential economic policies to support the development of the socialist economy via investment, taxes, credit, and so on. The cooperation between economic sectors was to be conducted under the principle of equality before the law.

2.2.3 Reforming the Economic Management Mechanism

At the Sixth Congress, the CPV was determined to abolish the bureaucratic centralism and State subsidies system in the formation of a synchronic planning mechanism based on the socialist business accounting, which is another name for a market economy. The new economic management mechanism centered on the planning, the relationship between currency and commodity prices, and other economic measures in combination with administrative and educational methods. The management was decentralized on the principle of democratic centralism, in which economic units were assured of the right to mastery of their businesses and finance. The State apparatus only performed administrative functions without intervention in the practical operations of economic units. The centralized management was only applied to the important issues regarding the whole country, while the local authorities had the right of initiative in the social-economic management within their domains.

2.2.4 *Solving the Urgent Problems of Distribution and Circulation*

Through the freeing of production capacity, the increase in the production of essential goods and goods would create substantial revenues for the budget. The State would strictly manage the supplies and goods produced and imported by the State enterprises and develop appropriate measures to control goods and money. The socialist commerce should be transformed into the business and improve service quality to dominate the market. The State would decide the pricing and management of prices according to the actual situation, ensuring the normal operation of production installations and the active participation of State enterprises in trade. In order to increase the volume of goods in circulation, it was necessary to extend the exchange of goods and abolish the prohibitions and division of markets based on the administrative boundaries. Speculative activities and illegal trade must be promptly detected and strictly penalized. The State must strengthen the control of money circulation and increase the non-cash transactions which would significantly facilitate the production and businesses (Dang Cong san Viet Nam 2006).

2.3 The Amendments and Supplements of the Doi Moi Policy

The Sixth National Congress of 1986 provided the initial orientations and guidelines for the Doi Moi in Vietnam. The details of the Doi Moi policy were amended and supplemented in the CPV's subsequent congresses, focusing on the following changes:

2.3.1 *Recognizing the Market Economy*

The concept of market economy was first introduced at the Sixth Central Committee Plenum in March 1989. At the meeting, the Party General Secretary Nguyen Van Linh, who is considered as an architect of the Doi Moi in Vietnam, emphasized that "the market mechanism must be consistently applied in planning and economic policies. The market mechanism develops in an environment of free production and circulation of goods according to law. Domestic prices are inseparable from international prices. The State does not use administrative regulations to impose prices but uses economic policies, measures, and reserve forces to affect the supply-demand relations. All economic units must be shifted to a business mechanism" (Dang Cong san Viet Nam 2006). Then, at the Seventh National Congress in June 1991, the Party officially recognized that "The operation of national economy follows the market mechanism under the control of the State by laws, plans, policies and other tools" (Dang Cong san Viet Nam 2007). This economic model was labeled "socialist-oriented market economy" at the Ninth Congress in April 2001 (Dang Cong san Viet Nam 2016), and it has become the general economic model of Vietnam in the Doi Moi era.

The concept of socialist-oriented market economy was clarified at the Twelfth Congress in 2017. The Party laid down that "the socialist-oriented market economy that Vietnam has been building is an economy operating comprehensively and synchronically according to the rules of market, while entrusting its governance to socialism in accordance with each stage of the country's development. It is a modern and international integrated market economy under the governance of the socialist rule of law State led by the Communist Party of Vietnam, struggling for a strong country with prosperous people, democratic, just and civilized society." In the socialist-oriented market economy, the State plays a role in orientating, building, and perfecting the economic regime, creating a fair, transparent, and sound environment of competition, using the measures, policies, and resources of the State to orientate and regulate the economy, promoting production and business and protecting resources and environment. The market plays the chief role in effectively mobilizing and allocating resources, the main driving force to release production capacity. The State resources are allocated according to the strategies, planning, and plans following the market mechanism (Dang Cong san Viet Nam 2017).

2.3.2 *Developing a Multi-Sector Economy*

The Sixth Congress recognized the existence of several sectors in the Vietnamese economy. The role of each economic sector was further identified and analyzed at the subsequent congresses. Particularly, the Constitution of 1992 officially recognized that "the State develops a multi-sector commodity economy in accordance to the market mechanism under State management and according to a socialist orientation. The multi-sectoral structure of the economy with diversified types of production and business organizations is based on ownership by the entire population along with collective and private ownership, of which the first and the second are the cornerstones" (Quoc hoi Viet Nam 2013).

The Ninth Congress identified six sectors of Vietnamese economy, including the State-owned sector, cooperative sector, State capitalist sector or joint State-private sector, individual and small-owner sector, private capitalist sector, and foreign sector. At the Tenth National Congress in April 2006, the individual and small-owner sector and private capitalist sector were combined into the private sector. Thus, since 2006, the Vietnamese economy officially has five sectors, in which the State-owned sector remains a decisive role (Dang Cong san Viet Nam 2006). According to the Party Resolution made at the Twelfth Congress in 2017, Vietnam only applies one business legal system for all enterprises, regardless of the types of ownership and economic sector. Enterprises in all economic sectors operate according to market mechanism. They are equal and have a fair competition under the law. However, the State should create favorable conditions to promote the development of Vietnamese enterprises and entrepreneurs who would play the key and leading role in the course of industrialization, modernization, and international economic integration and ensure the economic independence and autonomy of Vietnam (Dang Cong san Viet Nam 2017).

2.3.3 *Expanding Foreign Trade*

After the Sixth Congress, a series of reform policies on the promotion and efficient management of import–export activities were introduced. In 1988, Vietnam passed the first Law on Import Tax and Export Tax which focused on reducing and eliminating import–export tax and quota. Trade barriers were gradually lifted, allowing State- and private-owned firms to sell their goods to any Vietnamese trade companies which had legal export permits. From 1991, private-owned Vietnamese companies could directly participate in foreign trade under certain conditions, such as having foreign trade contracts, delivery permits, and minimum working capital of US$ 200,000.[2] The foreign currency policy was also reformed to facilitate the import–export activities. Companies were granted the right of using foreign currency, which allowed them to retain foreign currency accruing from foreign trade for their reinvestment and local construction. The State regularly adjusted the exchange rate according to the international market. Overseas Vietnamese and foreigners were allowed to transfer and carry foreign currency to Vietnam freely. They could deposit money at the State Bank of Vietnam and withdraw money in Vietnam Dong at the market exchange rate. From 1988, Vietnam policies on money remittance and currency exchange were implemented according to international practices.

2.3.4 *Attracting Foreign Investment*

In 1987, Vietnam passed the first Law on Foreign Investment which allowed foreign capital to do business in Vietnam and recognized that foreign-invested businesses formed a sector of Vietnam's economy. The Law was subsequently amended in 1990 and 1992, 1996, 2000, 2005, and 2014. The 1990 Foreign Investment Law added 15 articles, creating favorable conditions for foreigners to invest in Vietnam and allowing Vietnamese partners to expand joint ventures with foreign countries. The 1992 Foreign Investment Law opened new forms of investment via Export Processing Zones and Build-Transfer-Operate contracts and decided that Vietnamese firms of all sectors had the right to do businesses with foreign partners. The 1996 Foreign Investment Law was amended in the direction of diminishing incentives for foreign direct investment. It removed import tax exception for some materials, equipment, and transportation vehicles in the process of business establishment. The 2000 Foreign Investment was amended and supplemented in the direction of creating more stability and openness.

In 2005, the Law on Investment and Law on Enterprises were promulgated in the context of Vietnam's acceleration to join the WTO and pursue stronger international economic integration. These laws covered not only foreign investment incentive policies, but also regulations on both direct and indirect investments to create a level playing field for all domestic and foreign investors.

Particularly, in 2014, the National Assembly adopted a new Law on Investment and a new Law on Enterprise, providing detailed policies on business investment activities in Vietnam as well as outward business investments from Vietnam. According to these laws, foreign investors or enterprises undertaking a project in Vietnam must have an Investment Registration Certificate provided by the relevant provincial-level State Investment Registration Authority. Prior to operation, they must also receive an Enterprise Registration Certificate issued by the provincial level State Business Registration Authority. Investors are entitled to make investments in any businesses that are not banned by the State. The list of banned investments is clearly provided in the appendix, mostly related to trade in specific narcotic substances, chemicals, specimens of wild flora and fauna, prostitution, human trafficking, human tissues and body parts, and business pertaining to human cloning. Investors have the rights to decide their business investment on their own in accordance with the law or access and make use of loan capital, assistance funds, land, and other resources as prescribed by law. The ownership of assets, capital, income, and other lawful rights and interests of investors are recognized and protected by the State of Vietnam. All investors are treated equitably and the State of Vietnam shall uphold international agreements on business investment to which it is a signatory.

The 2014 Law on Investment also provided a series of assurances for foreign investment in Vietnam. The assurance of asset ownership stipulated that lawful assets of investors shall not be nationalized or confiscated by administrative measures. In case an asset is bought or commandeered by the State of reasons of national defense and security, national interests, State of emergency, prevention, or recovery of natural disaster, the investor shall be reimbursed or compensated in accordance with relevant laws. The Law also provides investors with assurance of business investment, in which the State would not interfere in the practical operations and businesses of enterprises. An article on the assurance of the transfer of foreign investors' assets to abroad provided that foreign investors are permitted to transfer to abroad their capital and liquidations, income from business investment, money, and other assets under their lawful ownership after fulfilling all financial obligations to Vietnamese government. Upon changes of laws, investors shall enjoy new incentives if the new investment incentives are more favorable or shall keep enjoying the current incentives in case the new investment incentives are less favorable, unless regulations of law are changed for reasons of national defense and security, social order and security, social ethics, public health, or environmental protection. Disputes over business investments in Vietnam shall be settled through negotiation and conciliation or resolved by arbitration or by either Vietnamese or international courts.

Another important reform of the 2014 Law on Investment is the detailed policies on investment incentives and investment supports. Various forms of investment incentives are included, such as a lower rate of corporate income tax, and exception or reduction of import tax, land rents, land levy. The law specifies the list of businesses and administrative divisions for which projects of investments shall benefit from investment incentives. Moreover, beneficiaries of investment incentives also include projects in which the capital investment is at least 6000 billion Vietnam Dong distributed within three years from the day of issuance of the Certificate of Investment Registration, projects in a rural area that employ at least 500 workers, high-tech companies, science and technology companies, and science and technology organizations. In addition, investors also receive investment support from the State, including support for development of technical and social infrastructure, for training and development of human resources, for scientific research, and development, for market development, credit support, and so on. Particularly, the law specified the investment support for industrial parks, export processing zones, hi-tech zones, economic zones, such as developing infrastructure, housing, public facilities, and amenities for workers. In addition, the 2014 Law on Investment provides useful information on the forms of investments, procedures for decision on investment policies, procedures for issuance, adjustment and revocation of certificate of investment registration, guidance for project execution, and instructions for outward investment from Vietnam (Chinh phu 2014). In comparison with the first Law on Investment introduced in 1987, the 2014 Law on Investment is a huge improvement in the foreign investment policy of Vietnam, representing the earnest efforts of the Vietnamese government to attract foreign investment. Still, Vietnam's Law on Foreign Investment still has a number of shortcomings, and foreign investors have suggested that the Vietnamese government continue to amend the law in order to create a fairer and more competitive environment for investment (Nguyen Huong 2017).

2.4 Major Economic Achievements of Doi Moi

Despite the amendments of the Doi Moi policy, the major change it created has been market liberalization. The results of the Doi Moi reform started to manifest themselves at the end of the fourth five-year plan (1986–1990). The main economic objective of the plan was to increase the production of food, consumer goods, and export goods. The most visible achievement of the plan was the booming of agriculture production. Since 1989, agriculture production not only put an end to the country's persistent shortage of food, but also transformed Vietnam from a food importer to major world rice exporter. Inflation rate also fell from 300% in 1987 to 67.1% in 1991 (Giang Dang and Low Sui Pheng 2015), and 3.2% in 1997. It turned into slight deflation with the Asian financial crisis and then reached 3.8% in 2002. Annual economic growth rate in the period 1990–2000 was approximately 7–8% (Niimi et al. 2007). The poverty rate of households declined from approximately 60% in the early 1980s to 28.21% in 1999 (Tong cuc Thong ke 1999). GDP per capita increased between 1986 and 2018 from US$ 231.452 to US$ 2566.597 in current US$ terms (World Bank 2018a). Since 1990, the GDP growth rate of Vietnam remained between 5% and 8%, except 1997, the year of Asian financial crisis. Vietnam's GDP growth rate slowed down again in 2008 as a result of a global crisis, but soon recovered to 6.4% in 2010. From 2013, Vietnam's GDP has shown steady growth (Fig. 2.1).

In addition to economic growth, trade and investment liberalization has been also an important part of economic reforms in Vietnam. The process of trade liberalization contributed to the rapid growth in the exports and imports. Between 1986 and 1999, exports increased at an annual average rate of 14%, while imports increased over 23%. In 1999, the value of total exports from Vietnam totaled US$ 11,622 million, and total imports to the country reached US$ 11,540 million (Fig. 2.2).

Foreign investment started flowing into Vietnam after the implementation of the Law on Foreign Investment in 1988. On average, FDI inflows amounted to more than 5% of GDP in the second half of the 1990s (World Bank 2018b). In the period between 1988 and 1996, Vietnam's FDI increased at a relatively fast rate in term of both number of projects and registered capital, then went into a gradual decline in the late 1990s. In 1996, the sharp increase in the amount of registered FDI was mainly directed to two investment projects in the field of urban development in Hanoi and Ho Chi Minh City, with more than 3 billion USD for

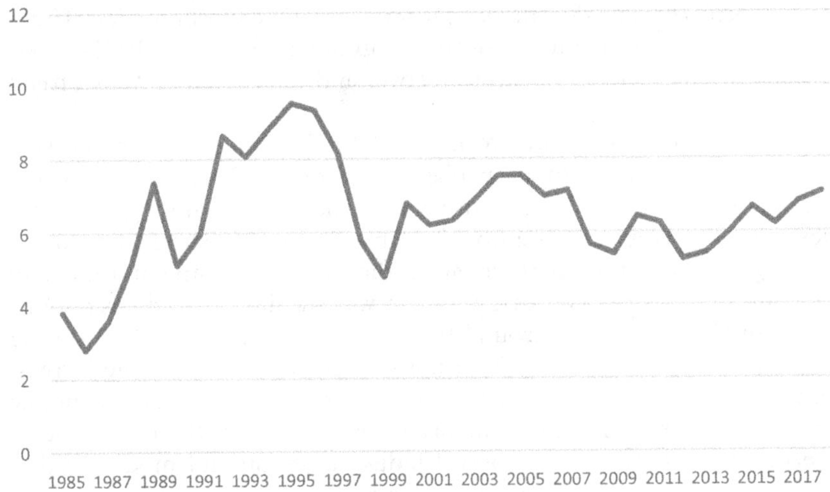

Fig. 2.1 Vietnam's GDP percent growth rate from 1985 to 2018 (*Source* World Bank 2018c)

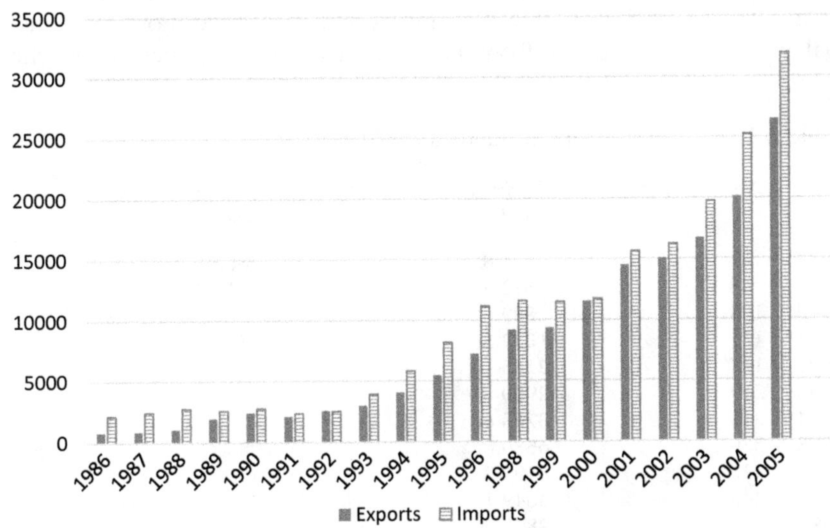

Fig. 2.2 Exports and imports in Vietnam from 1986 to 2005 (Million US$) (*Source* Tong cuc thong ke 2006)

the two projects. The decline of FDI flow into Vietnam in the late 1990s was mostly due to the impact of the Asian financial crisis in 1997–1998. FDI flows into Vietnam began to recover and followed an upward trend after 2000 (Table 2.1).

In the 1990s, more than two-thirds of foreign direct investment were from Asian countries. In particular, Singapore, Taiwan, Hong Kong, Japan, South Korea, and the British Virgin Islands were among the countries with the largest FDI into Vietnam (Tong cuc Thong ke 2000). Looking at the list of partners with the largest investment capital in Vietnam, it could be seen that Vietnam was starting to access economic and technological centers around the world. The increase in FDI during this period showed that Vietnam's business environment became increasingly transparent and attractive to foreign investors. In terms of economic sectors, the changes in FDI structure were in line with the requirements of economic reorganization toward industrialization and modernization in Vietnam. Since the 1990s, there has been a strong shift in the flows of FDI into the industrial, agricultural, and service sectors. FDI inflows into the agricultural sector accounted for a low proportion. In the early period, foreign investment projects mainly focused on hotel and office leasing, but in 1995 and 1996, FDI projects concentrated more on industrial production. Statistics from Foreign Investment Agency under the

Table 2.1 FDI in Vietnam in the period of 1988–1999

Year	*Number of projects*	*Registered capital (million USD)*	*Legal capital (million USD)*
1988	37	371.8	288.4
1989	68	582.5	311.5
1990	108	389	407.5
1991	151	1322.3	663.6
1992	197	2165	1418
1993	269	2900	1468
1994	343	3765.6	1729
1995	370	6530.8	2986
1996	325	8497.3	2940
1997	345	4649.1	2334.4
1998	275	3897	1805.6
1999	312	1568.3	693.3

Source Tong cuc Thong ke 2000

Ministry of Planning and Investment indicated that the proportion of FDI into the agricultural sector tended to decrease over time. In the 1990s, the proportion of FDI in agriculture, forestry, and fisheries accounted for about 5% and FDI into industry and construction accounted for 50% of total FDI, of which FDI into industries accounted for 38% of total FDI into Vietnam (Nguyen Trong Xuan 2002). The large inflows of FDI into industrial sectors were associated with the creation a large number of export processing and industrial zones in Vietnam. The system of industrial zones was established in 1991, starting with the establishment of Tan Thuan Export Processing Zone in 1991 and Linh Trung Export Processing Zone in 1992. The State Committee for Cooperation and Investment created several more industrial parks attracting investment from several countries, such as the Nomura Hai Phong industrial zone in collaboration with Japan, the Amata industrial zone in collaboration with Thailand and Japan, and five Vietnam-Singapore industrial parks in Binh Duong, Bac Ninh, Hai Phong, Quang Ngai, and Nghe An in collaboration with Singapore. The Vietnamese government has offered favorable incentives to investors in the establishment of industrial zones. Expenses incurred in investments for the construction, operation, or rent of apartment buildings and social infrastructure facilities for workers in industrial zones and economic zones would be deductible expenses when calculating taxable income. Investment projects focusing on the infrastructure development of industrial zones in areas with difficult socioeconomic conditions would get capital support from the central budget as well as local budgets. As of May 2018, Vietnam had about 328 industrial and export processing zones and 625 industrial clusters (Saigon dau tu 2018). The strong development of industrial zones has become a driving force in the process of industrialization and modernization in Vietnam.

2.5 Conclusion

The remarkable economic achievements of Vietnam over the last three decades have proved the accuracy of the Doi Moi policy implemented by the Communist Party of Vietnam since 1986. Before the adoption of the Doi Moi policy, Vietnam had lost four decades to warfare. Nonetheless, several attempts to reform the country's economy had been made by governments both in North and South Vietnam. Under the condition of escalated warfare, however, the economic policies targeted the needs of the war effort. The unification of 1975 did not bring an end to the system of command economy in Vietnam. In the difficult circumstance of the US embargo and the wars in northern and southern borders, the government of Vietnam chose to continue and extend the system of centrally planned economy, which they had successfully implemented in North Vietnam in the 1960s and early 1970s. Ten years of economic struggles and trials worsened the economic situation, which was about to collapse in the beginning of the 1980s. A radical reform toward the economic liberalization became indispensable, and thus in December 1986, the Communist Party of Vietnam inaugurated the Doi Moi.

The Doi Moi is a comprehensive reform program encompassing all aspects of life with the primary focus on the economic field. The Doi Moi policy has been regularly amended and supplemented by the CPV and the State of Vietnam in accordance with new circumstances, but its major focuses have remained on the decentralization of State management of the economy, the promotion of external economic relations to expand trade and attract foreign investment, and the recognition of the contribution of private sectors in the economy. The ultimate objective of the Doi Moi program is to accomplish the industrialization and modernization of Vietnam, transforming the country's economy from a centrally planned economy to a socialist-oriented market economy (Ngo Dang Tri 2016; Fford and de Vylder 1996).

Notes

1. Some information about economic transformation in Vietnam prior to the 1960s is taken from the project entitled "The collapse of a colonial economy" (code 601-01-2020-02) funded by the Vietnam National Foundation for Science and Technology Development (Nafosted).
2. In 1989, for instance, the number of goods subject to export tax was reduced from 30 to 12 while the number of goods subject to import tax was 80 compared to 124 in the previous periods. Trade quota were eliminated, except for 14 imported goods and 10 exported goods. (Dinh Cong Khai 2012).

References

Adam Fford and Stefan de Vylder. 1996. *From Plan to Market: The Economic Transition in Vietnam*. Boulder: Westview Press.

Chinh phu. 2014. Luat dau tu. 2014. http://vanban.chinhphu.vn/portal/page/portal/chinhphu/hethongvanban?class_id=1&_page=1&mode=detail&document_id=178136. Accessed March 16, 2020.

Dang Cong san Viet Nam. 2002. *Van kien hoi nghi lan thu 5, Ban chap hanh trung uong khoa IX*. Hanoi: Su That Publisher.

Dang Cong san Viet Nam. 2006. *Van kien Dai hoi dai bieu toan quoc lan thu X*. Hanoi: Chinh tri Quoc gia Publishers.

Dang Cong san Viet Nam. 2007. *Van kien Dang toan tạp. Tap. 51.* Hanoi: Chinh tri Quoc gia Publishers.

Dang Cong san Viet Nam. 2013. *Van kien Dai hoi Dang thoi ky Doi Moi (Dai hoi VI, VII, VIII, IX, X, XI)*. Hanoi: Chinh tri Quoc gia Publishers.

Dang Cong san Viet Nam. 2016: *Van kien Dang toan tap. Tap. 60.* Hanoi: Chinh tri Quoc gia Publishers.

Dang Cong san Viet Nam. 2017. http://tulieuvankien.dangcongsan.vn/van-kien-tu-lieu-ve-dang/hoi-nghi-bch-trung-uong/khoa-xii/nghi-quyet-so-11-nqtw-ngay-362017-hoi-nghi-lan-thu-nam-ban-chap-hanh-trung-uong-dang-khoa-xii-ve-hoan-thien-the-che-kinh-561. Accessed March 16, 2020.

Dang Phong. 2005. *Lich su kinh te Viet Nam.* Hanoi: Khoa hoc Xa hoi.

Dang Phong. 2009. *'Pha rao' trong kinh te vao dem truoc Doi Moi.* Hanoi: Tri thuc Publishing House.

Dang Phong. 2016. *Tu duy kinh te Viet Nam.* Hanoi: Tri thuc Publishing House.

Dang Phong and Thien Tran Dinh. 2012. *Bien nien cac su kien kinh te Viet Nam (1975–2008).* Hanoi: Khoa hoc Xa hoi.

Dean Forbes, Terence H. Hull, David G. Marr, and Brian Brogan. 1991. *Doi Moi: Vietnam's Renovation, Policy and Performance.* Canberra: Australian National University Press.

Doulas C. Dacy. 1986. *Foreign Aid, War, and Economic Development: South Vietnam, 1955–1975.* Cambridge: Cambridge University Press.

Dinh Cong Khai. 2012. Chinh sach thuong mai cua Viet Nam giai doan 2003 den nay. https://fsppm.fulbright.edu.vn/cache/MPP04-552-L14V-2012-11-16-16422311.pdf. Accessed March 18, 2020.

Edwin E. Moise. 1976. Land Reform and Land Reform Errors in North Vietnam. *Pacific Affairs* 49: 70–92.

Edwin E. Moise. 1996. *Tonkin Gulf and the Escalation of the Vietnam War.* Chapel Hill: University of North Carolina Press.

Giang Dang and Low Sui Pheng. 2015. *Infrastructure Investment in Developing Economies; The Case of Vietnam.* Singapore: Springer.

Kim Tran Hoang. 1996. *Kinh te Viet Nam; Chang duong 1945–1995 va trien vong den 2020.* Hanoi: Thong ke Publishing House.

Ngo Dang Tri. 2016. *Tien trinh lich su Dang cong san Viet Nam.* Hanoi: Thong tin va truyen thong.

Nguyen Huong. 2017. 30 Years of Foreign Investment Policy Improvement. https://www.vir.com.vn/30-years-of-foreign-investment-policy-improvement-54504.html. Accessed March 15, 2020.

Nguyen Trong Xuan. 2002. *Dau tu truc tiep nuoc ngoai voi cong cuoc cong nghiep hoa, hien dai hoc o Viet Nam*. Hanoi: Khoa hoc Xa hoi Publishers.

Pham Thanh Vinh. 1966. *L'Édification d'une Économie Nationale Indépendante au Vietnam*. Hanoi: Éditions en Langues Étrangeres.

Pham Thi Hong Ha. 2017. *Kinh te Viet Nam Cong hoa duoi tac dong cua vien tro Hoa Ky (1955–1975)*. Hanoi: Cong an nhan dan Publishers.

Pham Van Thuy. 2019. *Beyond Political Skin: Colonial to National Economies in Indonesia and Vietnam*. Singapore: Springer.

Quoc hoi Viet Nam. 2013. Hien phap nuoc Cong hoa xa hoi chu nghia Viet Nam nam 1992. http://quochoi.vn/60namqhvn/lichsuphattrien/Pages/noi-dung-va-y-nghia-hien-phap-dau-tien.aspx?ItemID=9. Assessed March 15, 2020.

Saigon dau tu. 2018. https://saigondautu.com.vn/kinh-te/ca-nuoc-co-328-khu-cong-nghiep-khu-che-xuat-625-cum-cong-nghiep-57590.html. Accessed March 18, 2020.

Tong cuc Thong ke. 1999. Ty le ho ngheo nam 1999 phan theo thanh thi, nong thon va theo vung. https://www.gso.gov.vn/Default.aspx?tabid=735. Accessed March 16, 2020.

Tong cuc Thong ke. 2000. *Nien giam thong ke 1999*. Hanoi. Thong ke Publishing House.

Tong cuc Thong ke. 2006. *Xuat nhap khau hang hoa Vietnam 20 nam Doi Moi 1986–2005*. Hanoi: Thong ke Publishing House.

Truong Chinh. 1988. *Doi Moi la doi hoi buc thiet cua dat nuoc va cua thoi dai*. Hanoi: Su that.

Vincent Edwards and Anh Phan. 2013. *Manager and Management in Vietnam: 25 Years of Economic Renovation (Doi Moi)*. London and New York Routledge.

World Bank. 2018a. Poverty Headcount Ratio at National Poverty Lines-Vietnam. https://data.worldbank.org/indicator/SI.POV.NAHC?locations=VN. Accessed March 16, 2020.

World Bank. 2018b. Foreign Direct Investment, Net Inflows (% of GDP)-Vietnam. https://data.worldbank.org/indicator/BX.KLT.DINV.WD.GD.ZS?locations=VN. Access April 5, 2020.

World Bank. 2018c. GDP Annual Growth-Vietnam. https://data.worldbank.org/indicator/NY.GDP.MKTP.KD.ZG?locations=VN.

Yoko Niimi, P.V. Dutta, and L.A. Winters. 2007. Trade Liberalization and Poverty Dynamics in Vietnam. *Journal of Economic Integration* 22 (4): 819–851.

CHAPTER 3

State-Owned Enterprises in Vietnam: Challenges Hindering the Privatization Process

Trung Q. Nguyen, Burkhard N. Schrage, and Victor L. Kane

Abstract This chapter provides an overview of the performance and progress of privatization of state-owned enterprises (SOEs) in Vietnam. Interviews with selected market participants in the SOE privatization process highlight key issues and obstacles that impede the process and pose clear opportunities for government reform to improve and speed up the process.

Keywords State-owned enterprise · Privatization · Equitization · Corporate governance · IPO

T. Q. Nguyen (✉) · B. N. Schrage
RMIT University Vietnam, Ho Chi Minh City, Vietnam
e-mail: trung.nguyen@rmit.edu.vn

V. L. Kane
Portland, OR, USA

R. Macdonald (ed.), *The Economy and Business Environment of Vietnam*, https://doi.org/10.1007/978-3-030-49974-7_3

3.1 Introduction

An "Equitization Program"[1] which sought to fully or partially privatize state-owned enterprises (SOEs) was central to the transition of the *Doi Moi* reform that was first formulated in 1986. The policy measures implemented in 1992 toward a change of ownership of SOEs from the state to private hands were motivated by two key reasons. First, SOEs continued to show overwhelming inefficiencies, both operational and financial. Second, SOEs crowded out private enterprises by accumulating capital and favored treatment from the government. This effect would be verified in Nguyen and Freeman 2009. The restructuring of ownership was believed to be cornerstone in achieving higher degrees of market efficiency and fair competition.

Equitization or privatization can be important for any firm considering entry into Vietnam because it introduces change into the business environment. Firms expecting to deal with state firms as suppliers or clients may find themselves dealing with a private firm. Other businesses may discover their competitive map has changed. Still other foreign companies may be interested in acquiring an SOE as it privatizes. In each case, an understanding of the evolving equitization process is useful.

3.2 SOEs in Vietnam

Vietnam's model of economic development is largely based on state-led industrialization inspired by Japan, South Korea and Taiwan and thus has accorded in the past an important role to SOEs. Current economic policies recognize the importance of the private sector and reinvigorate the push for privatization. Figure 3.1 shows that the number of the over 50% state-owned enterprises decreased from approximately 5700 to 2500 during the period from 2000 to 2017, a reduction by more than a half. SOEs that are minority state-owned increased fourfold in the same period, from 305 to 1167. In the same time period, privately owned enterprises increased 14-fold from 31,000 to 430,000. While state-owned companies make up less than 1% of total number of enterprises in Vietnam, they are large (see Fig. 3.2) and represent a considerable, albeit shrinking, portion of the economy (Fig. 3.3). The pace of the decrease has somewhat decelerated in the last decade and the latest data show the private sector with an approximate share of 66% in 2017. The continued influence of large state-owned enterprises is viewed as a way for the state to retain its authority

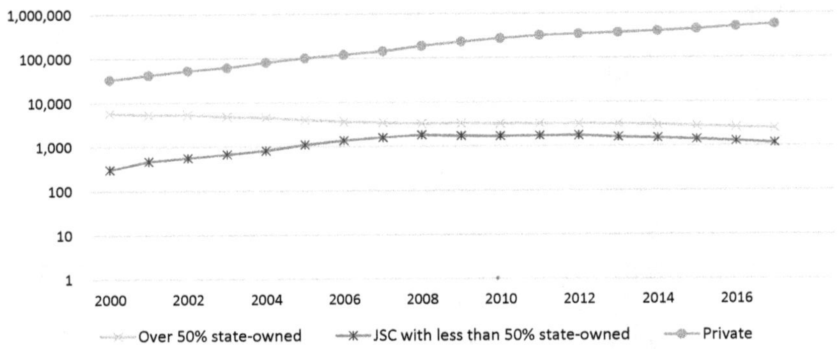

Fig. 3.1 Number of enterprises in Vietnam by ownership type (log-scale) (*Source* GSO Statistical Yearbook, multiple years)

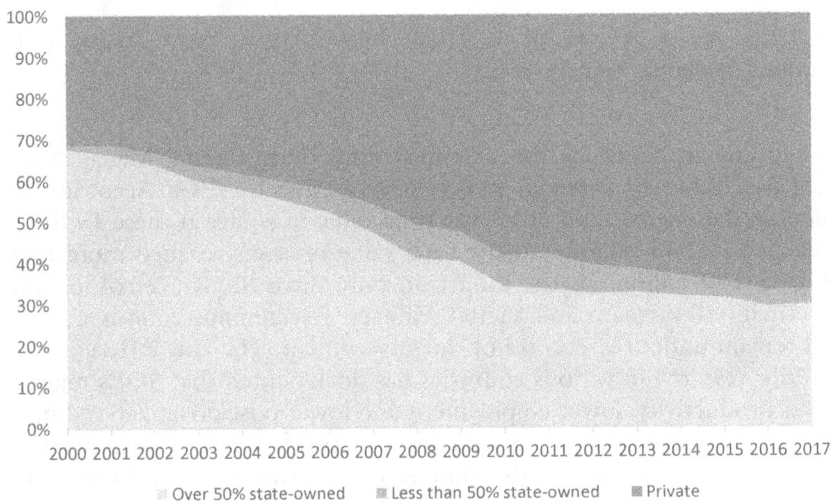

Fig. 3.2 Annual average capital per enterprise in 2017 (*Source* GSO Statistical Yearbook, multiple years)

through oversight and interference, especially in key industries, during the transition to increased market influence (Beeson and Pham 2012).

The Equitization Program consolidated SOEs into strategic State Economic Groups (SEGs) owned by various ministries. These SEGs are

Fig. 3.3 Assets by type of ownership from 2000 to 2017 (*Source* GSO Statistical Yearbook, multiple years)

owned and managed by the Committee for State Capital Management (CSCM). Table 3.1 provides an overview of these 19 SEGs. According to financial statements as of 2017, the total value of equity at these 19 SEGs exceeded US$43 billion and the total value of assets reached more than of US$ 100 billion. In the long run, only three SEGs (PetroVietnam, Electricity of Vietnam and Viettel Military Telecommunications Group) will remain under the control of the government (Ha Thu 2018).

Prior research in various countries has documented that SOEs register lower productivity, lower employment and lower post-privatization financial returns (e.g., Megginson and Netter 2001). While some studies in Vietnam have agreed with this finding (e.g., Truong et al., 2006), data from the General Statistics Office of Vietnam show that a typical Vietnamese SOE generates more profits than the typical private company (GSO 2018) (see Fig. 3.4). Of course, size is the real factor here. SOEs are on average much larger than private firms. Return on Capital Employed (Fig. 3.5) demonstrate that minority state-owned firms perform best, followed by privately owned enterprises. This pattern is consistent with the findings from Vaaler and Schrage (2009) which show that SOEs with less than 25% state ownership register highest returns

Table 3.1 State economic groups under the management of the committee for state capital management

No.	*State economic groups*	*Abbreviation*
1	State Capital Investment Corporation	SCIC
2	Vietnam Oil and Gas Group	PVN
3	Vietnam Electricity	EVN
4	Vietnam National Petroleum Group	Petrolimex
5	Vietnam National Chemical Group	VINACHEM
6	Vietnam Rubber Group	VRG
7	Vietnam National Coal-Mineral Industries Holding Corporation Limited	VINACOMIN
8	Vietnam Post and Telecommunications Group	VNPT
9	Vietnam Mobile Telecom Services One Member Limited Liability	MobiFone
10	Vietnam National Tobacco Corporation	VINATAB
11	Vietnam Airlines	
12	Vietnam National Shipping Lines	VINALINES
13	Vietnam Railways	VNR
14	Vietnam Expressway Corporation	VEC
15	Airports Corporation of Việt Nam	ACV
16	Vietnam National Coffee Corporation	VINACAFE
17	Vietnam Northern Food Corporation	VINAFOOD 1
18	Vietnam Southern Food Corporation	VINAFOOD 2
19	Vietnam Forest Corporation	VINAFOR

Source Adapted from Hai Minh (2018)

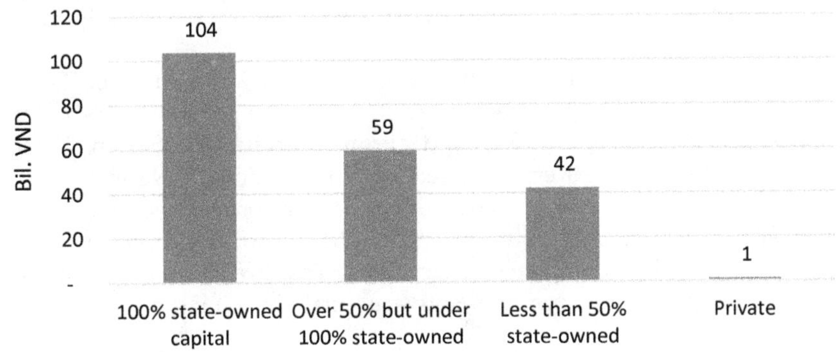

Fig. 3.4 Profit per enterprise in 2017, by type of enterprise (*Source* GSO Statistical Yearbook, multiple years)

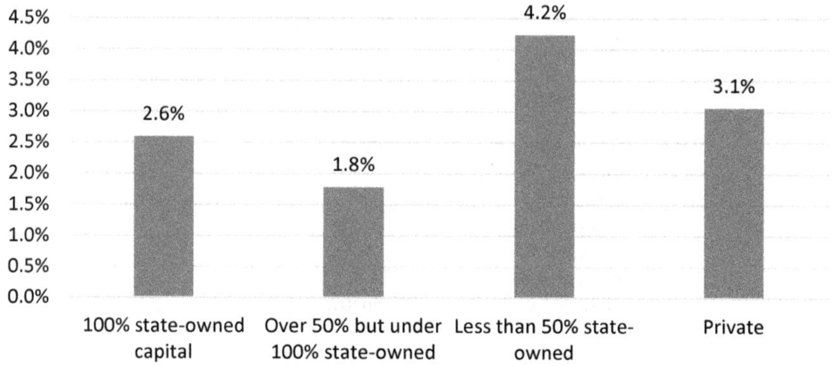

Fig. 3.5 Return on capital employed by ownership type (*Source* GSO Statistical Yearbook, multiple years)

following major investment decisions. As a matter of fact, the return on assets of the minority SOEs is more than double of that of the majority SOEs. The outperformance of the minority SOEs could be explained by two main factors (1) easier access to credit and (2) stronger influence from the private investors.

Despite the consensus on the importance and benefits of SOE privatization, the transfer of ownership of SOEs remains a work in progress. So far, the progress has not been satisfactory, and policy targets of reducing the influence of the state in the Vietnamese economy have rarely been met.

The latest wave of privatization—announced in 2015 with the Decision No.1233/QD-TTg of the Prime Minister—listed 405 SOEs to be equitized in the 2016–2020 period (Prime Minister 2015). In 2016, the new Vietnamese government led by Prime Minister Nguyen Xuan Phuc committed to the acceleration of the SOE reform. However, out of these 405 SOEs slated for privatization by 2020, as of December of 2019 fewer than 170 had completed the process. This low completion rate is grounded in political, procedural and structural challenges.

3.3 Challenges for the Privatization Process in Vietnam

The Vietnamese government, aware of the critical role of SOE equitization to the country's economic development, has provided support for the equitization process in the form of clear targets, measures and legal support (ADB 2015). The most recent direction from the government has reflected a more forward-thinking and stronger commitment from the government (Le 2017). Such efforts from the Vietnamese government have been positively perceived (Kim and Tru 2019). However, several issues in the overall equitization strategy appeared to hinder the pace of equitization itself and prevent the targets to be met on a timely basis (Le Thanh and Nhu Binh 2019).

This section presents several key challenges facing the privatization process, drawn from the findings of an in-depth qualitative study undertaken by the authors. The study consisted of twenty interviews with main stakeholders ("Market Participants") in Vietnam's SOE equitization, including representatives from brokerage firms, investment firms, law firms, auditing firms, government and the SOEs themselves. These interviews provided in-depth and multifaceted viewpoints on the barriers and facilitators of the SOE equitization process. Strategic challenges, resolved in terms of political will as well as motivated by incentives, governance issues and accountability, will be dealt with in turn over the following sub-sections.

3.3.1 Strategy

This sub-section outlines the prominent strategic setbacks from the perspectives of the market participants in our study. From their point of view, the overall strategy has been inadequate to provide sufficient incentives to meet the expectations of four key stakeholders: Central Government, SOEs, Advisors and Investors (Fig. 3.6). The main issues raised by the market participants and experts were: inadequate compensation for the advisors, unclear guidance for valuation method, rushed timeline and unattractive selection of firms on privatization offer.

3.3.1.1 Compensation Paid to Sell-Side Advisors Is Too Low

Professional advisors are believed to play a critical role in the successful equitization of SOEs. Financial consultants such as reputable investment

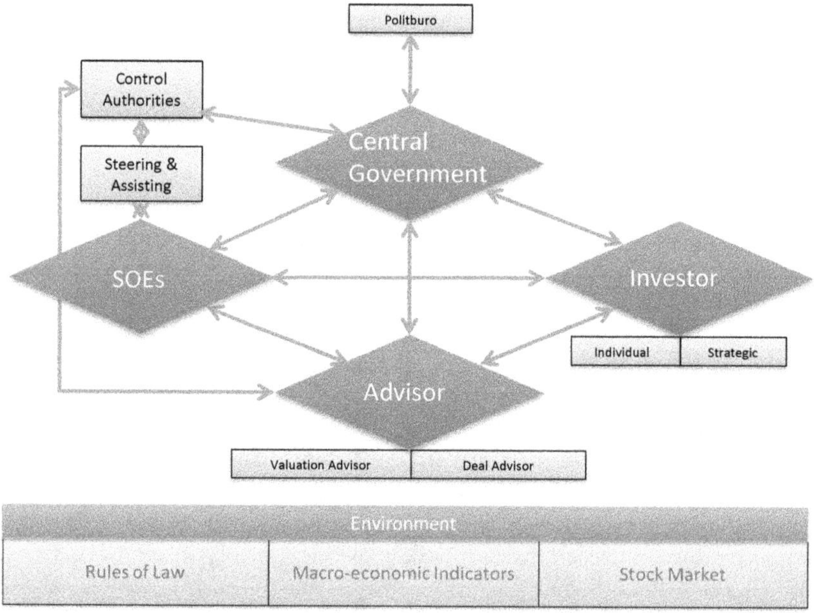

Fig. 3.6 Stakeholders in SOE equitization process (*Source* Authors' design)

banks or securities companies add value through their thorough understanding of the privatization process, especially in large and complex organizations (Gallo 1993). One of the most valuable services provided by these advisors is their objective assessment and valuation of the enterprise (Chen et al. 2014). Another advantage is the simplified procedure for investors to participate (Jagannathan et al. 2011). Overall, sell-side advisors such as investment banks, which have a unique set of skills, political and financial ties with stakeholders, will also boost the reputation of the IPO cases (Cook et al. 2006).

In successful cases of SOE equitizations in Vietnam, such as the case of a national air carrier, the role of professional advisors was clearly acknowledged from the SOE representatives. They mentioned reputable firms in the advisory industry such as Citigroup or Morgan Stanley as a critical factor in assuring the success of the IPO. Advisors like the Big Four accountancy firms should also be invited to assist in the large complex cases.

Notably, in most cases, the compensation paid to sell-side advisory services was perceived to be too low to motivate advisors. A broker shared that the advisory fee regulated in the decree was often not enough to cover costs and staff wages, and also not easily modified. Consequently, advisors did not have enough incentives to provide top-notch service to attract demand from the good investors. For the majority of equitized SOEs, the fee was out of their budget, and it was challenging to convince the government to approve success fee payment.

Besides the valuation advisors, the sell-side can also hire deal advisors to find a customized solution and develop sales options in order to increase the success chance of the IPO. This case-by-case strategy has been recommended in the past as a best practice for privatizing complex state enterprises (Welch and Fremond 1998). Rather than this method, the Vietnamese government prefers to stick to a one-size-fits-all approach, despite significant differences in firms operating in different sectors. A viewpoint shared by brokers and investment companies was that the government should hire experts specializing in the industry that the SOEs operate in, because their view is that different industries need different equitization processes.

Implementation details for the book-building method are often brushed aside. To price IPOs, the companies can apply three widely practiced approaches, such as public offerings, auction and book-building (Islam et al. 2006). While public auction can sell stakes at the highest prices to investors and maximize proceeds of SOE equitization for the government, this method focuses on only one criterion—price. In stock markets worldwide, book-building has become the de facto procedure by which businesses price their IPOs (Ganti 2019). It is arguably the superior approach (Kim and Tru 2019; Islam et al. 2006; Sherman and Jagannathan 2011). Valuation is arguably one of the most vital steps in equitization of SOEs in order to arrive at a win-win outcome for the sellers and buyers, in the case of SOEs, to avoid capital loss to the state and also to attract investors (Kim and Tru 2019). An appropriate method, clear procedure and proper implementation are important to speed up the process as well as to improve the transparency and attractiveness of the enterprises. Timing and transparency of the valuation were regarded as critical factors affecting investors' decisions, according to representatives from both SOEs and investment companies.

One of the advantages of book-building over the other IPO pricing mechanisms is enhanced transparency because in book-building an underwriter attempts to determine the IPO price based on the demand for shares from investors (Islam et al. 2006). A lawyer and broker interviewed in the study shared a similar viewpoint on enhanced transparency, since independent entities were allowed to determine the value of SOEs. Strategic investors could also research more about the company prior to the road shows, including company visits and management discussions to obtain information.

Another advantage is the convenience and efficiency for investors over the public auction method (Benveniste and Wilhelm 1997). Meanwhile, the auction method is prone to unexpectedly large fluctuations in the price discovery process and is likely to create more difficulties for investors, especially institutional investors (Sherman and Jagannathan 2011). A representative from an investment company commented that "Book-building should be the way to go for best practice in selling assets. It is one of the factors to facilitate the investors to go to the deal." Similar advantages were perceived by the participants of the SOE equitization in Vietnam, citing cases of Techcombank, Vincom Retail and Vinhomes about book-building application and its ability to provide reasonable price level that boosts investors' confidence.

In Vietnam, the most common method for turning SOEs into joint-stock companies is the auction (Kim and Tru 2019). The book-building method for pricing IPO of SOEs was introduced in decree 126/2017/ND-CP. The method is regarded as a positive change introduced by the government for the process of SOE equitization, but implementation of this method has not met expectations. Previous scholars have suggested that although book-building has its advantages, the key to success lies in using a policy of strategic pricing and allocation to offset the selling party incentive to prevent underpricing and to maximize returns from the IPO (Benveniste and Wilhelm 1997). How to apply it successfully in SOE privatization needs to be discussed in detail. It has been recommended that the central government should appoint credible underwriters for SOEs to choose for pricing their IPOs (Chen et al. 2014). Other suggestions mentioned by interviewed brokers and investors include a clear legal document on book-building to help guide and direct its practical application in the process of SOE equitization, or trials with the most capable SOEs to provide a case study for other firms.

3.3.1.2 Timeline Does Not Meet Investors' Needs

The timeline from the published prospectus to the IPO was perceived to be too tight and rushed. This is a significant hurdle especially for foreign investors who are not familiar with how the Vietnamese market operates and how the equitization works. In the case of big and complex SOEs, the timeline is too rushed compared to the international standard. The latest wave of equitization (2016–2020) included many large state corporations and economic groups, such as VNPT, Agribank, and Vinacomin, where sufficient time for preparation was needed (Le Thanh and Nhu Binh 2019).

According to brokers and investment firm representatives, one month of preparation for investors is clearly not enough, as the investors have to evaluate a substantial amount of evidence and submit many administrative documents. Foreign investors may also need more time to familiarize themselves with the Vietnamese market and the privatization process, as well as to wait for approvals and funds from their headquarters abroad. A broker stressed that the timeline is "not in accordance with international standards" and not sufficient for the investors to do their due diligence of SOEs, especially for state-owned conglomerates with extensive businesses and complicated structures. Time required also depends on how well-prepared and ready the SOEs are for the IPO:

> In other cases, if the documents are well organized and the roadshow is good, then the government can speed up the timeline. However, if the roadshow and documents are not well organized, then investors need more time to acquire and evaluate more information. Hence, the government should regulate the timelines to be more realistic and flexible on a case-by-case basis. (Investment Company)

Tendency of the State to hold onto majority shares of best performing large SOEs. The peak four years between 2003 and 2006 saw the privatization of nearly 60% of all SOEs, although these were mostly small and medium-sized enterprises (Le 2017). Although large SOEs also have been put into the equitization plan in recent years, the shares made available to the public are often very minor, which meant that private investors have often been reluctant to invest (Nguyen and O'Donnell 2017).

However, this strategy does not seem to work and could have slowed down the equitization process in Vietnam (Tran and Holloway 2014).

A significant negative relationship has been found between state ownership and the change in key performance measures of privatized firms (Truong et al. 2006). In other words, the higher the percentage of the state ownership, the less efficient the firms can be.

Holding onto the profitable SOEs might be counterproductive and hinder the potential of these firms. Meanwhile, getting rid of poorly performing SOEs has made privatization less attractive to investors and cannot bring high proceeds to the state budget. As one interviewee from an investment firm put it:

> No investor is going to pay a high price to buy shares of such SOEs, and keeping good SOEs would slow down the process of SOE equitization.

3.3.2 *Lack of Incentives and Political Will*

All parties need to pursue privatization in order for it to succeed. Resolve is currently weak. The reluctance to privatize SOEs has been found in among various stakeholders, including SOE managers and employees, the local government and the senior politicians in the Politburo. Also, the idea of state ownership has been a strongly endorsed view across Asia (Deutsch 1988). The emergence of SOEs in Vietnam was not only the product of a Communist economic system but also triggered by dominant political values of the wider region as well as by a colonialist history (Sjoholm 2006). At the time of reunification, the nationalization of firms was believed to be vital because private firms were unable to create adequate capital. The failure of the central planning economy during the first decade led to modifications in economic governance, including some degree of privatization. Similar to other transition economies, privatization in Vietnam has become a political arena where a number of actors fought to advance their specific interests (Turner et al. 2017).

3.3.2.1 *Lack of Meaningful Incentives for SOE Management and Employees*

Since the SOE is one of the key stakeholders in the equitization process, SOE managers' and employees' understanding and support of the equalization and divestment are viewed as having a significant impact on the speed and success of the process. Such postponement attitudes were found among SOE management (as summarized in a statement by the then Minister of Transportation, Dinh La Thang) that, although the local authorities accepted the equitization of the firm they are in charge, the executives "were using all means to ask for the state to hold dominant shares in the post-equitization businesses" (Han 2013).

SOE managers and employees have been unwilling to participate in the equitization process, creating a significant obstacle in previous phases of equitization (Vu 2003) (Lam An 2018). One of the reasons for this unwillingness among SOE management boards is the fear of losing their positions and the privileges availed by SOEs. Conventionally, SOEs enjoy preferred treatments in numerous areas such as land access, export quotas and tax, all of which would be abolished after equitization (Nguyen 2017). The SOE executives, staff and other vested parties have therefore been opposing the equitization initiative or trying to postpone it as long as possible.

Some interviewees believe that leaders and employees of some SOEs are reluctant and even prevent their SOEs from being privatized. Some SOE executives, besides the loss of benefits and privileges for the firm, also fear the loss of their positions of power in companies, especially when financial institutions invest and play a more active role in management (Thuy Dung 2018; Le Thanh and Nhu Binh 2019). Such conflict of interest is another reason for the slow pace of equitization of Vietnamese SOEs. The still mixed perception of the state sector's leading role among many executives has somehow been used as an excuse to justify their contention to retain their firms in the hands of the government (Vu 2003).

Throughout the interviews, the Employee Stock Ownership Plan (ESOP) was mentioned as an effective tool to gain support from SOE leaders and employees. Yet others mentioned that ESOPs may not provide sufficient incentives to attract employees to commit to the firms before and after equitization. Even though the government regulations provide for a 40% discount from the share price sold to management and main SOE employees, SOEs' leadership is still reluctant. This is because of the structure of ESOPs, which are equally distributed across all levels of employees, regardless of the position and responsibilities. As one broker commented:

> At SOEs, the government puts everything in the same rank, for example, security guards, administrative officers and the management are the same. They all get 100 shares of stock per year, which is not motivating for the management. In essence, there are no benefits differentiated in SOEs.

To further incentivize SOE employees, it was suggested by some interviewees that the government should give stock to employees based on their length of employment and/or their title or rank in the company. A grant of some monetary incentives to management and employees in the form of share bonuses of 1% or 2% of equity stocks was also raised.

Besides providing financial incentives, training and education targeted at the SOE management board could also foster their support. An investor emphasized that the SOE management should be aware of the importance of privatization for the economy, the community as well as their enterprises, in order to "encourage them to align with the private sector and have a more balanced view and private mindset."

3.3.2.2 Reluctance from the Local Government and Proprietor Ministries

SOEs in Vietnam can be classified into two groups, those owned by the local governments and those under central government's ownership (GSO 2012). Several SOEs at the city level are "cash cows," playing an important role in local government's budget. Consequently, the local representative body does not want to sell such businesses. In Ho Chi Minh City, for example, firms such as SATRA, Saigon Tourist and Ben Thanh Tourist are examples of these "cash cows," according to some of the investment companies in our study. Selling these SOEs to the public would mean that the local authorities would lose this source of income, while receiving little in return. At the central government level, the representative ministries are also hesitant to hand over their SOEs to private ownership, often citing national security or sensitive sectors as the reasons (Ha An 2019). An advisor to the Prime Minister observed:

> Demotivated SOEs and representative authorities normally have several excuses to delay or prevent equitizing their enterprises.

Privatization remains slow in both China and Vietnam, even as it was at the turn of the century (Morris et al. 2002). In particular, Vietnam has been remarkably slow, especially during 2018–2019. Full divestiture of state ownership from enterprises is also rare; instead, the state has favored alternative managerial reforms other than full transfer of ownership (Rama 2014). Interviewees believed the most important reason behind this "formalism" in divestment is the fear of losing the cash cows of the authorities both at provincial and national levels.

Lack of political will from senior politicians who could influence policymakers. Apart from reformists in the government who see the problems caused by the inefficiency of SOEs (Hai and O'Donnell 2017), there are still opponents to SOE reform who earn direct benefits from retaining state ownership and who are very influential and could assert considerable power over the enforcement of SOE equitization. Those of our interviewees who are close to the national government leaders felt that the senior politicians who could influence lawmakers seem to lack the political will to make a meaningful change to policy. From a political point of view, the government of Vietnam was hesitant to let go of state ownership because it was seen as a symbol of communism as well as an instrument of power and resources for making strategic decisions (Rama 2014). A common mindset among senior politicians was the belief that the equitization process could weaken socialism. A deputy Prime Minister was quoted saying: "If not SOEs, who will the government rely on?" (Beeson and Pham 2012, p. 551). This mindset essentially discourages those who could otherwise be active in promoting SOE equitization and making prompt decisions to clear the barriers in the government apparatus at lower levels.

Other market participants in our study indicated that the government should control only those relevant or critical sectors that contribute to public security and leave the other sectors for private ownership.

In addition, the government should have a more balanced view on the process to draw up a win-win scenario with the private sector in increasing enterprises' efficiency rather than maximizing profits of the government. Several of those interviewed noted the need for strategic decisions to clear up obstacles within the government's structure at lower levels. This responsibility should lie with the central government leaders in charge of SOE equitization in order to assert stronger push and monitoring of the representative authorities (ministry and local government who own the enterprises).

3.3.3 *Corporate Governance Issues*

Corporate governance is one of the key determinants of improvements in performance measures of privatized firms. Experiences of privatization in post-socialist states in Central and Eastern Europe have highlighted that a high standard of corporate governance practices is a necessary prerequisite for financially effective privatization (Mallin 2000). Better governance is also the key to establish shareholder rights in mixed-ownership companies and improved performance after privatization (World Bank 2014). For most Vietnamese SOEs, the weakness of corporate governance and lack of transparency in information disclosure, asset valuation and transaction were acknowledged by interviewees as hurdles for the privatization process.

3.3.3.1 Lack of Corporate Governance

In Vietnam, while the size and complexity of SOEs have been increasing, there is a persistent lack of effective mechanisms to hold the state firms accountable for their operation. This is an endemic problem and has been observed in previous studies. With many different actors participating in the same SOE, the separation of ownership and management responsibilities is very blurry (Sjoholm 2006). Vietnam still has a long way to go to build and enforce good corporate governance standards and board-level ethics and decision-making (Tran and Holloway 2014). While there is a general consensus on the necessity for standardizing corporate governance, the principle seemed to apply only for publicly listed companies and not for those with majority state ownership (Vu 2003). SOEs in Vietnam still lack the elements of sound corporate governance policies, such as a sound legal and regulatory framework, financial and fiscal discipline, a professional board of directors or a sound performance-monitoring system (World Bank 2014).

As many of the interviewees pointed out, the government should focus more on preparation prior to the IPO, including hiring advisors providing international services and applying procedures in accordance with international standards. Prospectuses that are more informative indirectly mean greater premarket due diligence, which reduces the reliance of the firms on book-building price and discourages underpricing (Hanley and Hoberg 2010). In other cases, there should be a restructure of the to-be-equitized SOEs to achieve better operational efficiency before equitizing (Babich and Sobel 2004). As an interviewee from an investment company put it

> To make SOEs more attractive, SOEs should put better governance policies and procedures in place, tidy up non-core & non-essential assets, get their books in order, and make sure that they are trying as much as possible to tidy up any historical non-transparent practices.

The lack of sound corporate governance in Vietnamese SOEs has resulted in poor operational performance metrics, making the SOEs unappealing for prospective investors. Indeed, SOEs have been shown to have much lower capital efficiency compared with firms in the private sectors (Truong and Weisblatt 2017). Poor governance and business decision making has turned some SOEs into multi-business conglomerates with unrelated extensions and bad managerial practices, and they are very frequently rife with corruption (Turner et al. 2017). As suggested by the interviewed market participants, SOEs with cumulative losses should first be merged with better performing ones or "re-engineered to improve operational performance.

3.3.3.2 *Poor Information Disclosure by SOEs*

A lack of clarity in information disclosure from the SOEs contributes to uncertainty regarding SOE's true performance and fair value (Kim and Tru 2019). While Decree No 81/2015/NĐ-CP mandated approximately 620 SOEs to disclose information, including financial and corporate management data, at least half of these firms failed to comply with information disclosure (Nguyen 2017). This poor disclosure of information has resulted in uncertainties for the strategic investors as well as the public (ADB 2015). For example, information in the prospectus prior to the IPOs was often insufficient to make informed investment decisions. Some interviewees noted that the standard template of the prospectus was too general with a low level of transparency compared to prospectuses in developed countries. Regarding the share price, price movement evaluation was also not transparent, causing doubts about price manipulation among investors. The lack of transparency has undermined the confidence of strategic investors, and in some cases caused them to revert the decision to invest in SOEs (Nguyen 2017). Yet, the hesitation to disclose information may come from the inherent inefficiencies and malpractices in the companies' operation. A lawyer we interviewed said:

> SOEs are not particularly keen to open the books and peel back the veil and let people really see what's inside the company, because maybe they know full well that there are a lot of things that foreigners would not feel comfortable with.

Improved disclosure of information would greatly enhance trust among investors as well as public sentiment (ADB 2015). In order to encourage investors to make investment decisions before the IPO, the equitized

SOEs should consider arranging prospective meetings and company visits for potential investors to provide them with fuller information. A broker recommended setting up an investor relations department to meet potential investors as required or to answer investors' questions and organize quarterly meetings with security and fund management companies. In a successful case of an equitized SOE, convenient information disclosure in the form of a virtual data room was provided by a Hong Kong advisory company specializing in virtual data, making it easy for investors to find any information about the companies. The quality of road shows should also be improved, together with the openness of managers to share information with investors. An interviewee from an investment company observed:

> Some management are very active and eager to meet investors to share information; others are overly conservative, especially when investors ask questions and the companies just answer with basic information.

3.3.3.3 Land Asset Valuation Is Complicated

One of the recognized obstacles to privatization is any technical difficulty such as disagreement over the value of assets, including land (Painter 2003). According to Vietnam Land Law 2013, land is collectively owned by all Vietnamese people, and the State represents the people to manage and grant the rights to use land. Hence, only the right to use the land but not land ownership are taken into the value of the firm due to the collective ownership. Furthermore, land ownership by foreigners is restricted by law, creating significant hurdles for the participation of foreign investors in investment in large SOEs. A broker we interviewed observed that, when public land is privatized, complicated issues arise regarding land ownership:

> When land is taken into company valuation in equitization and then enterprises are equitized, that means asset ownership would be shared to investors including land ownership.

Moreover, land granted to SOEs often makes up a large proportion of asset value. Some SOEs possess highly valuable pieces of real estate in central areas described as "golden land" (Phan 2018). SOEs enjoy favorable access to land, which provides significant advantages not only to carry out their main business operations, but also to access credit with enhanced collateral conditions as well as profitable opportunities for real estate businesses (Fujita 2017). Hence, the valuation of enterprise's assets sometimes is dramatically increased when the land is included in the property of an SOE, as shared by one of our interviewees. The IPO was recognized as a failure because the divestment of government was too large for domestic absorption, yet foreign investors are not interested due to the legal complication. It has been suggested that land should be excluded when evaluating the SOE's value, yet this is not a legally accepted practice. As an advisor to the Prime Minister pointed out in our interview:

> Perhaps, the government should take land from assets of SOEs and lease back to the enterprises after SOEs are transformed to JSCs, although currently, it is not legally supported to split land away from assets of SOEs. This action is necessary not only to solve the issue regarding foreign participation restrictions, but also to avoid unreasonably high valuation and usage of the land for purposes outside the core business of SOEs.

The complication of land asset valuation, together with the investigation of proper land use by some SOEs, appears to slow down the equitization plan even more. Not only is the valuation of SOEs, especially for larger SOEs, time consuming in the eyes of investors, it is also not transparent nor enacted according to international standards. SOEs continue to occupy most of the land reserved for business and exploit a substantial proportion of the new land provided by the government by leasing it clandestinely (Nguyen and Freeman 2009). Moreover, complex legal requirements and investigation of real estate management in SOEs further convolute the issue:

> There is a lot of investigation going on with respect to the sale of property by some SOEs before or after they go public. (Investment Company)

A broker in the study pointed to the simplification of valuation process as a way to speed up SOE equitization. Other advisors and SOE representatives agreed that the current valuation method is problematic. For example, some SOEs re-evaluate their assets to increase the chartered capital, a practice not acceptable for private companies. Asset-based valuation, according to an SOE representative, is disadvantageous because it is dependable on market value, and especially with land, the method gives out an unreasonably high figure. Efficiency-based valuation has also been mentioned as a credible alternative for asset-based method, in accordance with international standards. It is important that the IPO price be reasonably determined, so that the investors could make a profit and be confident with the IPO from state companies. An interview from an investment company argued:

> On the other hand, the starting price of shares also needs to be determined at an appropriate level which is not too high so the investors can make money from their investment, and not too low to avoid government capital loss. It is important for the investors to make money, because the following IPO will induce these investors to participate again.

3.3.3.4 Transactions Are Not Always at Arms-Length

Interviewees pointed out another factor which they believe impedes the SOE equitization process—namely group interests in SOE equitization. This seems to be the norm in Vietnamese SOEs as earlier studies such as Painter (2005) has also highlighted the problem. Cumbersome and fragmented management has created opportunities for problematic performance accountability and corruption (Painter 2008). Surreptitious transactions such as "backyard suppliers" (crony business dealings) are widespread in SOEs, as commented by one of the interviewees, an advisor to the Prime Minister:

> Nepotism and 'backyard' suppliers are common to these enterprises. These groups would lose such benefits after the enterprises are equitized, so they are not motivated toward equitization.

Kim and Tru (2019) also have observed that such groups naturally oppose equitization and attempt to delay the process to avoid losing favored treatment. Furthermore, crony business dealings in many SOEs tend to taint the image and thus the attractiveness of these enterprises for prospective investors (Truong and Rowley 2014). This was reflected in one of the interviews with a lawyer:

> The current manner of doing business at SOEs seems to be normal to SOEs and Vietnam companies and scares away foreigners. Specifically, the current approaches that some SOEs have informal ways of doing business and dealing with contracts to incentivize suppliers and customers. When SOEs stop following those approaches, they are not be able to maintain their business. That gives foreigners not-so-good an image of SOEs.

3.3.4 *Supervision and Accountability*

The last area for improvement for accelerating reform is the role of the government in supervision and accountability (Moreno De Acevedo Sánchez 2016). One of the imperative toolkits to facilitate privatization is to have in place a legal framework which makes clear the requisite responsibilities of each party to ensure the process is followed by SOEs and local authorities (Gray 1996). With respect to accountability, the state could coordinate with other participants in the system such as consultants, auditors and potential investors to have stricter oversight and discipline to hold SOEs accountable for the process. This could be achieved by designating key personnel responsible for the outcome and creating a clear set of key performance indicators for each party involved in the equitization process (Mallon 1994). Each of these points has been raised in our interviews with participants in Vietnam SOE privatization.

3.3.4.1 Law on Equitization Has Not Been in Place

An important step in the privatization process is to lay down the regulatory framework to standardize the process and hold the firms accountable before and after the privatization (Gilauri 2017). In Vietnam, the equitization program has been ongoing since 1992, and legal reform regarding equitization is also taking place at the same time. The situation was complicated for SOEs, since companies with at least 50% state-owned capital are expected to operate under both SOE and enterprise law (issued in 2005). By July 2010, the law on SOE was no longer effective while there were no details in the 2005 law on enterprises until amended in 2014. Absent a detailed law regulating SOEs, between 2011 and 2013, there were a total of 26 related Decrees and 11 Decisions and Directives issued regarding equitization (Wacker 2016). Despite the number of legal reform documents, their implementation has been stagnating and fragmented.

Recent legal changes in the latest wave of equitization (2016–2020) were perceived as more realistic and open, with practical policies such as allowing independent parties to determine the value of SOEs, and granting strategic shareholders the right to study the firms before the road shows, including company visits and consultation with management to obtain information. However, there is still room for improvement, particularly with regard to the restrictions of foreign participants. Past studies have provided evidence supporting the technical, managerial and financial advantages of foreign ownership for the domestic firms in developing markets (Bailey and Jagtiani 1994; Douma et al. 2006). In Vietnam, foreign ownership in privatized companies is still limited. The percentage of foreign ownership in listed companies was capped at 49% and will only be removed by the end of 2019, with the continued exception of some sectors such as banking, aviation and pharmacy (Nikkei 2018). Such policies were viewed as rigid and unfair. A broker observed in his interview:

> Policies regarding selling stakes to strategic investors are still conservative, lack flexibility and have not been attractive in the eyes of both domestic and international investors.

3.3.4.2 Delay in Or Absence of Stock Market Listing

In the past, since equitized SOEs were not obliged to become publicly listed companies, most SOEs postponed trading on the stock exchanges to avoid having to disclose information (Truong and Weisblatt 2017). An investment company representative in the study remarked that SOEs want to avoid listing since they do not want to prepare financial reports and be forced to be transparent and under the spotlight of the public. Many SOEs are believed to be overstaffed, inefficient and frequently abuse their privileges and monopolistic advantages "that may well evaporate after being equitized," according to an interviewed investor. The fear of losing these privileges disincentivizes the management of SOEs and makes them reluctant to communicate and engage in equitization.

To solve this issue, the government released Decision 126/2017/ND-CP, which mandated the equitized enterprises to complete all procedures to be listed on the Unlisted Public Company Market (UPCoM) within 90 days after IPOs finish. Compared to previous regulations, the Decree sets strict requirements on the public listing of equitized SOEs, which have been perceived as a positive improvement that draws attention of more investors. Following this, Vietnam raised US$2.6 billion from just five IPOs in 2018 and became Southeast Asia's top market for IPOs in 2018, partly because of the push from the government to privatize large SOEs such as PetroVietnam Power, Viet Nam Rubber Group and Viet Nam Southern Food Corp (Mehta 2019).

Nevertheless, the key informants in the reform remained less enthusiastic about the enforceability of the mandatory listing requirement. Given the SOEs' close ties with the government, it is possible for them to request a special mechanism to extend the process or not to be included in the bourses. As a result, some large equitized SOEs took several years after the auctions just to be listed on UPCOM Stock Exchange, a mezzanine market that has very little oversight, compared to other two—the Ho Chi Minh Stock Exchange (HoSE) and the Hanoi Stock Exchange (HNX). The government should put in place policies to advance the equitized companies to two main stock exchange markets, especially HoSE which is more attractive to foreign investors due to greater liquidity and better oversight. This mechanism can be achieved with stricter requirements and enforcement of listing criteria (Li 2015), as in the following suggestion from one investment company interviewee:

> Listing criteria should be advanced, especially for big SOEs, if they go to UPCOM that looks like two big fish in a small pool, they should come to HoSE instead.

3.3.4.3 Lack of Centralized Decision-Making Body in Central Government

It is common in Vietnam that SOEs are representatively owned by local or central authorities, besides the management body, creating a complex structure with no clear directive for decision-making (Painter 2003). This complex structure gives rise to several coordinating challenges during the equitization process since there is no main decision-maker in this process (Truong and Rowley 2014). In many cases, the SOEs also set up a steering committee in charge of equitization, which is comprised of members from the SOE and representative authorities, yet oftentimes this committee lacks the expertise and motivation to make the final decisions. Instead, they delay the process and play the "blame-game." One lawyer interviewed illustrates this with an example:

> A completed proposal from cities such as Ho Chi Minh City was sent to a representative ministry in Hanoi and was stuck there for months. In addition, several decisions on promoting and connecting with the investors depends on the steering committee, which is comprised of members from SOE and representative authorities. In many cases this steering committee does not have the expertise, capability and the power to make the final decision and delays are the result. In this context the blame-game usually occurs.

In an attempt to centralize the reform, the government has set up the State Capital Management Committee (SCMC) to oversee the equitization process. While replacing the current representative committees with a single centralized SCMC is a positive move, the centralized committee's capability to accelerate privatization depends on having skilled leaders and experts with relevant experience from both the public and private sectors. Charged with a critical responsibility, the management team of this committee would decide the future of this nationally high prioritized process. The SCMC should be directed by the government to formulate a detailed plan and proactively push for results, with identified personnel to be in charge of the outcome.

Divestment from the already equitized SOEs has not been paid much attention by government, since most of the effort has been concentrated on the IPO. The lack of government supervision has resulted in slow divestiture, often lagging behind schedule (Gainsborough 2009). A mix of reward and penalties should be applied to accelerate divestment from non-core industries that do not require state involvement. For the remaining SOEs, the government should consider a comprehensive reform of management teams and business operations.

3.4 Conclusion

Privatizing SOEs will remain a challenging task for the government of Vietnam. Given the large share of SOEs in the country's GDP as well as the increasingly important role of private enterprises in Vietnamese economy, it is high time to re-evaluate the equitization processes, from start to finish. It requires leadership and collaboration from both the state and the SOEs to enhance every step of the equitization, from improving corporate governance, market valuation, prospectus development and road show preparation, to IPO completion and initial issuance of share on the stock markets. Equally important is understanding the challenges confronting market participants in their interactions with government and SOEs, and coming up with substantive reforms to make the process more efficient, transparent and accountable.

Foreign businesses contemplating entering the Asian market by acquisition of minority or controlling ownership of a former SOE in Vietnam should monitor opportunities and attempt to address the various challenges, for example, by providing incentives for current SOE employees.

Acknowledgements The content of this chapter was developed based on a study conducted from May–August 2018 by the authors at RMIT University Vietnam. The authors would like to thank VinaCapital for their funding for the aforementioned study and Nguyen Thu An for her research assistance work.

Note

1. In this chapter, we use the terms and concepts "privatization" and "equitization" interchangeably.

References

ADB. 2015. State-Owned Enterprise Reform in Viet Nam: Lessons Learnt and Future Directions. In *Background paper prepared for the Viet Nam Public Finance Partnership Group High Level Meeting*. Hanoi, Vietnam: Asia Development Bank.

Babich, V., & Sobel, M. J. 2004. Pre-IPO Operational and Financial Decisions. *Management Science*. https://doi.org/10.1287/mnsc.1040.0252.

Bailey, W., & Jagtiani, J. 1994. Foreign Ownership Restrictions and Stock Prices in the Thai Capital Market. *Journal of Financial Economics*. https://doi.org/10.1016/0304-405x94)90030-2.

Beeson, M., & Pham, H. H. 2012. Developmentalism with Vietnamese Characteristics: The Persistence of State-Led Development in East Asia. *Journal of Contemporary Asia*, *42*(4), 539–559. https://doi.org/10.1080/00472336.2012.706481.

Benveniste, L. M., & Wilhelm, W. J. 1997. Initial Public Offerings: Going by the Book. *Journal of Applied Corporate Finance*, *10*(1), 98–108. https://doi.org/10.1111/j.1745-6622.1997.tb00130.x.

Chen, C., Shi, H., & Xu, H. 2014. The IPO Underwriting Market Share in China: Do Ownership and Quality Matter? *Journal of Banking and Finance*. https://doi.org/10.1016/j.jbankfin.2014.05.028.

Cook, D. O., Kieschnick, R., & Van Ness, R. A. 2006. On the Marketing of IPOs. *Journal of Financial Economics*. https://doi.org/10.1016/j.jfineco.2005.08.005.

Deutsch, A. 1988. The Question of Privatization in the Market Economies of Southeast Asia. *Southeast Asian Affairs*, *1988*(1), 51–59. https://doi.org/10.1355/seaa88d.

Douma, S., George, R., & Kabir, R. 2006. Foreign and Domestic Ownership, Business Groups, and Firm Performance: Evidence from a Large Emerging Market. *Strategic Management Journal*. https://doi.org/10.1002/smj.535.

Fujita, M. 2017. Vietnamese State-Owned Enterprises Under International Economic Integration. *RIETI Discussion Paper Series*.
Gainsborough, M. 2009. Privatisation as State Advance: Private Indirect Government in Vietnam. *New Political Economy*, *14*(2), 257–274. https://doi.org/10.1080/13563460902826013.
Gallo, L. G. 1993. The Value-Added of Investment Bankers in Privatizations. *Columbia Journal of World Business*, *28*(1), 196–205. https://doi.org/10.1016/0022-5428(93)90066-x.
Ganti, A. 2019. Book Building. *Investopia*. https://www.investopedia.com/terms/b/bookbuilding.asp.
Gilauri, N. 2017. Privatizing State-Owned Enterprises. In *Practical Economics* (pp. 113–124). Cham: Springer International Publishing. https://doi.org/10.1007/978-3-319-45769-7_6.
Gray, C. W. 1996. In Search of Owners: Lessons of Experience with Privatization and Corporate Governance in Transition Economies: Policy Research Working Papers. *Policy Research Working Papers- World Bank Wps*.
GSO. 2012. Doanh nghiệp và c s s n xuất kinh doanh cá th (Enterprise and Individual Business Establishment). In *Vietnam Statistical Yearbook 2012* (pp. 193–348). Hanoi: General Statistics Office of Vietnam (GSO).
GSO. 2018. Doanh nghiệp , Hợp tác xã và C s kinh t cá th phi nông nghiệp (Enterprise, Cooperative and Non-farm Individual Business Establishment). In *Vietnam Statistical Yearbook 2018* (pp. 287–469). Hanoi: General Statistics Office of Vietnam (GSO).
Ha An. 2019, September 5. TS. Vũ Đình Ánh: "Mua lại c ph n ACV đi ng ợc tất c các ch tr ng l n từ tr c đ n nay." *BizLIVE.vn*. https://bizlive.vn/kinh-doanh/ts-vu-dinh-anh-mua-lai-co-phan-acv-di-nguoc-tat-ca-cac-chu-truong-lon-tu-truoc-den-nay-3519450.html. Accessed 4 December 2019.
Ha Thu. 2018, May 30. Vietnam to Retain Three State Economic Groups by 2020. *The Hanoitimes*. Ha Noi.
Hai Minh. 2018. *Committee for State Capital Management to Make Debut*. Viet Nam Government Portal. http://news.chinhphu.vn/Home/Committee-for-State-Capital-Management-to-make-debut/20189/34783.vgp.
Hai, N. M., & O'Donnell, M. 2017. Reforming State-owned Enterprises in Vietnam: The Contrasting Cases of Vinashin and Viettel. *Asian Perspective*, *41*(2), 215–237.
Han, T. 2013, October 25. SOE Equitization Is Slow Due to Managers' Fear of Losing Their Positions (C ph n hoá doanh nghiệp nhà n c chậm trễ vì s p sợ mất ch c?). *Đời Sống & Pháp Luật*. Hanoi, Vietnam. https://www.doisongphapluat.com/kinh-doanh/doanh-nghiep/co-phan-hoa-doanh-nghiep-nha-nuoc-cham-tre-vi-sep-so-mat-chuc-a6513.html.
Hanley, K. W., & Hoberg, G. 2010. The Information Content of IPO Prospectuses. *Review of Financial Studies*. https://doi.org/10.1093/rfs/hhq024.

Islam, K. M. Z., Siddiquee, M., & Rahman, M. I. 2006. Book-Building System: Will It Really Help to Build the Market? *Journal of Business Research*, *8*(June). https://papers.ssrn.com/sol3/papers.cfm?abstract_id=928137. Accessed 2 December 2019.

Jagannathan, R., Jirnyi, A., & Sherman, A. E. 2011. Why Don't Issuers Choose IPO Auctions? The Complexity of Indirect Mechanisms. *NBER Working Paper Series*. https://doi.org/10.2139/ssrn.1330691.

Kim, K., & Tru, N. A. 2019. Reform of State-Owned Enterprises in Viet Nam to Increase Performance and Profit. In *ADBI Working Paper 999*. Tokyo: Asian Development Bank Institute. https://www.adb.org/publications/reform-state-owned-enterprises-viet-nam-increase-performance-and-profit.

Lam An. 2018. Slow Privatization in State-Owned Enterprises Due to Fear of Lossing Position. Retrieved from https://bizlive.vn/doanh-nghiep/doanh-nghiep-nha-nuoc-cham-co-phan-hoa-vi-lanh-dao-lo-mat-ghe-3467317.html.

Le, H. H. 2017, July. Vietnam's New Wave of SOE Equitization: Drivers and Implications. *Perspective: Researchers at ISEAS - Yusof Ishak Institute - Analyse Current Events*, *57*, 1–8. https://www.iseas.edu.sg/images/pdf/ISEAS_Perspective_2017_57.pdf.

Le Thanh & Nhu Binh. 2019. C ph n hóa doanh nghiệp nhà n c: khó đ đ ờng - Tu i Tr Online. *Tu i Tr* . https://tuoitre.vn/co-phan-hoa-doanh-nghiep-nha-nuoc-kho-du-duong-20190824083042997.htm. Accessed 4 December 2019.

Li, J. 2015. OTC Stock Market in China—The New Venture Capital Exit? *Asian Journal of Law and Economics*. https://doi.org/10.1515/ajle-2014-0002.

Mallin, C. 2000. Developments in Corporate Governance in Central and Eastern Europe. *Corporate Governance: An International Review*, *8*(1), 43–51.

Mallon, R. D. 1994. State-Owned Enterprise Reform Through Performance Contracts: The Bolivian experiment. *World Development*. https://doi.org/10.1016/0305-750x(94)90062-0.

Megginson, W. L., & Netter, J. M. 2001. From State to Market: A Survey of Empirical Studies on Privatization. *Journal of Economic Literature*, *39*(2), 321–389. https://doi.org/10.1257/jel.39.2.321.

Mehta, H. 2019, February 28. Reality Bites in Vietnam's March Towards Privatisation. *The Business Times*. Singapore. https://www.businesstimes.com.sg/opinion/reality-bites-in-vietnams-march-towards-privatisation. Accessed 10 December 2019.

Moreno De Acevedo Sánchez, E. 2016. State-Owned Enterprise Management Advantages of Centralized Models. *IADB*.

Morris, J., Hassard, J., & Sheehan, J. 2002. Privatization, Chinese-Style: Economic Reform and the State-Owned Enterprises. *Public Administration*. https://doi.org/10.1111/1467-9299.00308.

Nguyen, T. H. 2017. Privatization of State-Owned Enterprises in Vietnam: Opportunities and Challenges. *Datarama*. https://medium.com/@dataramatech/privatization-of-state-owned-enterprises-in-vietnam-opportunities-and-challenges-5e418c69afec.

Nguyen, M. H., & O'Donnell, M. 2017. Reforming State-Owned Enterprises in Vietnam: The Contrasting Cases of Vinashin and Viettel. *Asian Perspective*, *41*(2), 215–237. https://doi.org/10.1353/apr.2017.0011.

Nguyen, V. T., & Freeman, N. J. 2009. State-Owned Enterprises in Vietnam: Are They "Crowding Out" the Private Sector? *Post-Communist Economies*, *21*(2), 227–247. https://doi.org/10.1080/14631370902778674.

Nikkei. 2018, October 10. Vietnam to Remove 49% Foreign Ownership Cap on Listed Companies. *Nikkei Asian Review*. Ho Chi Minh City.

Painter, M. 2003. The Politics of Economic Restructuring in Vietnam: The Case of State-owned Enterprise "Reform." *Contemporary Southeast Asia*, *25*(1), 20–43. https://doi.org/10.1355/cs25-1b.

Painter, M. 2005. The Politics of State Sector Reforms in Vietnam: Contested Agendas and Uncertain Trajectories. *Journal of Development Studies*. https://doi.org/10.1080/0022038042000309241.

Painter, M. 2008. From Command Economy to Hollow State? Decentralisation in Vietnam and China. *Australian Journal of Public Administration*, *67*(1), 79–88. https://doi.org/10.1111/j.1467-8500.2007.00570.x.

Phan, N. 2018, September 24. "Đất vàng" hãng phim truyện Việt Nam bị "thâu tóm" th nào? (How Was the Golden Land of the Vietnam Film Studio Acquired?). *Ti n Phong*. Ha Noi. https://www.tienphong.vn/dia-oc/dat-vang-hang-phim-truyen-viet-nam-bi-thau-tom-the-nao-1327109.tpo. Accessed 3 December 2019.

Prime Minister. 2015. Decision No.1233/QD-TTg. Approving Import Management Scheme by 2020 in Conformity with International Commitments. Hanoi, Vietnam.

Rama, M. 2014. Viet Nam. In R. E. Looney (Ed.), *Handbook of Emerging Economies* (pp. 339–363). New York: Routledge. https://doi.org/10.30875/feecd05f-en.

Sherman, A. E., & Jagannathan, R. 2011. Why Do IPO Auctions Fail? *NBER Working Paper Series*. Cambridge, MA. https://doi.org/10.2139/ssrn.874344.

Sjoholm, F. 2006. *State Owned Enterprises and Equitization in Vietnam. East*. Stockholm, Sweden. http://swopec.hhs.se/eijswp/papers/eijswp0228.pdf.

Thuy Dung. 2018. S p lo mất gh ; khi n doanh nghiệp nhà n c chậm c ph n hoá. *Lao Động Online*. Hanoi. https://laodong.vn/doanh-nghiep-doanh-nhan/sep-lo-mat-ghe-khien-doanh-nghiep-nha-nuoc-cham-co-phan-hoa-750571.ldo. Accessed 5 December 2019.

Tran, T. H. L., & Holloway, D. A. 2014. Developments in Corporate Governance: The Case of Vietnam. *Corporate Ownership and Control*, *11*(3C), 219–230.

Truong, D. L., Lanjouw, G., & Lensink, R. 2006. The Impact of Privatization on Firm Performance in a Transition Economy—The case of Vietnam. *Economics of Transition*, *14*(2), 349–389.

Truong, N., & Weisblatt, B. 2017. *SOE Reform Contributes to Bright Outlook for Economy*. Viet Capital Securities.

Truong, Q., & Rowley, C. 2014. Post-State Capitalism. *The Oxford handbook of Asian business systems*, 283.

Turner, M., Michael, O., & Kwon, S. H. 2017. The Politics of State-Owned Enterprise Reform in South Korea, Laos, and Vietnam. *Asian Perspective*. https://doi.org/10.1353/apr.2017.0009.

Vaaler, P. M., & Schrage, B. N. 2009. Residual State Ownership, Policy Stability and Financial Performance Following Strategic Decisions by Privatizing Telecoms. *Journal of International Business Studies*, *40*(4), 621–641. https://doi.org/10.1057/jibs.2008.104.

Vu, Q. N. 2003. SOE Equitization in Vietnam: Experiences, Achievements, and Challenges. *Southeast Asian Affairs*. https://doi.org/10.1355/seaa03t.

Wacker, K. M. 2016. Restructuring of the SOE Sector in Vietnam: Where Do We Stand and What Are the Challenges Ahead? In *Vietnam Forum 2016 "Vietnam: Thirty Years of Doi Moi and Beyond."* Singapore: ISEAS. https://doi.org/10.2139/ssrn.2828197.

Welch, D., & Fremond, O. 1998. *The Case-by-Case Approach to Privatization: World Bank Technical Papers*. The World Bank. https://doi.org/10.1596/0-8213-4196-0.

World Bank. 2014. *Corporate Governance of State-Owned Enterprises: A Toolkit*. The World Bank. https://doi.org/10.1596/978-1-4648-0222-5.

CHAPTER 4

Participating and Upgrading in Global Value Chains: The Case of Small and Medium Enterprises in Vietnam

Trung Q. Nguyen, Hiep Cong Pham, and Robert McClelland

Abstract This chapter defines small and medium-sized enterprises and global value chains in a Vietnamese context. It provides some historical perspectives and outlines its position and performance in this area relative to other Southeast Asian countries. The critical factors for participating and upgrading of small and medium-sized enterprises in global value chains are addressed, outlining the role of lead firms, small and medium-sized enterprises competitive advantages and institutional factors. There is a discussion on challenges for Vietnamese participation and upgrading in global value chains and also this includes an account of a medium size group missing in small and medium enterprises, corporate governance, innovation capability, the macroeconomic environment, access to formal credit, and logistics infrastructure. The chapter concludes with outlining some of the obstacles faced and recommendations for government in

T. Q. Nguyen (✉) · H. C. Pham · R. McClelland
RMIT University Vietnam, Ho Chi Minh City, Vietnam
e-mail: trung.nguyen@rmit.edu.vn

R. Macdonald (ed.), *The Economy and Business Environment of Vietnam*, https://doi.org/10.1007/978-3-030-49974-7_4

developing absorptive capacity, assimilating and exploiting the knowledge and information from lead firms, comments on national logistics capacities, and future sustainable development.

Keywords Small and medium-sized enterprise · Global value chains · Vietnam · FDI · Lead firm · Institutional factor

4.1 Introduction

A value chain is defined as "the full range of activities which are required to bring a product or service from conception, through the intermediary phases of production, delivery to final consumers, and final disposal after use" (Kaplinsky and Morris 2000: 4). However, one must also consider Research and Development as well as conception. A value chain may be contained within one firm and one country, or it may extend across several firms and several countries (Lim and Kimura 2009). Large firms participate in value chains, as do small and medium-sized enterprises (SMEs). Participation in global value chains (GVCs) has benefited SMEs globally. Beyond the immediate benefits of business opportunities and financial flows into the host country, GVC participation, mainly through the channel of foreign direct investment (FDI) for developing countries, can enable local SME suppliers to enhance managerial skills, improve product quality, innovate production and business processes, renovate working conditions and shift to more sustainable business practices. These benefits have been confirmed as spillover effects on productivity and technology by studies on FDI impacts (OECD-UNIDO 2019).

There have been significant economic changes in Vietnam since the war in Vietnam ended in 1975, particularly since the early 1990s. The nation would surprise visitors by seemingly transforming every time they return. The most common and general factor cited for the country's transformation is the shift in its economic model, gradually transitioning from a command economy to a more market-based economy, known as *Doi Moi* since 1986. For many, Vietnam is seen as a success story of poverty eradication and economic integration. Data from the World Bank (2019) shows the average economic growth rate for the period from 1990 to 2018 of Vietnam was 6.78%, making it among the fastest-growing economies in the world. Its active international economic integration and the development of domestic private sector play a critical role in this process. A challenge facing the country is how to better link the domestic private sector with the value chains of foreign-invested enterprises.

4.2 Economic Integration and Domestic Private Sector Development

The relationship with the United States normalized in 1995 and by the end of 2019 twelve bilateral and multilateral free trade agreements were signed. The free trade deal most expected, between Vietnam and the European Union (EU), was recently ratified by the European Parliament in early 2020 (European Parliament News 2020). It is expected to be effective in July 2020, making Vietnam the only developing country in Asia that has secured an ambitious trade agreement with the EU. For many years, Vietnam has been an attractive destination for international investors. By the end of 2018, there were 16,178 foreign-invested enterprises operating in Vietnam, accounting for about 3% of the enterprise population (Ministry of Planning and Investment 2019). The foreign-invested enterprises have been successful in boosting international trading activities in Vietnam. In 2019, out of US$ 263.5 billion of Vietnam's total exports, 69% is from the FDI sector (Phuong 2019). As a matter of fact, Vietnam is one of the most open economies in the world, and several local enterprises have joined in the global value chains of several lead firms. The problem remains, however, that Vietnamese firms contribute only a small proportion in export value of the foreign-invested firms. In other words, the linkages between the FDI sector and local firms are weak, and the FDI firms have been mainly exploiting low labor cost and other preferential policies, such as on tax and land. In 2019, import volumes from the FDI account for 58% of total imports of Vietnam (see Fig. 4.1) (Phuong 2019), which demonstrates that the suppliers for these firms remain largely outside the country. When foreign-invested enterprises consider only to utilize low-cost labor or natural resources and acquire other key materials from overseas suppliers, they are not deeply rooted in the host country.

After 1975, private enterprises in Vietnam were banned until *Doi Moi*. Since the early 1990s they have started to develop in tandem with the privatization of the state-owned enterprises (see Chapter 3). This sector has increasingly proven to be the backbone of the economy. According to the White Book on enterprises of Vietnam, by 2019 approximately

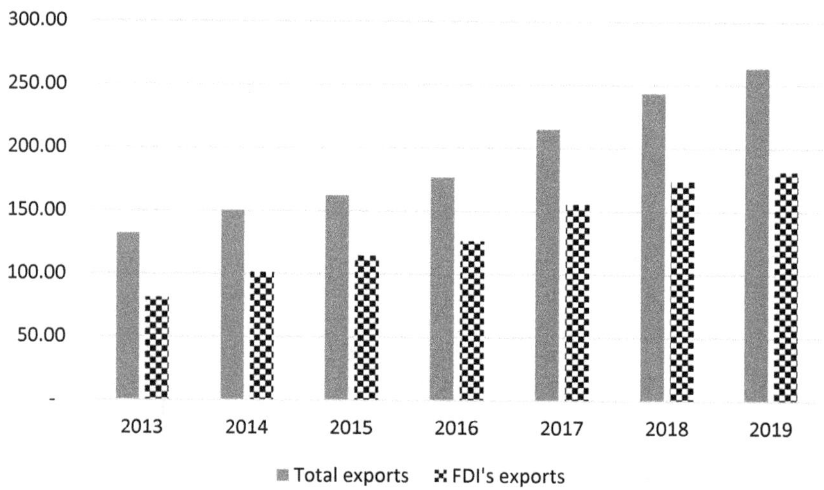

Fig. 4.1 Exports from FDI in total exports of Vietnam ($US billion) (*Source* GSO multiple years)

96.5% of 715 thousand operating enterprises in Vietnam were domestic private enterprises (Ministry of Planning and Investment 2019). Similar to other Asian countries, SMEs in Vietnam took a large share of total number of domestic private enterprises (98%), contributing about 45% of the GDP (Phung 2019). However, these firms can only join in low-value-added links in value chains, such as assembling. Although there have been improvements, lead firms in Vietnam such as Samsung Electronics once struggled to find capable local suppliers for simple electronic parts in their production line (Dinh and Ngoc 2015). In 2017, only 21% of Vietnamese SMEs were linked with global supply chains, much lower than 30% in Thailand and 46% in Malaysia. Similarly, the localization rate of Japanese enterprises in Vietnam only reached 34%, while that figure was 68% in China and 57% in Thailand (ADB 2017). A recent survey shows better signs of local sourcing for intermediates from foreign manufacturers; however, Vietnam remains low in comparison with other peer countries in the region (see Fig. 4.2).

While Vietnam has achieved initial successes with its economic integration and private sector development, it is facing challenges to sustain these successes with the low-value-added exports and the disconnection

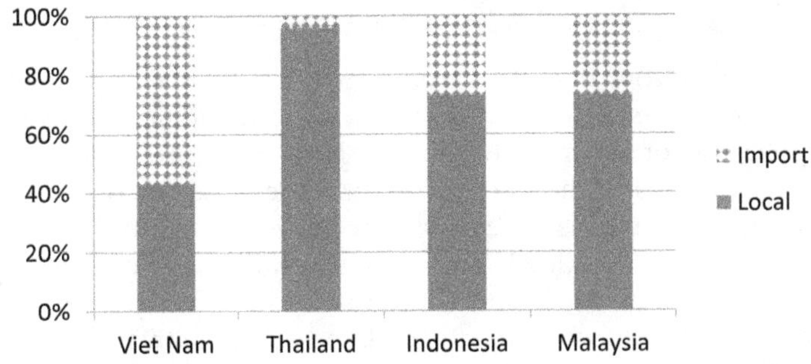

Fig. 4.2 Intermediates sourced locally by foreign manufacturers (*Source* OECD-UNIDO 2019)

of the local SMEs and the FDI. Recent studies, however, show that small firms can have more active roles to play in GVCs, given the rise of the digital economy (World Bank and World Trade Organization 2019). This chapter provides an overall picture of GVC and the SMEs integration in the context of Vietnam. It first specifies critical factors for the participating and upgrading of SMEs in GVCs. The subsequent sections proceed to provide a better understanding of challenges facing SMEs when integrating and upgrading in GVCs. The analysis in this chapter enhances the understanding of the lead firms, the local SMEs, and the policymakers about their roles in a GVC.

4.3 Critical Factors for Participating and Upgrading of SMEs in a GVC

In developing countries, integration into the GVC is necessary and important to convert unproductive labor in agricultural activities to better-pay jobs in the manufacturing sector. However, SMEs joining the GVCs should target upgrading as the ultimate goal. The notion of upgrading emphasizes the ability to deliver products or services with greater value-added, or to move into more skilled activities (Pietrobelli and Rabellotti 2006). In other words, the challenges for SMEs in developing countries should not only be about participating but also moving up in the GVCs tiered structure as this can afford more sustained growth (Ponte and Ewert 2009). This includes both more often assembly as well as moving into product design and final marketing.

4.3.1 Lead Firms

A GVC is usually controlled by a lead firm. This lead firm's main services or production inputs are often supplied by contracting firms, which are in turn supplied by other firms, forming a tiered structure (Abonyi 2005). The higher a firm is in the tiered structure, the closer it connects to the lead firm, the more sophisticated tasks the contracting firms have to carry out, resulting in higher added value. Firms in the lower tiers tend only to perform simple functions that add little value to the final product/service and therefore can be more easily replaced (Abe 2009). Notably, the highest value creating activities take place in the two extremes of the chain, namely research, design, and development at the beginning, and marketing, branding, and after sales service at the end. It is no surprise that these tasks are often performed by the lead firms themselves. Production, manufacturing, and assembly form the lowest value-added activities in the value chain, but require a high employment rate (Humphrey and Schmitz 2000). These stages are often outsourced to firms in developing countries, which lack technical capability but provide a plentiful supply of low-cost labor (Kano 2018).

The role of lead firms in promoting GVC integration for local SMEs is executed through their decisions in chain governance type and production strategy, as well as decisions contributing to FDI spillover effects. Productivity gain resulting from the diffusion of knowledge and technology from foreign investors to local firms and workers often involves a range of endowments, from technology transfer to tacit knowledge, such as managerial expertise, know-how, and working practices (Alfaro and Johnson 2012).

4.3.2 SMEs Competitive Advantages

Advances in technology and efforts from governments in developing countries to reduce barriers for international trade have generated market chances for firms of all sizes in these countries. Similarly, participating and upgrading in GVC of lead firms opens up opportunities for SMEs, but at the same time it means these firms must enhance their competitiveness if they are to survive and grow in a competitive marketplace (OECD and ERIA 2018). Researchers from World Bank (2017) contend that in order to upgrade their participation in GVCs, local firms, especially the SMEs, must increase their productivity and access the necessary knowledge and technology. Similarly, a joint study by OECD and World Bank (2015) makes it clear that an absence of competitive edge is one of the biggest hindrances for GVC upgrading. Unfortunately, SMEs internal capabilities are often weak, making it difficult to build the necessary competitive edge. Thus, for example, the size of firms can limit cost advantages in many industries since SMEs can hardly take advantage of economies of scale. Similarly, resource constraints make it hard for these firms to reap the productivity benefits of labor division. In addition, other problems including lack of skills and expertise in organization, difficulty in access to finance, and weak innovation culture are found to be the challenges for SMEs to expand their participation in GVC (ADB 2016).

A downside of lacking local competent suppliers is that lead firms would turn elsewhere to find suppliers for reliable and suitable inputs to their production. This can significantly limit local SMEs' chances to engage and ultimately upgrade within a GVC. SMEs are, therefore, advised to develop capacities such as entrepreneur competencies, good corporate governance, absorptive capability, application of government rules on FDI, and innovative culture which enable them to be more competitive, innovative, and resilient (Abor and Adjasi 2007; Junge et al. 2016; Kadarusman and Nadvi 2013; Pfeifer 2014).

4.3.3 Institutional Factors

Conducive business environments are influenced by institutional factors, mainly through policies and laws. Countries that possess a favorable and fair business environment are often able to attract FDI and support SMEs to participate and upgrade in GVCs. Where "shocks" exist in the market, under the forms of quality standards, environmental laws, macroeconomic shifts and social movements, GVC upgrading is more likely to happen (Pipkin and Fuentes 2017). In the absence of institutional factors, governments are unable to introduce and enforce regulations, especially in those areas related to local SMEs and the lead firms operating in the country. For example, inward FDI is widely believed to drive the GVC participation (Abe and Proksch 2017; Ahmed and Kumar 2018). But in order to attract FDI, countries need to consider gradually improving environmental factors such as growth potential, labor market flexibility, infrastructure facilities, innovation capability, and clearly defined property rights (Rana and Chia 2017). Countries that present a favorable business environment to foreign investors often have a better chance for their

SMEs to participate and upgrade in GVC trade. This may not however be fully sufficient. Institutional factors can therefore either encourage or discourage firms to innovate (Schneider 2013) which in turn influences their ability to participate in GVCs.

4.4 Challenges for Vietnamese SMEs Participating and Upgrading in GVCs

Most activities of Vietnamese firms in a GVC have mainly focused on the assembly of final products from imported materials (OECD-UNIDO 2019). As a result, there is plenty of room for development for participating in other high value-added activities of the supply chain. Key initiatives can be taken through investments in upstream processing of the goods, for which Vietnamese firms possess a certain level of comparative advantages such as agribusiness, garments, and wood production. Nevertheless, unlike downstream activities that firms in Vietnam have been performing, upstream activities require intensive capital, technical knowledge, and skilled labor (Ignatenko et al. 2019). This challenge can be addressed through the linkage with global lead firms. As an attractive destination of FDI inflow, there are great opportunities for local firms to take the spillover effect in terms of knowledge and skills from global lead firms, which benefit the upstream in GVCs. Nevertheless, there remains much to be done with both local SMEs and the relevant institutional factors before the potentials can be realized. The subsequent sections will discuss firm size distribution, corporate governance, and the innovation capability of SMEs, as well as macroeconomic environment, access to credit, logistics infrastructure in the context of Vietnam.

4.4.1 The Medium Size Is Missing

Despite the fast growth of domestic private enterprises, there are concerns in the firm size distribution of this sector. Accordingly, the medium size seems missing as firms of this size account for a tiny part of the total SME population.

The majority of these SMEs are very small (micro) or small. Figure 4.3 shows that micro and small enterprises account for 75 and 23% of the total SMEs in 2017, respectively. In other words, there is a missing middle classification in the size structure of SMEs in Vietnam as only 2% of SMEs have a medium size. For the further details of the definition of SMEs, Table 4.1 summarizes the government resolution 39/2018/NĐ-CP in 2018.

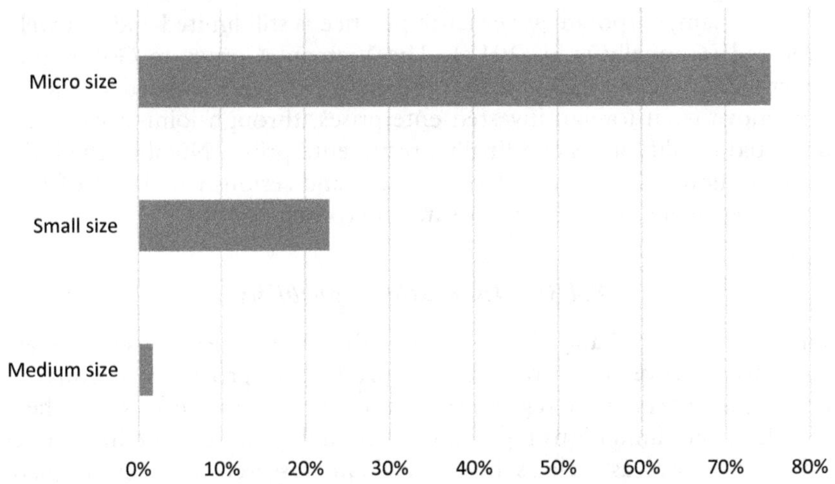

Fig. 4.3 Firm size distribution of SMEs in Vietnam (*Source* General Statistics Office of Vietnam 2018)

Table 4.1 Definition of SMEs in Vietnam

Size	*Indicator*	*Sector*	
		Agriculture, forestry and fishing, industry and construction	*Trade and services*
Micro-size	Number of employees	≤10	≤10
Small size	Number of employees	11–100	11–50
Medium size	Number of employees	101–200	51–100

Source Government of Vietnam (2018)

4.4.2 *Corporate Governance*

More stringent standards have been put into assessing criteria of supplier selection by lead firms in GVCs (World Bank 2017). As a result, it is urgent for Vietnamese firms, especially SMEs, to reform their corporate governance practices if they want to integrate more deeply into GVCs under emerging FTAs with the EU and other countries, which generates pressure and motivation for constructing higher standard of business practices (Vietnam News 2019).

In Vietnam, corporate governance practice is still limited and not well-embraced (Connelly et al. 2017). The Vietnam Corporate Governance report (VCCI 2016) indicates that the quality of governance decreases as firms move from foreign-invested enterprises, through joint-stock firms, to limited liability firms and finally private enterprises. Notably, the independent audit is implemented very strictly and seriously in 100% of FDI enterprises, while only 25% of private enterprises do this.

4.4.3 Innovation Capability

Data from World Bank (2017) shows that Vietnamese businesses are trying to improve their products and production processes to equal or surpass their peers in the region. However, the data also reveals that there are still certain limitations regarding firms' ability to innovate in product and in processes as well as better facilitate research and development (R&D) activities.

First, the analysis of product innovation rates for different types of businesses in Vietnam shows that medium and large enterprises innovate more than small businesses and joint ventures with foreign partners tend to be more creative, as is also seen in other Southeast Asian countries (OECD and World Bank 2015). From the resource-based view, this scenario is clear for understanding as SMEs tend to possess less capacity to offer gradual renovation in their products compared to large enterprises and firms with great support from foreign collaboration. The World Bank report (2017) reveals that about 23% of Vietnamese enterprises claimed to have introduced a new or improved product over the past three years. This is much lower rate compared with peer countries. For example, Cambodia and the Philippines claim over 30%, while Thailand, Laos and Malaysia are significantly higher. One important question arises at this point concerning the main motivation for the product innovation of Vietnamese enterprises. It is found that product innovation in Vietnam is mostly to cut costs, rather than to introduce entirely new features (World Bank 2017).

Second, similar to product innovation, process innovation of Vietnamese enterprises is still facing limitations. Surveys on improvements in their production processes, delivery, maintenance, procurement, and accounting suggest that SMEs in Vietnam need to pay extensive attention to the automation of current manual work and the adoption of new technologies or production methods similar to other countries (Pham and Matsunaga 2019).

Third, the level of expenditure on R&D of Vietnamese enterprises is relatively low (1.6% of annual revenue), lower than those of Laos (14.5%), Philippines (3.6%), Malaysia (2.6%) and Cambodia (1.9%). Moreover, there are only 26% of medium and large firms declaring expenditures on R&D, while only 9% of small businesses on R&D. On the other hand, 20% of Vietnamese businesses declare training for their employees to develop new products or processes, which is higher than Laos, Malaysia, and Thailand although lower than the Philippines and Cambodia (World Bank 2017).

4.4.4 *Macroeconomic Environment*

The improvements in several macroeconomic factors have fostered the business environment for attracting FDI into Vietnam (OECD-UNIDO 2019). Firstly, the rapid economic growth has helped expanding the size of Vietnam's domestic market. This creates incentives for foreign firms, who are seeking for market expansion opportunities in developing economies. Secondly, the active economic integration in regional and global markets has enabled more support from partner countries and attracted more international investors. The exporting market opportunities for Vietnamese firms have been widened by key free trade agreements (FTAs) such as the Comprehensive and Progressive Trans-Pacific Partnership (CPTPP) and the European Union Vietnam Free Trade Agreement (EVFTA). To illustrate, CPTPP has opened the gateway for Vietnam enterprises to several international markets such as Australia, Brunei, Canada, Chile, Japan, Mexico, New Zealand, and Peru (Viet 2016). Similarly, Vietnamese products will soon benefit from easier entry to 27 countries in the EU thanks to the EVFTA. However, the success of global integration depends largely on firm capacity and other institutional factors to take advantage of those opportunities (Lema et al. 2018).

4.4.5 *Access to Formal Credit*

The participation of SMEs in GVCs also faces the challenge of difficulty in financial access to facilitate their production cycle as most lead firms delay payment 30 to 90 days for payment (Lunati 2008). The limitation of financial resources also inhibits SMEs' ability to grow fast and adopt new advanced production technologies. In this section, we observe how Vietnamese SMEs have struggled with accessing formal credit sources to sustain their businesses.

Lack of access to finance is the top obstacle according to 21.8% of Vietnamese firms responding to a World Bank survey (2018a). More firms in Vietnam complained about access to finance than is the case in peer countries (ibid.). Furthermore, the Enhancing Enterprise Competitiveness and SME Linkage report indicated that, regarding the rate of firms with access to formal credit and overdraft facilities, Thailand and Malaysia both outperformed Vietnam (Akhlaque et al. 2018). Also, in this report, it is well noted that foreign-invested enterprises are generally more productive than domestic firms in Vietnam, which can be explained by easier access to finance and technology with support from their parent firms. This may lead to an unequal distribution of financial resources, undermining the competitiveness of Vietnamese firms (World Bank 2018a). Dang and Chuc (2019) stated that SMEs have a much lower chance to acquire bank loans than large enterprises. Only 200,000 out of 507,000 SMEs in Vietnam have bank loans. The total outstanding loans for SMEs in Vietnam account for only 22% of the credit provided for the whole country's economy, compared to 35% in Thailand and 25% in Bangladesh (World Bank 2018a).

For a deeper understanding of difficulties in accessing finance, faced by Vietnamese SMEs, it is essential to look at historical SOE blocking and underlying root causes. Going back to the survey of CIEM, ILSSA & UNU-WIDER (2016), there are major concerns that prevent banks from lending to SMEs including insufficient collateral provided by SMEs, poor business plans, unaudited book-keeping systems. First, nearly 80% of banks in Vietnam insist that secured assets are a prerequisite for credit assessment (Le and Nguyen 2019). This is considered a luxury that most SMEs in Vietnam cannot afford. Second, a large number of Vietnamese SMEs do not show clear business plans. Their plans are mostly spontaneous, seasonal, and exposed to many risks, which makes them fail to gain the trust of banks. Third, other strict requirements to get credit such as business operating minimum years required and financial reporting as tools for banks to control the credit risk are also crucial barriers for SMEs (Dang and Chuc 2019).

In summary, access to finance has been the most pressing issue for SMEs as they are trying to invest in developing capacity, skills, and technology needed to upgrade production, increase competitiveness at home and abroad markets. SMEs should be more proactive in reforming their business practices to be trusted by the banks and should aim to get credit granted rather than waiting for supporting policies from the government.

Chapter 6 discusses SME access to credit under the heading "Credit Availability for Domestic Firms and Joint Ventures."

4.4.6 *Logistics Infrastructure*

Finally, high logistics cost is a hindering factor of Vietnam's economic growth. According to VNA (2018), logistics costs amount to 20.9% of Vietnam's GDP. This is higher than other countries in the world such as Germany (8.5%), Singapore (9.5%), India (13%), and Brazil (12%) (World Bank 2018b). Of the total logistics cost, transport costs make up to 59% and unofficial costs account for 5 to 10% (Lam et al. 2019).

Logistics services in Vietnam have made remarkable improvements as testified by a 25-fold level increase in the National Logistics Competency Index (LPI), from 64th in 2016 to 39th in 2018 (World Bank 2018b). However, Vietnam still needs to continue to take more efforts at the national level to strengthen the logistics industry as well as minimize costs in this field. Reducing logistics costs will improve the cost of operating businesses in Vietnam and thereby contribute to economic growth (Lam et al. 2019).

In Vietnam, road freight plays a key role in freight transport, with the market share (in tons) having grown rapidly in recent years, from 66% in 2006 to 77% per year in 2016. In terms of transport distance, road freight increased from 20.5 trillion ton-km in 2006 to 56.6 trillion ton-km in 2016, equivalent to nearly 11% compound annual growth rate (highest among all transport types) (GSO 2018). The problem is that the cost of this current major transport mode is relatively high. According to calculations by the Ho Chi Minh City Transport Association, in addition to fixed fees, road tolls are even higher than fuel costs for the same transport distance because of frequent toll stations (Mai and Phuong 2019). A government official commented: "Around the gateways of Ho Chi Minh City, from NH1 to Binh Duong, Dong Nai, Tay Ninh or to Western provinces, there are so many toll stations, mostly located on the exclusive roads, costing a lot for businesses. Currently, a truck has to pay more than 17 million dong /year (US$735 / year) for road maintenance fees" (Mai and Phuong 2019).

The high cost of freight transport within the borders of Vietnam raises another issue that prevents lead firms from buying from local suppliers. They will opt for supplies from other countries with cheaper ocean freight even for a much greater distance.

4.5 Conclusion

This chapter has examined major determinants of SMEs' participation in GVCs as a base for discussing the potentials and challenges for Vietnamese SMEs to further upgrade and integrate in GVCs. Lead firm provides motivation for SMEs internal competitiveness and therefore institutional factors are crucial for nudging host country's SMEs toward higher value-added activities in GVCs. It is essential to develop an effective collaboration between lead firms, local SMEs and the government to constitute a better business environment that fosters innovation, technology transfer, and mutual benefits of all parties involved in the GVC activities. Vietnam clearly has the potential to be a new global value hub, with an adequate pool of natural resources and a young labor force.

Though with high potential, Vietnamese SMEs and the institutional agencies still face significant obstacles to deeper integration into GVCs. There are inhibiting factors within SMEs, such as low corporate governance standards, low innovation capability, and insufficient access to formal credit. The government needs to develop effective policies while creating a clear, transparent, and favorable environment for global lead firms to invest in high-value industries within Vietnam. The government can still create affordable conditions for SMEs to develop absorptive capacity through acquiring, assimilating, and exploiting the knowledge and information from lead firms. It is this knowledge-intensive linkage with lead firms that will help Vietnamese SMEs to participate in higher value-added business activities. Last but not least, the government needs to increase national logistics capacities in order to cope with the ever-increasing transport needs, at competitive rates, for future sustainable development.

References

Abe, M. 2009. Globalization of Production and the Competitiveness of SME in Asia and the Pacific: Trends and Prospects. *Studies in Trade and Investment, 65*, 33–57.

Abe, M., & Proksch, M. 2017. Supporting Participation of Asia-Pacific SME in Global Value Chains. *Journal of Korea Trade, 21*(2), 86–106.

Abonyi, G. 2005. *Integrating SME into Global and Regional Value Chains: Implications for Subregional Cooperation in the Greater Mekong Sub Region*. Bangkok: UNESCAP.

Abor, J., & Adjasi, C. K. 2007. Corporate Governance and the Small and Medium Enterprises Sector: Theory and Implications. *Corporate Governance: The International Journal of Business in Society, 7*(2), 111–122.

ADB. 2016. *Asian Development Outlook 2016: Asia's Potential Growth*. Asian Development Bank. Retrieved from https://www.adb.org/sites/default/files/publication/182221/ado2016.pdf. Accessed January 23, 2020.

ADB. 2017. *Asian Development Outlook 2017: Transcending the Middle-Income Challenge*. Retrieved from https://www.adb.org/sites/default/files/publication/237761/ado-2017.pdf. Accessed February 4, 2020.

Ahmed, F., & Kumar, P. 2018. Toward a National Participation Index for Developing Countries in the Global Value Chains: A Graph Theoretic Modelling Approach. *Journal of Modelling in Management, 13*(2), 475–494.

Akhlaque, A., Ong Lopez, A. B. C., & Coste, A. 2018. *Vietnam: Enhancing Enterprise Competitiveness and SME Linkages—Lessons from International and National Experience*. Retrieved from http://documents.worldbank.org/curated/en/974911528477201878/Vietnam-Enhancing-enterprise-competitiveness-and-SME-linkages-lessons-from-international-and-national-experience. Accessed January 9, 2020.

Alfaro, L., & Johnson, M. 2012. Foreign Direct Investment and Growth. In *The Evidence and Impact of Financial Globalization*, ed. Gerard Caprio (pp. 299–309). London: Elsevier.

CIEM, ILSSA ,& UNU-WIDER. 2016. *Characteristics of the Vietnamese Business Environment: Evidence from an SME Survey in 2015*. Hanoi: Central Institute for Economic Management of Vietnam.

Connelly, J. T., Limpaphayom, P., Nguyen, H. T., & Tran, T. D. 2017. A Tale of Two Cities: Economic Development, Corporate Governance and Firm Value in Vietnam. *Research in International Business and Finance, 42*, 102–123.

Dang, L. N., & Chuc, A. T. 2019. *Challenges in Implementing the Credit Guarantee Scheme for Small and Medium-Sized Enterprises: The Case of Viet Nam*. ADBI Working Paper Series (No. 941). Retrieved from https://www.adb.org/sites/default/files/publication/496271/adbi-wp941.pdf. Accessed December 21, 2019.

Dinh, B., & Ngoc, L. 2015. *Samsung Challenges Vietnamese Suppliers*. Retrieved from https://nhipcaudautu.vn/biz-tech/samsung-thach-thuc-nha-cung-ung-viet-3279282/. Accessed January 23, 2020.

European Parliament News. 2020. *Parliament Approves EU-Vietnam Free Trade and Investment Protection Deals*. Press Release. Retrieved from https://www.europarl.europa.eu/news/en/press-room/20200206IPR72012/parliament-approves-eu-vietnam-free-trade-and-investment-protection-deals. Accessed February 14, 2020.

General Statistics Office of Vietnam. 2018. *Results of the 2017 Economics Census*. Hanoi: Statistical Publishing House.

Government of Vietnam. 2018. *Decree Detailing Articles to Support Small and Medium Enterprises*. Hanoi.

Humphrey, J., & Schmitz, H. 2000. *Governance and Upgrading: Linking Industrial Cluster and Global Value Chain Research*. IDS Working Paper 120. Retrieved from https://opendocs.ids.ac.uk/opendocs/bitstream/handle/20.500.12413/3466/Wp120.pdf?sequence=1. Accessed January 2, 2020.

Ignatenko, A., Raei, F. & Mircheva, B. 2019. *Global Value Chains: What Are the Benefits and Why Do Countries Participate?* IMF Working Paper 19/18, International Monetary Fund, Washington, DC.

Junge, M., Severgnini, B., & Sørensen, A. 2016. Product-Marketing Innovation, Skills, and Firm Productivity Growth. *Review of Income and Wealth, 62*, 724–757.

Kadarusman, Y., & Nadvi, K. 2013. Competitiveness and Technological Upgrading in Global Value Chains: Evidence from the Indonesian Electronics and Garment Sectors. *European Planning Studies, 21*(7), 1007–1028.

Kano, L. 2018. Global Value Chain Governance: A Relational Perspective. *Journal of International Business Studies, 49*(6), 684–705.

Kaplinsky, R., & Morris, M. 2000. *A Handbook for Value Chain Research* (Vol. 113). Brighton: University of Sussex, Institute of Development Studies.

Lam, Y. Y., Sriram, K., & Khera, N. 2019. *Strengthening Vietnam's Trucking Sector*. Washington, DC: World Bank.

Le, C. H., & Nguyen, H. L. 2019. Collateral Quality and Loan Default Risk: The Case of Vietnam. *Comparative Economic Studies, 61*(1), 103–118.

Lema, R., Rabellotti, R., & Sampath, P. G. 2018. Innovation Trajectories in Developing Countries: Co-evolution of Global Value Chains and Innovation Systems. *The European Journal of Development Research, 30*(3), 345–363.

Lim, H., & Kimura, F. 2009. *The Internationalisation of SME in Regional and Global Value Chains*. Retrieved from https://pdfs.semanticscholar.org/5299/4acb261cb6d841f2b7d7eee6eb82dd4dc571.pdf. Accessed February 2, 2020.

Lunati, M. 2008. Enhancing the Role of SME in Global Value Chains. *Staying Competitive in the Global Economy*, 65–101.

Mai, H., & Phuong, M. 2019. *Logistics Costs in Vietnam Are Costliest in the World*. Retrieved from https://thanhnien.vn/tai-chinh-kinh-doanh/phi-logistics-cua-viet-nam-thuoc-hang-dat-do-nhat-the-gioi-1014492.html. Accessed January 14, 2020.

Ministry of Planning and Investment. 2019. *The White Book About Vietnamese Enterprises 2019*. Hanoi: Statistical Publishing House. Retrieved from http://trungtamwto.vn/download/18754/Sach%20trang%20DN%20VN%202019.pdf. Accessed January 9, 2020.

OECD & ERIA. 2018. *SME Policy Index the SME Policy Index Boosting Competitiveness and Inclusive Growth*. Jakarta and Paris: OECD Publishing.

OECD & World Bank. 2015. *Inclusive Global Value Chains: Policy Options in Trade and Complementary Areas for GVC Integration by Small and Medium Enterprises and Low-Income Developing Countries*. Retrieved from https://www.oecd-ilibrary.org/content/publication/9789264249677-en. Accessed February 4, 2020.

OECD-UNIDO. 2019. *Integrating Southeast Asian SME in Global Value Chains: Enabling Linkages with Foreign Investors*. Retrieved from https://www.oecd.org/investment/Integrating-Southeast-Asian-SMEs-in-global-value-chains.pdf. Accessed January 10, 2020.

Pfeifer, C. 2014. The Nexus Between Top Managers' Human Capital and Firm Productivity. *Applied Economics Letters, 22*, 1–5.

Pham, T. T. T., & Matsunaga, N. 2019. Product and Process Innovation of Micro, Small and Medium Manufacturing Enterprises in Vietnam. In *Innovation in Developing Countries*, ed. Nobuaki Matsunaga (pp. 23–51). Singapore: Springer.

Phung, T. D. 2019. *Supporting Vietnamese SME in Their Current Development*. Retrieved from http://tapchitaichinh.vn/tai-chinh-kinh-doanh/ho-tro-doanh-nghiep-nho-va-vua-viet-nam-phat-trien-trong-giai-doan-hien-nay-314736.html. Accessed January 10, 2020.

Phuong, C. 2019. *Socio-Economic Panorama 2019*. Retrieved from https://vietstock.vn/2019/12/buc-tranh-toan-canh-kinh-te-xa-hoi-nam-2019-761-721953.htm. Accessed January 12, 2020.

Pietrobelli, C., & Rabellotti, R. 2006. *Upgrading to Compete: Global Value Chains, Clusters, and SME in Latin America*. Washington, DC: Inter-American Development Bank.

Pipkin, S., & Fuentes, A. 2017. Spurred to Upgrade: A Review of Triggers and Consequences of Industrial Upgrading in the Global Value Chain Literature. *World Development, 98*, 536–554.

Ponte, S., & Ewert, J. 2009. Which Way Is "Up" in Upgrading? Trajectories of Change in the Value Chain for South African Wine. *World development, 37*, 1637–1650.

Rana, P. B., & Chia, W.-M. 2017. *Jumpstarting South Asia: Revisiting Economic Reforms and Look East Policies*. Oxford: Oxford University Press.

Schneider, B. R. 2013. *Hierarchical Capitalism in Latin America*. Cambridge: Cambridge University Press.

VCCI. 2016. *Annual Report on Vietnamese Enterprises 2016—Topic of the Year: Corporate Governance*. Retrieved from http://vbis.vn/wp-content/uploads/2017/05/VCCI-2017-B7.pdf. Accessed February 5, 2020.

Viet, P. Q. 2016. Opportunities and Challenges When Vietnam Joins TPP. *Issues in Economics and Business, 2*(1), 28–46.

Vietnam News. 2019. *Local Firms Need to Improve Capacity When Joining EVFTA*. Retrieved from https://vietnamnews.vn/economy/522085/local-firms-need-to-improve-capacity-when-joining-evfta.html#egvgm35tlJQAMIL 6.97. Accessed February 7, 2020.

VNA. 2018. *High Logistics Costs Hinder Vietnam's Economic Growth*. Retrieved from https://en.vietnamplus.vn/high-logistics-costs-hinder-vietnams-economic-growth/141370.vnp. Accessed January 8, 2020.

World Bank. 2017. *Vietnam: Enhancing Enterprise Competitiveness and SME Linkages—Lessons from International and National Experience*. Retrieved from http://documents.worldbank.org/curated/en/214681506064742480/pdf/119861-WP-VitNamTngcngNnglcCnhtranhvLinKtcaDoanhnghipVavNh-PUBLIC-VIETNAMESE.pdf. Accessed January 17, 2020.

World Bank. 2018a. *Enhancing Enterprise Competitiveness and SME Linkages in Vietnam*. Paper presented at the AmCham Supplier Day 2018, HCMC. Retrieved from https://chambermaster.blob.core.windows.net/userfiles/UserFiles/chambers/2917/File/Presentation/2018/181004_AmCham_Supplier_Day_2018/World-Bank-SME-Linkages-Brian-Mtonya-EN.pdf. Accessed December 14, 2019.

World Bank. 2018b. *Logistics Performance Index 2018*. Retrieved from https://lpi.worldbank.org/international/global/2018. Accessed January 12, 2020.

World Bank. 2019. *World Development Indicators*. Washington, DC: The World Bank.

World Bank and World Trade Organization. 2019. *Global Value Chain Development Report 2019: Technological Innovation, Supply Chain Trade, and Workers in a Globalized World (English)*. Washington, DC: World Bank Group.

CHAPTER 5

Marketing in Vietnam

Nghĩa Huỳnh Phước

Abstract This chapter describes Vietnamese consumers, the retail system in Vietnam, and advertising trends. It relates the rise of digital commerce in Vietnam as well as the growing importance of CSR for company image, particularly as regards sustainability.

Keywords Retail · Consumer · Gen Z · Advertising · E-commerce · Sustainability

5.1 Introduction

This chapter provides a first introduction to marketing in Vietnam, with an emphasis on retailing and consumer behavior. After a brief history of marketing conditions in Vietnam, this chapter describes Vietnamese consumers, both as regards demographics and as regards the main categories of consumers. A description of the retail system in Vietnam follows, covering both the ever-important traditional markets and the recent

N. H. Phước (✉)
University of Economics Ho Chi Minh City, Ho Chi Minh City, Vietnam
e-mail: nghia.hp@ueh.edu.vn

R. Macdonald (ed.), *The Economy and Business Environment of Vietnam*, https://doi.org/10.1007/978-3-030-49974-7_5

consolidation of brick and mortar outlets. The latter are coming under pressure, as digital commerce is growing in Vietnam more quickly than in most Western nations. The final section provides an overview of how many large businesses are actively pursuing sustainability.

5.2 Genesis of the Marketplace in Vietnam

In the late 1980s and early 1990s, 80% of Vietnam's population lived in rural areas and 90% of the population worked at small-scale agricultural production. Industrial production provided job opportunities for only about 5% of the working-age population. Further, this industrial production came mostly from state-owned enterprises, with almost no international trade and virtually the entire economy controlled by state-owned enterprises. Misconceived monetary policy brought inflation above 300%, peaking at 700% in 1986. As a result, people's spending, saving and consumption were paralyzed. The consumer economy was almost non-existent. There was little place for creative marketing as the needs of consumers were limited to essential goods. Most consumers had almost no disposable income, and even for those few that could spend more, there remained the shortage of products and services.

The eventual implementation of Đổi Mới (particularly the Foreign Investment Law in 1987 and the Private Enterprise Law in 1990) and the cessation of the embargo on Vietnam in 1993 opened a new dawn of business oriented to customer value, with a business competitive environment and free enterprise-oriented search for innovative market solutions. Private business, both foreign and domestic, gradually occupied the decisive role in the economy, both satisfying consumption needs and triggering new desires, with local businesses competing with each other and some even building international brands. Currently, private firms are the most dynamic force in marketing solutions in Vietnam. Although they still only contribute 40% of GDP, they account for 80% of transactions, and attract 51% of the labor force. Foreign enterprises (both 100% foreign-owned and joint ventures) have been bringing a new marketing breath into Vietnam's economy over the past 30 years, with global experience, superior marketing capacity, innovative media platforms and long-term brand strategy. Many have quickly become market leaders and "giants" in key industries.[1]

5.3 Consumers in Vietnam

The population has grown 12% in the past 10 years. Today, Vietnamese consumers are deeply segmented and highlighted by a new middle class emerging since 2010. Generation Z is leading the trend and has great influence. In addition, the cohort above 50 years old is growing and will account for nearly 20% of the population in the next two decades. The number of people over 65 years old is 8% and will increase to 9% in the next 10 years. Nearly 40% of the Vietnamese population of 96 million people is living in urban areas (GSO 2019). Women account for 51% of the population and households number 30 million with an average of 3.5 persons per household. Currently, nearly 70% of the population earns an income. The largest agglomerations of households are in Southeast Vietnam, the Red River Delta (where Ha Noi, Hai Duong, Hai Phong and other larger cities are located) and the Mekong Delta regions.

There are over 22 million Vietnamese from 0 to 14 years old (2019), a new generation of consumers. See Fig. 5.1 for population cohorts. This population structure makes Vietnam an attractive market for the coming decades.

The characteristics of Vietnamese consumers are clearly revealed in their consumption behavior. In 2019, Vietnam sales of fast-moving consumer goods (FMCG) have grown 11.5% compared to the previous

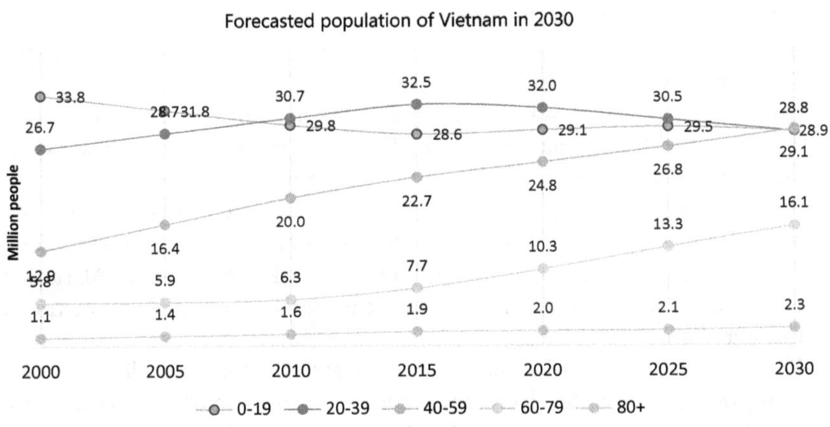

Fig. 5.1 Vietnam's population growth and forecasting to 2030 (*Source* Euromonitor International, and data from GSO national statistics 2019)

year. Although witnessing a slight decline in major cities, the FMCG sector has enjoyed an increase of 6–7% in annual spending, especially in confectionery, soft drinks and home care. In the first quarter of 2019, the FMCG market in rural regions achieved double the growth over the same period last year. The demand for consumer products is changing toward high-quality goods imported directly from the USA, Japan and the EU. Many imported products with high quality, creativity and unique features have captured the middle-class Vietnamese and are gradually gaining attention (FMCG Monitor 2019 from Kantar Worldpanel).

There has also been a shift from traditional channels to online channels since 2015. The size of online shopping on e-commerce (for both B2B and B2C) is $7 billion in 2019 and it is forecasted that the number will increase to $13 billion by 2025 (growing over 30% annually) (Google Temasek Bain 2019). Vietnamese people spend an average of 450 USD/year for online shopping and 66% of population use mobile phones (Digital Marketing 2019 Report). Before 2015, Vietnamese people only used the Internet to search for information about products and services. By 2020, they were also making online decisions for buying electronics, sporting goods, cosmetics, tools and equipment, offices, household goods and fashion products; even sanitary equipment and machinery were being bought online. The key to this shift is the role of payment solutions. From 2017 to 2019, the size of Vietnam's consumer credit market has increased by 67% per year. Consumer credit will play a decisive role in the attractiveness of consumption in Vietnam in the next 5 years as predicted by the largest representative of this segment in Vietnam—Home Credit.

Hallyu, the Korean wave, has had a strong influence in Vietnam. Researchers and the media stated that the three-phase coverage strategy of the Korean wave was successful The first stage is the coverage of dramas, the second phase is connecting music (K-pop) with the actors and the final stage is bringing products from Korea to conquer Vietnamese consumers. The Vietnamese Z generation warmly welcomes Korean values. Attracted by the Korean way of life, they formed the need to learn Korean, travel to and even study in Korea.

The growth of a middle class and their strong domestic demand and consumption are new development steps in Vietnam market (World Bank 2019). The middle class accounts for 20% of the population and is forecast to be 30% of the population by 2030. Most of this class earns from non-farm sectors and the private economy. They earn over 2000 USD/month

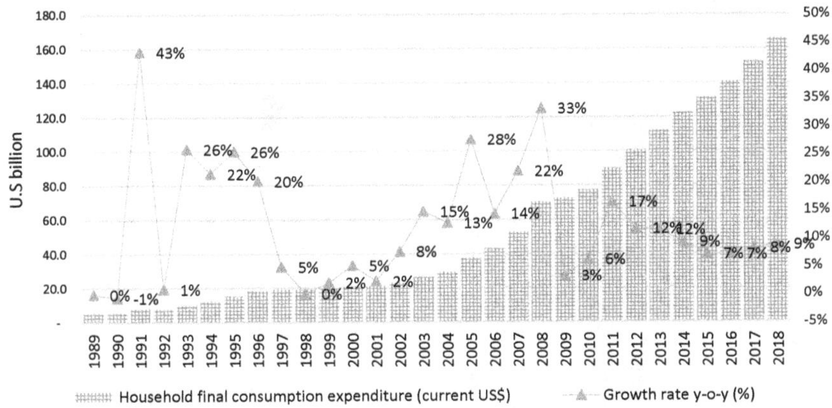

Fig. 5.2 Vietnam: Household final consumption expenditure 1988–2018 (*Source* World Bank national accounts data, and OECD National Accounts data files)

and spend over 15 USD/day. Many high-end fashion brands are present in Vietnam to serve this emerging "rich" group, and services arise for high-income groups such as study or travel abroad by children (see also Retailing in Vietnam 2017 for a projection over the next 10 years). Many businesses are exploiting this trend, investing in the business of importing high-class products from Europe, the USA and Japan—categories that domestic producers do not provide. In addition, businesses also invest in unique high quality and strong reputation products such as cigars, traditional coffee machines from Italy and premium cheeses from France. See Figs. 5.2 and 5.3.

5.4 The Transformation of Retail Systems in Vietnam

The traditional retail system is still a mainstay in the distribution system in Vietnam. For a long time, consumer behavior has been formed by the practice of exchanging agricultural goods at the market (wet markets selling fresh meat, fish, and seafood, dry markets selling vegetables as well as garments and other dry goods). This was the first place that people traded retail and negotiated deals for every need. The markets are held in a specific time frame and are not only an important retail

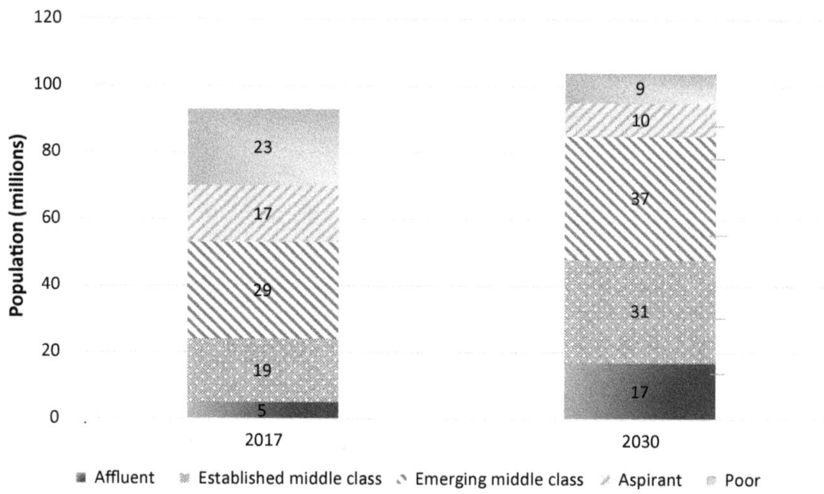

Fig. 5.3 Changes in population grouped by disposable income (*Source* Consultancy Asia 2018)

place but also a cultural feature of the Vietnamese people. They function as both retail markets and simultaneously a wholesale market for street vendors and others who distribute and supply throughout the country. According to statistics, in Vietnam there are currently 9000 official markets and these constitute 60% of retail sales of Vietnamese consumer goods. These markets are found throughout the country, even in large urban centers such Ho Chi Minh City and Hanoi. Currently, the role of traditional markets is being fiercely contested by new retail models and the emergence of e-commerce. However, in the future these markets will continue to affect the Vietnamese people because of their unique purchasing habits. Although in some ways they are less convenient than online shopping, they are superior sources of fresh food for morning breakfast, for example. In this sense, they may survive online rivalry better than Western-style brick-and-mortar retail outlets. FMCG enterprises cannot ignore the traditional market network if they want to penetrate deeply into the Vietnamese market.

Still, the traditional market is not the only retail channel in Vietnam. There are also many diverse retail formats such as grocery retail, restaurants and specialized stores. There are around 300,000 grocery stores,

200,000 restaurants and 150,000 cafes (GSO 2019). Sectors such as bakery, beverage, alcoholic beverages and packaged foods have used these channels as pillars of their distribution strategy. However, traditional retail still plays the leading role in Vietnam. This stems are from multiple factors, such as war history, geographical conditions, the subsidy period from 1975 to 1986. The obvious strength of this channel is pervasive distribution throughout Vietnam, with convenient access from every alley, meeting the needs of low-income people. There are even many markets that form a "sell on credit" culture for regular buyers. Critically, however, the disadvantage of the traditional market is its difficulty in applying modern technology in the distribution system.

Private and foreign enterprises providing retail services in Vietnam have had a great impact. In 1997, the government allowed Cora supermarket (France) to operate in Vietnam. And in 2001, they gave the wholesale model of Metro (Germany) permission to operate in Vietnam. As a member of WTO, foreign companies could open retail outlets in any industry by 2017. Vietnam fully opened to retail services by 2017, including retail banking. The retail industry in Vietnam reached 142 billion dollars in 2018 and is expected to reach 180 billion dollars by 2020, with a series of global retail groups entering the market. These non-traditional forms of retail such as supermarkets and convenience stores have grown 50% in 10 years. The more than 1000 supermarkets, 150 shopping centers, 6000 convenience stores account for 30% of the retail industry. In big cities and provincial cities, consumers have been moving to shopping malls, supermarkets, convenience stores and specialized stores instead of buying groceries in the traditional markets (Deloitte 2019).

Logistics costs account for 15% of the selling price. Warehouse conditions and logistics services for the distribution system are affecting distribution costs in terms of market connectivity. Another equally complex aspect is the retail space. The cost of premises accounts for 3–5% of the cost, with the rental prices increasing rapidly in big cities. Even the rental cost in shopping malls or supermarkets has increased rapidly, making urban retailing more and more expensive. In contrast, the traditional retail model in the provinces has more advantages in terms of rent (FiinGroup 2019).

The supply chain is also a difficult matter for traditional channels to deal with. Currently, retailing in Vietnam needs to go through a large intermediary role such as an exclusive distributor so traditional retail models have to buy through intermediaries with poor discounts.

In contrast, supermarkets do not need to go through intermediaries, so they have the advantage of price and promotions. Understanding these problems, many international retailers enter the market and bring their international supplier partners into Vietnam, but in reply Vietnamese suppliers will offer a high discount for these supermarkets to access to retail industry.

Another issue related to retail in Vietnam is the cash paying habit of Vietnamese people: 80% of consumers prefer to spend cash. Although over the past 5 years, 30% of consumer transactions used credit cards and e-wallets, these behaviors only occurred in big cities. (Q&Me 2018) The development of delivery service by motorbike encourages consumers to use credit payment. In addition, the development of technology allows for delivery services such as Giaohangnhanh or Ahamove. Many logistics service companies also offer direct delivery solutions across the country. This makes the model of sales and products distribution no longer too dependent on traditional retail points.

In the last decade, a harsh competition between international retail groups and domestic retail businesses has emerged, with a series of notable mergers and acquisitions taking place. M&As in Vietnam's retail are estimated to total US$8 billion from 2013 to 2019. Even large foreign-owned vendors such as Metro and Auchan that had entered Vietnam earlier, and then had to sell themselves to new systems, also foreign-owned, such as Aeon, Mega Mart, Lotte Mart. In addition, convenience store systems have increased rapidly in numbers over the past 10 years. As of early 2020, there are nearly 5000 stores grouped in 4 large systems: Vinmart+, Green Department Store, Saigon Coop and Circle K. All this has quickly changed consumption habits as well as the marketing solutions. The most obvious manifestations of this are the introduction of seasonal sales promotions, loyalty card programs, consumer brand activation activities, discount days (such as Black Friday) or products specifically designed for supermarket/convenience store sales channels.

The future of retail in Vietnam will surely change in the direction of more technology and added services (Vietnam retail store statistic 2019). That is the reason why marketers need to build online experience and combine customer interaction solutions on the multichannel platform. Brands need to consider online platforms more. In addition, brick-and-mortar stores lacking convenient services will be replaced by online sales solutions, delivery services or modern shopping centers with a variety of entertainment facilities. Marketers employing smart interactive tools at the point of sale are also trends to "optimize the data" of customers.

5.5 Communication and Media to Moving Digital

The total advertising expenditure in Vietnam (including Internet) is 2.6 billion USD. However, there are still unspecified advertising budget expenditures that account for more than another 2.5 billion USD. Since 2004, budget spending on all advertising channels in Vietnam has increased nearly 5 times (Kantar Worldpanel, 2019). Vietnam has 859 newspapers in print media, 135 electronic newspapers and more than 258 information pages (which are similar to online newspapers), 268 radio channels and 67 television channels (VTV is the national channel and the rest are local channels), with 18,000 professional journalists and nearly 1000 press agencies.

TV channels still account for 50% of the budget for advertising. Many brands tend to switch to the Internet, but FMCG brands still spend a lot of their budget on TV channels because they focus on the rural market, where consumers are still spending most of the time on watching TV. The Internet accounts for 43% of budget spending and is the main communication channel for urban markets while the budget for online channels in rural markets is just over 25% of the budget. In addition to TV and Internet as the main channels, out of home (OOH) advertising accounts for only 5% of the budget, print accounts for 7% and radio has remained at almost the same level for nearly 10 years.

The highlight of media in Vietnam in the last 5 years is the increase in the budget of brands for digital and mobile channels. Compared to other Asian countries, this budget is still very small. But this is a remarkable move compared to the past in Vietnam. Instead of relying mainly on TV and print media, now media budget in Vietnam has dramatically shifted to digital and mobile and accounted for more than 40% of the total budget, becoming the current main channel of brands and marketing campaigns. According to eMarketer, the total of all Vietnamese firms' budgets for digital advertising is 500 million USD and including 311 million USD for digital advertising (Vietnam digital advertising 2018). In particular, social media advertising, search advertising and banner advertising account for 70% of digital advertising activities. For the interface, mobile has accounted for 39% of the advertising budget and will increase to 48% by 2023 (ibid.). Nearly 70% of this budget is spent by firms in three main industries services and retail (Table 5.1).

Table 5.1 Advertising spending in Vietnam from 2004 to 2018 by channels (million US)

Channels/years	*2004*	*2010*	*2015*	*2018*
TV	166.4	436	969	1295
Newspapers	51	60.5	52	52
OOH/Outdoor	18	20	31	38.5
Internet	0.3	3	20	35
Magazines	26.5	37	32	32
Cinema	1	0.3	1.7	2.6
Radio	0.6	1.4	1.9	2.4

Source Statista Research Department 2020

Vietnamese behavior in viewing media has changed rapidly. In 2019, Kantar Worldpanel Vietnam reported that 98% of Vietnamese households watch 2.5 hours of television every day while OOH reaches 98% of viewers and often affects 9 minutes a day. Print newspapers have a lower access level. Only 33% of households read newspapers and it only takes 12 minutes a day. In contrast, online behavior has increased significantly, taking up nearly 6 hours per day. In addition, 46% of Vietnamese people are using smart mobile devices to participate in social networking, view services and read news. Typical pages are kenh14.vn, ngoisao.net, phimmoi.net, etc.; social networking sites including Facebook, Linkedin, Pinterest and online shopping sites like Tiki, Lazada, Sendo and Shopee.

Many marketers and entrepreneurs suppose that over the past 5 years, the media industry in Vietnam has undergone a dramatic transition and transformed strongly. In Vietnam, media channels are under control of the authority of the Party and the government. Setting up media channels is very difficult. Although public and private organizations can set up a newspaper, a television channel, or a web page, their operation is then under the central management of the state agency.

The world's top 20 advertising companies are present in Vietnam and control almost 70% of the advertising market (adbrand.net 2019). Advertising in Vietnam has many creative approaches and many campaigns to revive many local and global brands. And perspectives on persistent creative messaging strategy are influencing brand communication solutions. The global campaigns of Coke, Nivea, Vim, Omo or Samsung are all innovative global solutions. In addition, local brands such as Bitis

Hunter, Dienmayxanh, Vinamilk or Tiki campaigns also bring new wind in the way of conveying creative messages.

The enormous power of the Z generation, along with the rise of mobile devices and digital media, has forced marketers to find ways to create messages adapted to Vietnamese gen Z. Major brands must design solutions to bring increasingly interesting and unique experiences. And using influencers or key opinion leaders is an effective solution because they are successful, well-known with representative images that can influence customers. Currently, favorite Vietnamese influencers are Son Tung M-TP (Oppo, Bitis, Goviet …), Chipu (Tiki, nova, Huawei, Dove …), football player Xuan Truong (Pepsi, Revive) or beauty blogger Kaity Nguyen (Vivo, Sunplay, Rejoice, Tiktok …). The celebrities have started to "catch" the needs of the marketer so they have been increasing their influence and using their image associated with the brand on Facebook. Many players, actors, singers and artists, as well as other individuals, have also started building content production solutions on articles, images and videos to attract the attention of viewers. Currently, influencers are divided into different types of services or groups of people related to specific brands or categories. For instance, there are influencers in kitchen group, hot mom group, English group, beauty group and other retail services. Most of them have their own social channels and use creative solutions to attract the attention of regular viewers as well as to attach to the appearance of a certain brand.

Brands require creativity and endless evolution in communication as well as reinforcement of the message. In Vietnam, that evolution may not come to all brands. Although some brands have a budget for long-term projects, the majority of them focus their budget on seasonal campaigns. Tet holiday (lunar new year) is the most remarkable example. Brands in Vietnam spend 30% of their annual budget on media activities for this period. Marketers in Vietnam need to adapt quickly to provide media activities both in the state dominated media and in new digital solutions.

5.6 The Growth of E-Commerce in Vietnam

In 2001, the term "e-commerce" appeared in Vietnam and brought new solutions to the sales model. Initially, this concept was known primarily through the application of information technology advances to commercial and business transaction solutions such as email and Web sites.

Information technology was initially considered as useful only for advertising. In the last 5 years, however, all aspects of marketing have become digitized, and online transactions have grown 20–30% in recent years (Ministry of Industry and Trade Vietnam 2018).

In 2005, 95% of enterprises were using e-commerce transactions, more than 40% of enterprises were using Web sites including an estimated more than 100,000 Web sites with commercial transactions (Vecom 2019). This was the time when many e-commerce exchange vendors (Lazada, Zalora, Vatgia, NhomMua or Hotdeal,...) were considering the integration of mobile features, having anticipated the era of shopping with mobile devices. Accompanied by the strong development of both fiber optic and 4G infrastructure, social networks have increased the feasibility and ease of online transactions. Many sales utilities offered by Facebook, Zalo (a service of VNG corporation of Vietnam similar to WeChat and WhatsApp) and YouTube (for reviewing products) make it more and more convenient to search information, exchange information, and conduct transactions quickly. As of 2015, 51% of shoppers researched online before purchasing products or services (Google 2015). Although there remain many risks compared to traditional purchases, it is obvious that social networks have been contributing significantly to the success of e-commerce in Vietnam.

However, e-commerce in Vietnam only developed strongly in the B2C segment while B2B transactions have just begun to grow (Vecom 2019). What makes B2C e-commerce grow more significantly is the fact that consumers can easily use Internet to search for information or access e-commerce platforms. It can be seen that e-commerce becomes a new distribution incentive that integrates benefits for customers. In addition, e-commerce changes shopping habits, shifts the shopping process to a more technological basis.

A number of domestic and foreign businesses have begun to develop cross-border e-commerce models. E-commercial sites such as Shopee (Singapore), Lazada (launched in Singapore with German and Swedish funds, now property of Alibaba), Tiki (Vietnam, and has acquired Lazada operations in Vietnam) and Cho Tot (Vietnam) are widely trusted by many consumers. Online sales continue to account for 30% of sales of many businesses and are a key sales channel in the field of distribution and retail of consumer goods. Internet usage rate is high. Up to 85% of the Vietnamese population spends an average of nearly 7 hours a day online (Nielsen 2018). There are more than 90% of smartphone users in urban areas and 50% in rural areas. Besides, more than 55% of Vietnamese consumers admit they are willing to use network connection for a faster and easier shopping experience. 35.8 million people use social networks with an average of 24.7 hours per week for reading news, buying and selling goods. The number of shoppers in Vietnam on e-commerce platforms is 49.8 million and will increase to 51.1 million in 2019 for a total market size expected to reach up to 10 billion USD (Statista 2020).

Information and communications technology (ICT) also brings online payment solutions for e-commerce, offering consumers a variety of payment options: payment via bank, by e-wallet, advance payment or cash on delivery (COD) payment or. Vietnam has issued over 106 million debit and credit cards (an increase of 3.4 times compared to the end of 2010) (State Bank report 2018). About e-wallet services, there are six organizations: MService, Banknetvn, VNPay, BankPay, Vietnam Online, VietUnion. In addition, Vietnam bank system has launched more convenient services such as Internet banking, mobile banking, cross-border card payment, online payment. Brands visible in e-commerce transactions include Visa, Master, American Express, JCB (can pay more than 60 Web sites connected to OnePay payment gateway), pay via Samsung, Apple, Adayroi. Payments are also made COD. The trend of multi-channel sales emerged strongly in 2018. Nearly 97% of stores were selling on two or more channels by 2018, and 54% of stores sell at least on five different channels, especially on the main channels such as Facebook, brick and mortar stores, Web sites, e-commerce platforms, agents or collaborators (Sapo 2018).

Logistics is a challenge for e-commerce in Vietnam. Costs estimates vary widely from 15% to nearly 25% of GDP (Blancas et al. 2014; see VietnamNet 2017 for a recent estimate of 16–17%). The capacity of Vietnamese carriers is low and connectivity between regions is still weak. The lack of connection between e-commerce enterprises and logistics enterprises is a further weakness. Some enterprises may create the initial connection but remain ineffective due to a lack of professionalism, and failing to fully appreciate the role of technology. These enterprises need to proactively cooperate with each other. There is also a vacuum that needs to be filled by associations related to e-commerce, logistics as well as state management agencies on trade and logistics in the locality.

5.7 Sustainability

Corporate social and environmental responsibilities impact the image customers have of the firm. In addition, they are the subject of international development recommendations of ILO, OECD and other organizations, and of various national action programs in Vietnam. Serious issues include deforestation (considered a red alert), water pollution (due to deforestation, hydroelectric projects and pollution), air pollution in urban areas, and mangroves in the Mekong Delta.

In 2008, the Taiwanese corporation Vedan admitted discharging waste polluting the Thi Vai River. This became a hot topic. After 10 years of litigation, Vedan was fined and had lost its place as the dominant monosodium glutamate brand in Vietnam—most supermarkets refused to sell its products. Recently, when another Taiwanese firm, Formosa Plastics, polluted the marine environment and had to pay US$500 million in compensation, environmental issues and sustainable development in businesses became one the most noticeable topics of marketers and administrators, especially the awareness of corporate social responsibility (CSR). Currently, many companies have a CSR strategy evolving around sustainable development with 3 representative values including employee sustainability/talent development; products for human health and environmental friendliness. On the basis of this strategy, many businesses in Vietnam, especially foreign businesses, are aiming for sustainability, and their marketers implement many solutions to increase community value and make business strategy more effective. Aside from ethical motives, the impact of social media on a firm's reputation requires top management to adopt a solid CSR stance.[2]

A serious environmental problem affecting Vietnam today is plastic waste, which is an even greater problem in Vietnam than in most other countries. The central government has taken action and asked all organizations to work on solutions and initiatives to address reduction and pursue total recycling. Recognizing the urgent problem, a PRO Vietnam packaging recycling alliance was established including: Coca-Cola, FrieslandCampina, Lavie Vietnam, Nestle Vietnam, Nuti-Food, Suntory Pepsico, Tetra Pak, TH Group, URC Vietnam, Annam group and Saigon Coop. They will focus on recycling plastic packaging to meet the goal of fully recycling all plastic materials produced by these 12 companies by 2030. Other firms that have taken visible measures include Prudential Vietnam, Aviva, Mondelez Kinh Do and Vietnam Airlines.

5.8 Conclusion

This chapter has provided an introduction to marketing in Vietnam. A basic description of the Vietnamese consumer preceded a discussion of the retail channel. This led to a discussion of advertising as well as electronic commerce. Digital and electronic commerce is less developed but growing more quickly in Vietnam than the other large ASEAN countries, although 70% of transactions occur in Ho Chi Minh City and Hanoi (Dang 2020). This must be an important component of any firm's marketing plan in Vietnam. Corporate social responsibility and in particular sustainability is a sensitive issue in Vietnam given the track record of some foreign firms and the impact of social media in propagating concern.

Notes

1. After the near 20-year embargo that the USA had imposed after the cessation of its war in Vietnam, international integration began when Vietnam joined ASEAN in 1995. See Chapters 1 and 2 as well as Ministry of Industry and Trade of the Socialist Republic of Vietnam 2020 for current announcements and Deprez (2018) and Herr et al. (2016) for retrospectives.
2. Many foreign businesses in VN have implemented practical activities as part of their CSR strategies. HSBC has set aside 9 billion VND to encourage employees to participate in the Future First project to provide environmental guidance to children. Honda has instructed 70,000 children on traffic safety. Intel provided US$9.5 million USD to the Higher Engineering Education Alliance Program (HEEAP) and Cargill helped transfer breeding techniques to 1.5 million farmers. In addition, Samsung invested in the Digital Hope project and renovated libraries for 50 schools and national libraries. Suntory PepsiCo Vietnam launched the Mizuiku project focusing on educating children about the protection of clean water sources under the connection with the original project in Japan (so far, the Vietnam project has organized 400 classes for 5000 students, 16 festivals and 15 tours and developed 8 reverse osmosis water filtration systems. Moreover, Suntory Pepsico Vietnam has pledged to reduce water usage by 70%, reduce electricity consumption by 42% and save 8000 tons of plastic in 10 years. Coca-Cola in Vietnam implemented the Ekocenter project to build solar water kiosks to provide clean water to the community (as of December 2019, providing 1 million liters of clean water and training more than 3000 women). Nescafe Plan is a project to help improve sustainable farming capacity of 28 million coffee trees for 200,000 farmers. The project achieved a 30% increase in farmers' income and a sustainable ecosystem and environment.

References

Adbrand.net. 2019. Top Advertisisng Agancies Worldwide. https://www.adbrands.net/top-advertising-agencies-index.html.

Blancas, Luis C., John Isbell, Monica Isbell, Hua Joo Tan, and Wendy Tao. 2014. *Efficient Logistics a Key to Vietnam's Competitiveness*. Washington, DC: The World Bank.

Consultancy Asia. 2018. BCG Reports Highlights the Growing Upper Wealth Classes of Asean. BCG. https://www.consultancy.asia/news/1660/bcg-report-highlights-the-growing-upper-wealth-classes-of-asean. Accessed February 2020.

Dang, Hoang Linh. 2020. Vietnam's Booming E-Commerce Market-Analysis. ISEAS. https://www.ssi.com.vn/index.php/en/individual-customer/economic/news/518713.

Deloitte. 2019. Retail in Vietnam 2019. https://www2.deloitte.com/vn/en/pages/consumer-business/articles/vietnam-consumer-retail-2019.html. Accessed February 2019.

Deprez, Sophie. 2018. The Strategic Vision behind Vietnam's International Trade Integration. *Journal of Current Southeast Asian Affairs* 37 (2): 3–38.

Euromonitor International. 2015. Vietnam in 2030-the Future Demographic.

FiinGroup. 2019. Vietnam Logistic Market. http://www.biinform.com/Reports/19B6C-vietnam-logistics-market-2019-preview-.html. Accessed August 2019.

FMCG Monitor. 2019. Kantar Worldpanel. https://www.kantarworldpanel.com/vn/news/FMCG-Monitor-December-2019. Accessed February 2020.

Google. 2015. The consumer Marometer 2015 Report. https://www.thinkwithgoogle.com/tools/consumer-barometer/.

Google Temasek Bain, E-Conomy SEA. 2019. https://www.blog.google/documents/47/SEA_Internet_Economy_Report_2019.pdf.

GSO. 2019. 2019 Census Report. General Statistics Office of Vietnam.

Herr, Hansjörg, Erwin Schweisshelm, and Truong-Minh Vu. 2016. *The Integration of Vietnam in the Global Economy and Its Effects for Vietnamese Economic Development*. Global Labour University.

Ministry of Industry and Trade of the Socialist Republic of Vietnam. 2018. International Integration.

Nielsen. 2018. Spotlight on Vietnam Market Landscape. https://www.nielsen.com/apac/en/insights/article/2018/spotlight-on-vietnam-q1-2018/. Accessed March 2019.

Q&Me. 2018. Vietnam E-commerce Market. https://qandme.net/en/report/vietnam-ec-market-2018.html.

Sapo. 2018. Global Business Reports in Ecommerce. https://www.sapo.vn/blog/sapo-cong-bo-ket-qua-khao-sat-toan-canh-kinh-doanh-2018/.

Statista. 2020. Advertising Spending in Vietnam from 2004 to 2018 by Channels (Million US). Statista Research Department. https://www.statista.com/statistics/257580/advertising-spending-in-vietnam-by-medium/. Accessed February 2020.

Vecom. 2019. Vietnam E-business Index Reports. https://www.vecom.vn/tai-lieu/bao-cao-chi-thuong-mai-dien-tu-viet-nam-2019.

Vietnam E-commerce Association. 2019. Vietnam E-Business Index Report.

VietnamNet. 2017. Vietnam's Logistics Cost Make Up 20.8% of GDP. https://english.vietnamnet.vn/fms/business/192227/vietnam-s-logistics-costs-make-up-20-8–of-gdp.html. Accessed February 14, 2020.

World Bank. 2019. Vietnam's Development over the Past 30 Years Has Been Remarkable. https://www.worldbank.org/en/country/vietnam/overview. Accessed October 18, 2019.

CHAPTER 6

Financial Services in Vietnam

Van-Hong Vu

Abstract This chapter offers an overview of the financial services in Vietnam. As such, it is an introduction useful both for financial firms seeking to gain a foothold in the Asian market and for any firm planning a presence in Vietnam that would require it to avail of local financial services. This chapter covers the four main topics. The first part introduces the inventory of the financial services in Vietnam and how banking works in Vietnam. The second part presents the Vietnam Securities market. Fintech and Payment in Vietnam will be covered in the third part of this chapter. Finally, the insurance market in Vietnam will be presented to close this chapter.

Keywords Bank · Credit · Payment · Securities · Fintech

V.-H. Vu (✉)
Department of Business Management, Yncrea Hauts-de-France, Lille, France
e-mail: van-hong.vu@yncrea.fr

R. Macdonald (ed.), *The Economy and Business Environment of Vietnam*, https://doi.org/10.1007/978-3-030-49974-7_6

6.1 Introduction

Modern financial services did not exist in Vietnam before the mid-1980s. Liberalisation and deregulation of the sector started in the early 1990s. Nonetheless, financial services are large for a low-middle-income country, with assets of more than 200% of Vietnam's GDP[1] in 2018.

6.2 Relevant Legislation and Inventory of Financial Services in Vietnam

Under the Ministry of Finance of Vietnam (henceforth MFV), three central government agencies manage and oversee financial services. First, the State Bank of Vietnam (SBV) organises and supervises the credit institutions (bank and non-banking institutions), Fintech businesses and payment systems. Second, the State Securities Commission (SSC) controls the operations of securities market. Finally, the Insurance Supervisory and Authority (ISA) directly supervises insurance activities (Fig. 6.1).

On March 1988, the Decree No. 53/HDBT issued by the Council of Government laid the foundation for a new banking system in Vietnam, transforming it from state-controlled to market-oriented operations. In May 1990, the MFV issued the ordinance on the SBV and ordinance on

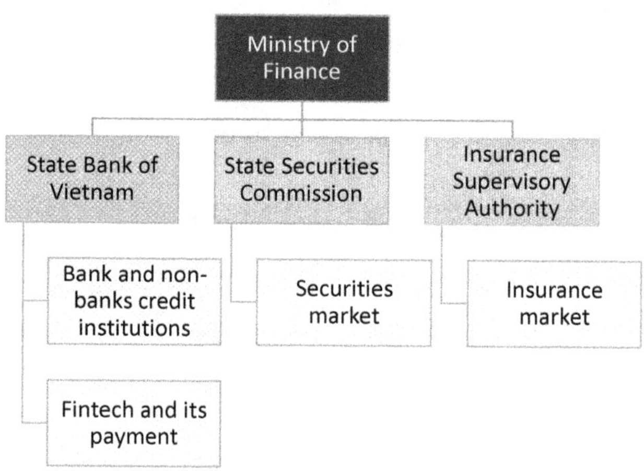

Fig. 6.1 Financial services and their supervision in Vietnam 2019 (*Source* Author's consolidation across the data files of MFV, SBV, ISA and SSC)

banking, credit co-operatives and finance companies, officially changing the banking system of Vietnam to a two-tier system:

- The SBV implements the governmental management of currency trading and banking.
- Commercial banks and non-banking institutions perform currency trading, payment, foreign exchange and banking services.

From 1990 to present, the National Assembly has issued a series of legislations for financial institutions: the Law on Credit institutions of 2/12/1997 and its revision in 2003, the Law on the State Bank of Vietnam (2010), the Law on Credit Institutions (2010) and various supplementing decrees.

SBV operates the electronic/paper clearance and interbank electronic payment systems. In addition, there is a bank card switching and clearing system, a securities clearing and settlement system and internal and bilateral payment systems operated by credit institutions. The Vietnam Securities Depository (VSD) conducts the securities settlement payment exclusively, in which all the transaction must be conducted via banks. There are about 19,100 Automatic Teller Machine (ATM) and 278,400 electronic payment systems involving electronic funds transfers using the payment card and payment terminal of point of sale (POS/EFTPOS/EDC) nationwide. The value of transactions via ATM and other devices is USD113 billion via ATM and USD24.44 billion via other devices such as POS/EFTPOS/EDC (Table 6.1).

6.3 The Operation of Credit Institutions in Vietnam

6.3.1 The Structure of the Credit Institution System

The credit institution system has been restructured recently, especially for the state-owned commercial banks (SOCBs). The CI system comprises 07 SOCBs, 28 joint stocks commercial banks (JSCBs), nine 100% foreign-owned commercial banks (FOCBs) and 2 joint venture commercial banks (JVCBs). Also, there are two policy banks (banks that help implement government policies such as the Viet Nam Bank for Social Policies) and one co-operative bank. The policy banks are subsidised and guaranteed by the State budget; therefore, they are exempt from taxes and

Table 6.1 Payment transactions via ATM and POS/EFTPOS/EDC, value: USD billion, 2013–2019

Year	*ATM*		*POS/EFTPOS/EDC*	
	Number of equipment ('000)	*Transaction value*	*Number of equipment ('000)*	*Transaction value*
2019	19.1	113	278.4	24.4
2018	18.3	99.5	273.6	19.3
2017	17.6	85.9	268.8	14.1
2016	17.5	72.4	263.4	10
2015	16.9	62.6	223.4	7.7
2014	16.1	49.6	172	6.4
2013	15.3	39.8	129.7	5.1

Source Author's consolidation across data files from the department of payment and settlement of SBV

other state budget remittances. The Co-operative Bank of Vietnam aims to support the operation of the people's credit funds system, playing a role in regulating capital. Concerning the non-banking institutions: there are 16 financial companies, ten leasing companies and 51 fund management companies. There are also four microfinance institutions and 1166 people's credit funds among the CIs (Fig. 6.2).

The commercial bank sector dominates the financial systems, with its assets reaching USD 482.9 billion, equivalent to 200% of GDP and 95.3% of financial institutions assets in 2019 (GSO 2019). The "Big Four" SOCBs in term of total assets, the outstanding loans and the deposits from clients are: Vietnam bank for agriculture and rural development (Agribank), Joint Stock Commercial Bank for Investment and Development of Vietnam (BIDV), Vietnam joint-stock commercial bank for industry and trade (Viettin) and Joint-stock commercial bank for foreign trade of Vietnam (Vietcombank). The non-state banking segment has proliferated and accounts for 41% of the total banking assets. Most foreign banks began operating in the 1990s with a licence to open branches; these international operations primarily serve companies from their homelands and take place in the major cities (Table 6.2).

Vietnam has been quite late in implementing the Accord by the Basel Committee on Banking Supervision (Basel II) standards. Fourteen years after the initial publication of Basel II, in 2016 the SBV set a deadline of 31 January 2021 for 17 commercial banks to meet Basel II norms under a national banking development strategy.

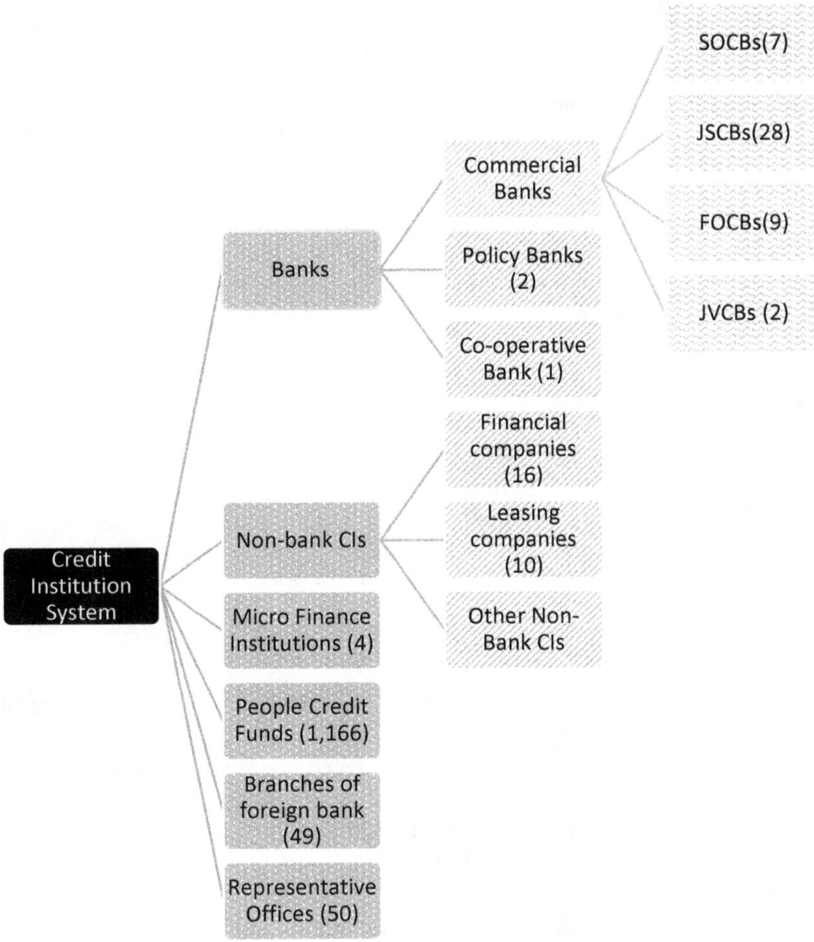

Fig. 6.2 System of formal credit institutions by June 30, 2019 (*Source* Author's consolidation across the data files of MFV, SBC and SSC)

6.3.2 Basic Account Services and Loans Payment

The performance outlook of Vietnam's banking system in terms of loans to customers seems positive over the last decade. For the period from 2013 to 2018, the compound annual growth rate (CAGR) of the loans to customers (based on the principal amounts outstanding at the end of

Table 6.2 Total assets and employed capital of credit institutions in Vietnam as of November 30, 2019, value: USD billion

Categories of CIs	*Total assets*		*Capital adequacy ratio, %*	*Ratio of short-term funds using for mid- and long-term loans, %*
	Value	*Growth rate, % for the same period in 2018*		
SOCBs	206.5	6.1	10.6	29.69
JSCBs	201.4	10.6	10.6	30.99
JVCBs, FOCBs, foreign banks' branches	52.2	14.9	24.5	–
Finance and leasing companies	0.8	16	19	35.72
Policies and Co-operative banks, People's Credit Funds	15.0	–	–	–
Whole system	482.9	9.1	12.2	27.15

Note Excluding microfinance institutions. Total assets are calculated on the basis of the Circular 49/2014/TT-NHNN
Source Data source are from the credit institutions' chart of accounts in December 2019 of SBV

each fiscal year) of the banking systems is 14.2%, with a total amount of USD296 billion in 2018, equivalent to 133% of the GDP. Deposits from customers in the banking system also achieved a similar growth rate. The CAGR of the outstanding deposits from customers is 13.9% over the same period with the deposit value of USD 321.8 billion, equivalent to 145% of GDP in 2018 (Figs. 6.3 and 6.4).

The commercial banks developed payment services on multiple traditional distribution channels and on new channels such as online banking, mobile and SMS banking and card payment services. Statistics from 35 commercial domestic banks in 2018 show that the commercial banks prefer to lend in the short term rather than the medium and long term (Fig. 6.5).

The ratio of Vietnam non-performing loan (NPL) per total outstanding loans by quarter reported by credit institutions stood at 1.9% in June 2019, compared with the ratio of 2.2% in the first quarter of 2019. The monthly average of NPLs reached 4.2% from 2012 to 2015 with an all-time a peak of 4.93% in September 2012[2] (Figure 6.6).

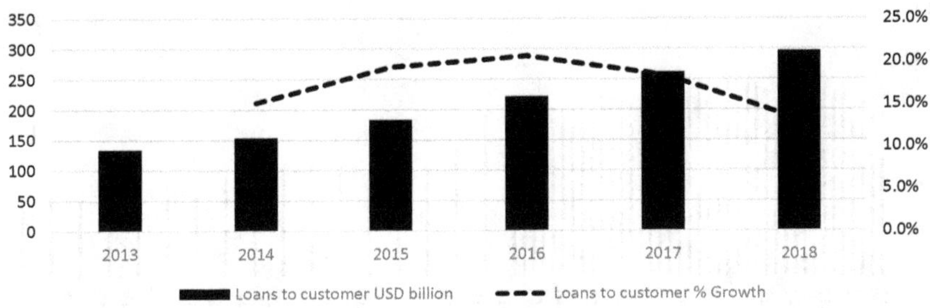

Fig. 6.3 Bank loans to customer in value, USD billion 2013–2018 (*Source* Author's consolidation across the data files of Bureau Dijk)

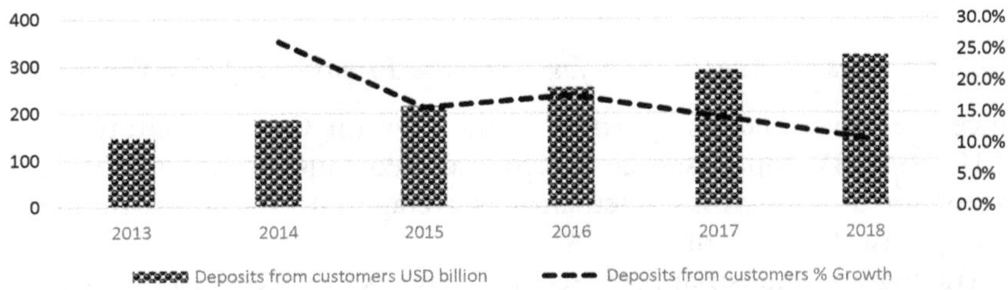

Fig. 6.4 Bank deposits from customer value: USD billion 2013–2018 (*Source* Author's consolidation across the data files of Bureau Van Dijk)

Fig. 6.5 Vietnam 35 domestic commercial banks–Loan portfolio in term of payment, % share, 2018 (*Source* Author's consolidation across data files of Bureau Van Dijk and banks' financial statements)

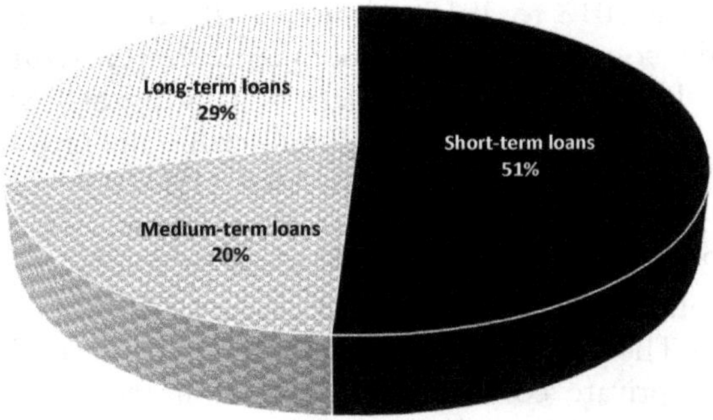

The commercial banks implement three interest rate tariffs: for business loans in Vietnam dong, for business loans in foreign currencies and for consumer loans in Vietnam dong.

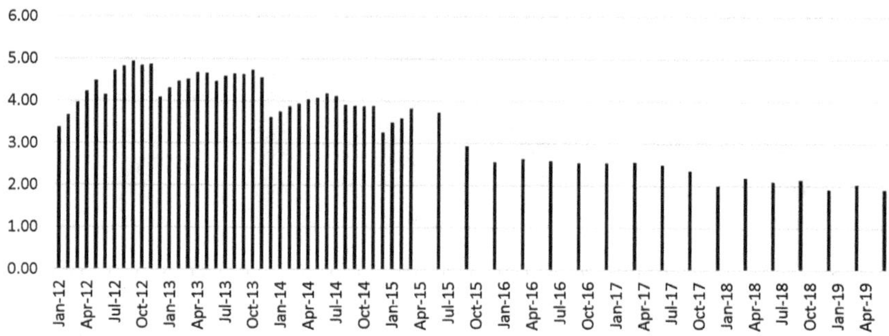

Fig. 6.6 Ratio of Vietnam NPLs over total outstanding lending by Cis by quarter, in %, 2012–2019 (*Source* Author's consolidation across data files of SBV)

6.3.3 *Credit Availability for Domestic Firms and Joint Ventures*

Since the government's approval of the Law on Credit Institutions in 2010, the SBV supervised all the formal credit institutions in Vietnam except for policies banks. Vietnam has average rates of access to credit among East Asian countries.

Trading and industrial firms seem to have better access to credit than businesses in other economic sectors. By the end of October 2019, the total credit was USD 71.9 billion for trading firms and USD 61.1 billion for industrial firms. However, the CAGR of the credit for trading firms was at 73%, nine times higher than the CARG of credit for industrial firms from 2013 to 2018. Although 90% of the population of Vietnam live in the countryside and work in agriculture, credit for the sector of the agriculture, forestry and fishery remain low at USD 28.2 billion, accounting about 8.8% of the loans for all economic sectors in 2019 (Table 6.3).

The SOCBs group provided USD20.9 billion to state-owned enterprises (SOEs) in 2018, accounting for 25% of its outstanding loans in 2018. The JSBCs are more likely to lend more to the non-SOEs with the total loan of USD 54.9 billion in 2018 (Fig. 6.7).

The loans for small and medium-sized firms (SMEs), partnership or private corporate entities amounted to only USD 1.6 billion and accounted for only 1.3% of the total outstanding loans of the 25 commercial banks in 2018. SMEs access to external finance is generally difficult, especially bank financing (Le and Wang 2005). The loans that SMEs do access are always short-term loans, with interest rates higher than most

Table 6.3 Credit by economic sectors in value, USD billion, 2013–2019

Economic sector	*2013*	*2014*	*2015*	*2016*	*2017*	*2018*	*2019*	*CAGR, % 2013–2019*
Agriculture, forestry and fishery	14.6	15.6	18.6	22.2	25.5	26.7	28.2	12.0
Industry	38.8	40.9	43.4	47.5	56.6	57.3	61.1	8.0
Construction	13.8	15.2	18.1	20.2	25.8	28.0	30.5	14.0
Trade	2.7	29.8	33.1	40.1	52.2	62.7	71.9	73.0
Transportation and telecommunications	5.1	5.4	6.1	7.9	9.7	8.6	8.9	10.0
Other activities	4.0	51.9	66.9	82.3	90.7	105.1	119.5	76.0
Total	139.1	158.8	186.2	220.2	260.5	288.4	320.2	13.0

Source Author's consolidation across data files from SBV

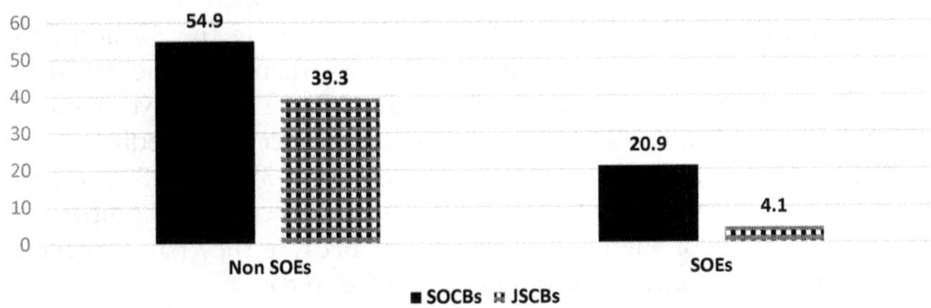

Fig. 6.7 Loan portfolio by type of borrowers of 25 commercial banks, in USD billion, 2018 (*Source* Author's consolidation across data files from banks' financial statements)

comparators (VCCI 2014). World Bank-IFC's Enterprise Survey data shows that SMEs' characteristics and collateral requirements are a major constraint in SME lending, with a 218% collateral-to-loan ratio (World Bank 2014). As mentioned in Chapter 4, part of the problem resides in many SMEs being unable to comply with basic documentation. SMEs generally encounter corrupt practices, in particular having to pay "tips" to extortionary bank officials (PCI 2015). Lending to SMEs thus tends to depend on inter-organizational and interpersonal banking relationships (Le 2013)

6.3.4 *Credit Availability for Foreign-Invested Enterprises (FIEs)*

FDI plays an essential role in the Vietnam economy, contributing 20.28% to GDP and providing 8.4% of the annually employed population (15+ years) in 2018 (GSO 2018). By the end of 2018, the accumulation of total implemented capital for effected projects is USD 195.9 billion, accounting for 57% of the total registered capital of registered projects.

As its original FDI concept, Vietnam focuses on attracting FDI rather than developing the credit market for FIEs. FIEs usually receive loan support from their parent companies or through the foreign banks located in Vietnam. However, many FDI enterprises, especially SMEs, now try to obtain credit from local Vietnamese banks to fund operations.

Foreign banks lead the FDI loans sector with USD 8.6 billion, or 60.8% of the sector's value in 2018, among them Korean and Japanese banks are very active in lending activities to their compatriots.

The overall credit balance structure for FIEs among the 35 domestic commercial banks in Vietnam is usually less than 1% due to their constraints on the resources. However, the "Big Four" have a credit balance between 1 and 5% of the outstanding balance (the credit balance for FIEs of Viettin and Vietcombank accounts for 5.5% and 6.3%, respectively). A large portion of FIEs has better access to credit in comparison with the same size of Vietnamese enterprises because they have excellent financial results and clear investment plans (Fig. 6.8).

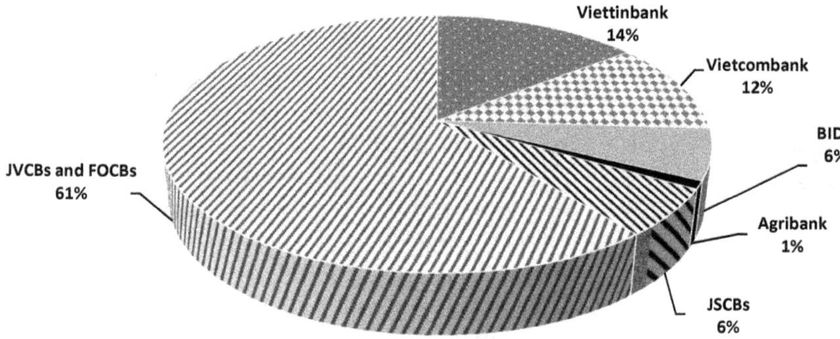

Fig. 6.8 Outstanding bank loans balances segmentation by value, % share, 2018 (*Source* Author's consolidation across data files from banks' financial statements)

The Law of Securities approved by the National Assembly in January of 2020 has lifted the general cap limitation on the ownership by foreign investors in the public offering of securities and creates equal rights in access to the securities market between Vietnamese businesses and FIEs. Fourteen years after, the first foreign business was listed in Vietnam; the number of listed FIEs still stands below ten. Some FIEs delisted due to their undesired performance or problems with tax evasion.

Investing in the form of share purchase increased sharply in recent years and constitutes a more significant proportion of total foreign investment. In the first 11 months of 2019, the total newly registered, adjusted and contributed capital of foreign investors was nearly 31.8 billion USD, up 3.1% as compared to the same period in 2018. The implemented capital of the FDI projects is estimated at USD 17.6 billion, up 6.8% over the same period in 2018 (VAFIE 2019).

As for foreign capital flows in through mergers and acquisitions, Asian investors are mainly interested in Vietnamese enterprises operating in the field of finance and technology, logistics, real estate and retail. Recently, the wave of FDI transfers from China to Vietnam escalated to evade tax punishment over the US-China trade war, creating a great demand for industrial park infrastructure.

6.4 Securities, Insurance and Fintech

The second part of this chapter covers the securities market, Fintech and payment and the insurance market in Vietnam.

6.4.1 Securities Market

History and Development

In July 2000, the Ho Chi Minh City Stock Exchange (HOSE) launched its first operation in Ho Chi Minh City with two listed enterprises and two trading sessions per week. The Hanoi Stock Exchange (HNX) started after five years in March 2005, and the operations of VSD centre officially operated from May 2006. The Securities Law takes effect from January 1, 2021, replacing the Securities Law No. 70/2006/QH11 and Law No. 62/2010/QH12, which states the SSC's authority in managing and supervising the securities market comprehensively.

Vietnam's securities experienced the highest growth among the securities markets in the South-East Asian Region in 2019 with a market capitalisation of nearly USD 241.4 billion, equivalent to 101% of country GDP.

Operations and Structure

Markets

Vietnam's **stock markets** have experienced at least five development stages with different ups and downs. During the first stage from 2000 to 2005, the market index leapt from 100 up to 570 points after one and half years but dropped quickly to 200 index points in early 2002 and further went down to 130 index points in April 2003. The market continued with this "frozen stage" until 2005. From 2005 to 2007, it grew rapidly, peaking at 1170.1 points in March 2007. The bubble burst from 2007 to 2009, with the lowest index point of 236 in February 2009. The market was unstable from 2009 to 2015. Since 2017 till now, the market seems to have developed sustainably (Fig. 6.9).

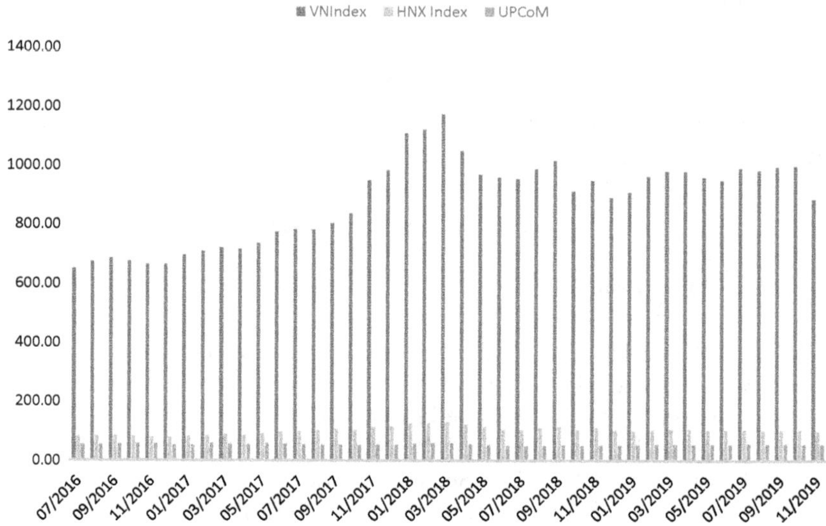

Fig. 6.9 Vietnam securities index, by index, 2016–2019 (*Source* Author's consolidation across data files of State Securities Commission)

The market capitalisation value of the stock market for listed companies is USD 161 billion, the equivalent of 61% of the country's GDP in 2019. Presently, there are 748 listed stocks and listed investments funds on the HOSE and the HNX. By November 30, 2019, HOSE held 59% of the market capitalisation value. Also, 862 stocks are registered and traded on the UPCoM exchanges, with the total listing and trading of 97.3 billion securities, an increase of 14% in compared with the end of 2018.

The **bond market** mainly comprises government bonds (accounting for 84–85% of market share), while corporate bonds are still very uncommon. Government bond futures derivative products started operating in July 2019 adding to investors a hedging tool. There are 515 bonds listed with a total market value of USD 151 billion by the end of 2019. There are still some challenges for the corporate bond market in Vietnam such as the small market size, the legal framework, the diversification of the products and the dominance of the commercial banks.

The **derivatives market** started operation in August 2017, with the first product of the VN-30 Index futures, but it has shown impressive development in both the number and value of contracts. Presently, there are around 15,000 trading accounts, double the number of the initial month of operation. However, most accounts belonged to individual investors, while accounts of the domestic institutional investors were at a very modest level, mainly focused on dealing activities.

The **covered warranty** only started operation in the second half of 2019. By the end of November 2019, according to the SCC, there are 0.122 billion registered covered warranties at the HOSE with 39 registered securities companies.

Exchanges

The two trading centres HNX and HOSE for listed companies are not entirely self-regulated, and still under the management of the MFV and SCC. Cross-listing is not allowed between these two exchanges. Margin trading is permitted, but short-selling is not allowed. The HOSE is a trading platform for relatively large corporation's securities, and the HNX is mainly for the smaller and medium corporate size.

The establishment of UPCoM in 2009 aimed to gradually narrow the grey market of unlisted public companies and to improve the transactions and liquidity of equitized but not yet listed stocks of SOEs and public companies. At the end of 2019, there are 862 companies registered in UPCoM with a total capitalisation of more than USD39.8 billion.

Investor accounts
The average growth rate of the number of investor accounts is 4–6% over the last two years. By the end of August 2019, there are 2,321,049 investor accounts. Of these, 98.66% are private investor accounts, most of which are retail. Only 0.57% are organizational investor accounts, both domestic and foreign.

Securities companies and investment fund management companies
By the end of 2019, there were 89 securities firms, most of them members of the stock exchanges. These securities firms, according to their registered licences, can provide the services related to securities trading, financial advisory, brokerage, underwriting—the legal capital for each of the business activities is stipulated by the law, including the registered capital. There are 48 investment fund management companies operating (SSC 2019). There were three registered **closed-end funds** and two **exchange-traded funds** in the securities market of Vietnam by the end of 2019. The reduced number of closed-end funds resulted from previous constituents reaching the end of their lives, transforming to open-ended funds or restructuring in some other way.

6.4.2 The Insurance Market

Introduction

Many large insurers consider Vietnam as a strategic expansion of their regional and global footmarks. In 2018, the growth rate for the insurance sector reached 25%, with total posted premiums of USD 7 billion—about 3% of GDP.

Before 1992, the Vietnamese government didn't consider the insurance industry as a business activity; therefore, insurance was treated as a method to share the risks between the SOEs and to comply with international transaction's obligations. The Degree No 100/CP, dated December 18, 1993, allowed the formation of insurance businesses other than SOEs. After nearly 20 years of operations, the Law of Insurance Business has been amended and supplemented by different laws and decrees, developing a comprehensive legal context for the insurance in Vietnam (Fig. 6.10).

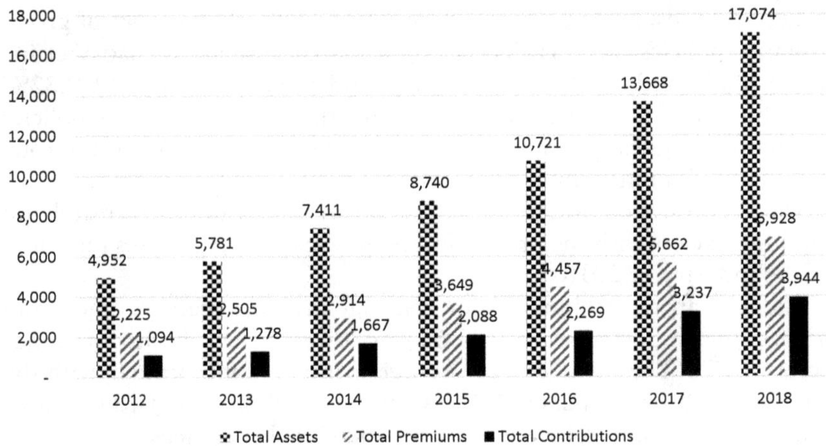

Fig. 6.10 Vietnam insurance market performance in value: USD Million, 2012–2018 (*Source* Author's consolidation across data files of ISA)

Operations and Structure

Market participants

Vietnamese and foreign organisations that contribute capital to form an insurance enterprise must meet strictly specific financial and non-financial terms and conditions indicated by line of business and other related laws and degrees. By the end of 2018, the market was covered by 64 players, including non-life insurers (property and casualty), life insurers, reinsurers and insurance brokers.

Market size

The **non-life insurance** market was still highly concentrated within the "Big Five" domestic insurers with total gross premiums of nearly 52% of total insurance market in 2019. The other 25 insurers and branch of the foreign insurers had a contribution to premium income of 42%. Credit and Financial risks, Fire and Explosion Insurance, Liability Insurance achieved high growth rates in recent years. The claims payment ratio (the gross claims payment divided by total premiums for the year) ranges from 30 to 40% during the last five years, with a peak of 42% in 2018.

The **life insurance** market: The average growth rate of the new life insurance policies written is 15% during 2013–2018. In 2018, the number of individual insurance policies reached 2,247,830; the number of group insurance policies was 331. The top five market leaders are Bao Viet life (17.8%), followed by Dai-ichi (17.4%), Prudential (16.68%), AIA 9.32%) and Chubb (3.56%). The premium of investment-liked products policies counted the highest premium proportion which was 62.55% of the total market premium in term of new business

The areas of operation from the **reinsurance** activities focus mainly on non-life business with the proportion of 90.73% total premiums reinsured for the industry in 2018.

The insurance premium of the brokerage activities mainly comes from the non-life insurance sector (82.6%), followed by the health insurance sector of 17%. The **insurance brokerage** market is concentrated, with the four foreign brokers Marsh, AON, Grass Savoy Willis and Jardine Lloyd Thompson accounting for more than 95% of brokerage fees.

By the end of 2018, the number of **insurance agents** reached 899,071, an increase of 21% compared to the previous year, of which 760,723 were life insurance agents (an increase of 21.5%) and 138,348 were non-life insurance agents (an increase of 18.5%).

Bancassurance (insurance sold by banks) in Vietnam has high growth potential backed by an increase of the middle- and high-income earners, as well as the better local awareness of insurance. About 51 banks in the market who cooperate with the underwriters of both in life and non-life insurance make up 15–17% of life insurance's revenue in Vietnam annually.

6.4.3 *Fintech and Digital Innovations in Vietnam*

Introduction

Vietnam currently ranks second among Association of South-East Asian Nations (ASEAN) member states in terms of Fintech development, behind Singapore. The total Fintech transaction market value was approximate of USD 7.7 billion in 2019, with a CARG of 12.2% for transaction value from 2019 to 2023. This part highlights recent trends for digital payment, lending, financing, banking, blockchain application, and other Fintech services (Fig. 6.11).

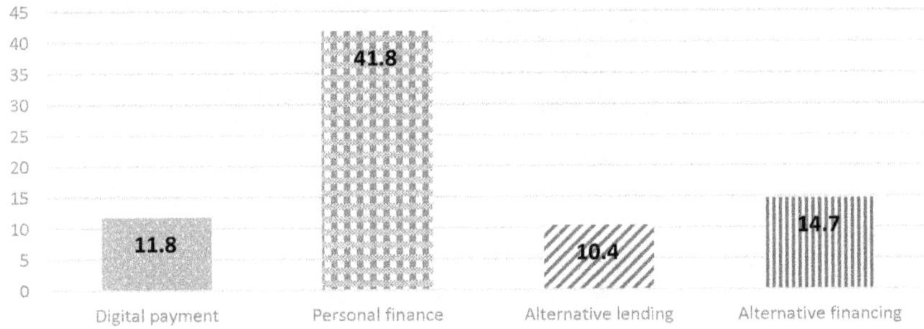

Fig. 6.11 CARG of Fintech transaction value segmentation, in %, 2019–2023 (*Source* Data files from Statista Digital Market Outlook 2018)

Payments

Mobile payments are the most popular Fintech segment, in which the wide range of payments services are offered to its users. Two notable brands in providing the financial services through mobile phone technology are M-Service and Vietnamese start-up Moca. M-Service is the developer of mobile payments application MoMo with nearly 10 million downloads by October of 2018. By December 31, 2019, there were 31 non-financial intermediate payment companies licensed by the SBV to provide financial and payment services. The key digital payment players include independent start-ups as well as subsidiaries of extensive media and communication conglomerates such as VNPT, FPT and Viettel (Fig. 6.12).

Decree number 101/2012/ND-CP dated November 22, 2012, and the amended decree 80/2016/ND-CP, dated July 1, 2016, apply to non-cash payment service providers, payment intermediary services providers and users. Complexities in legacy payment services in Vietnam have propelled the demand for consulting services, which, in turn, is likely to accelerate the growth of the services segment of the digital payment market.

POS Management and Facilitators

Hottab is a new start-up in Hanoi that provides a cashier/POS solution provider and a comprehensive F&B management system with supplier

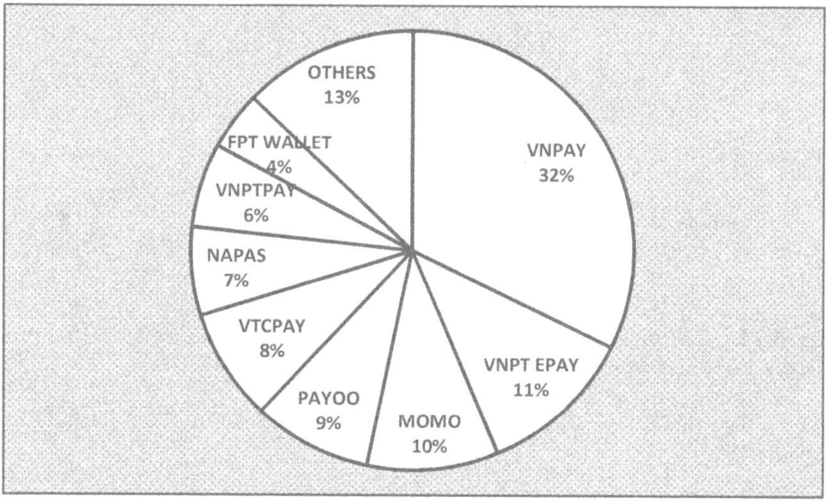

Fig. 6.12 Top 8 Fintech payment companies and its market share in term of service revenue, % share, 2018 (*Source* Author's consolidation across data files of Bureau Van Dijk and companies' financial statements)

integration, the marketplace and loyalty management. Two other POS management platforms are Softpay and Ibox.

Digital Lending

Peer-to-peer lending (P2P) experienced a period of fast growth, starting in 2005 being run by most P2P lending companies in Vietnam with two categories: personal credit and SME lending. The P2P credit is restricted to connecting lenders and borrowers (investors). The P2P lending service providers act as intermediaries to connect lenders and borrowers and are not allowed to mobilise capital. Financial institutions will not be allowed to take part in this segment.

The P2P lending remains a new way of accessing finance in Viet Nam while the specific laws regulating the activity is on a preliminary stage. Some companies falsely advertise profits or provide inaccurate information related to risks when participating in the service or even apply the law of the jungle to NPL borrowers. There is no regulation in regard to the responsibilities of the P2P lending platform in case of NPLs.

Personal digital lending has faced challenges of its own over the last few years due to the fierce competition with personal borrowing from the CIs. Observations from the market show that digital lenders are taking advantage of opportunities to diversify their scope of activities, both in terms of the process of loan application and approval and in terms of new products.

Timo Bank is the first *and only 100%* digital bank in Vietnam, which is operated by the Vietnam Prosperous Commercial Bank. Timo Bank provides all traditional banking services through mobile banking applications on smartphones or at the website, all *at no cost.*

Crowdfunding

Crowdfunding is a relatively new concept that reached the Vietnamese recently. The four types of crowdfunding in Vietnam include the equity-based crowdfunding, reward-based crowdfunding, lending-based crowdfunding and donation-based crowdfunding. Personal business relationships play an essential role in Vietnamese culture, which makes it difficult for people to invest in a "stranger" over the Internet. Another obstacle is the Vietnamese legal system, which has not defined specific laws about crowdfunding yet.

Blockchain and Its Application

In general, there are two main branches of blockchain in Vietnam. Firstly, Vietnamese start-ups and subsidiaries of foreign blockchain firms are outsourcing the production solutions in these technologies to international customers from overseas. Secondly, one part of the companies is researching its application for use in agriculture, travel, supply chain, transport and e-government. Despite the booming number of companies and recent successes, the investment in blockchain start-ups is still at an early stage.

The Vietnamese government is very prudent on the issue of cryptocurrencies. The government entirely bans official transactions using digital or virtual currency following an alleged fraud of USD 658 million related to cryptocurrency that scammed 32,000 investors in Vietnam (Decree no 10/CT-TTG dated 11/4/2018).

6.4.4 *Other Services*

Financial leasing services started taking root in Vietnam's soil since the mid-1990s. However, Vietnam's financial leasing industry remains in the stage of experimentation, facing problems like imperfect regulations, regional development imbalance and limited financing channels. As at December 2018, there were ten registered leasing enterprises with the total assets which are approximate to USD 1.2 billion.

The **consumer finance** market had total balances of outstanding loans of USD 111.7 billion in 2018, in which retail banks and consumer finance companies account for 93% and 7% of the market share, respectively. With extensive retail networks, banks target customers with a good credit history, while target clients of credit consumer companies are new and unbanked customers.

Investment banking is at its initial stages in Viet Nam and focuses on domestic deals with medium-sized transaction value.

There has been **venture capital** in Vietnam since at least 1995, but the stock of capital available began to increase significantly in the first decade of this century with the arrival of foreign actors. As of January 2020, there are more than 70 venture capital companies, most foreign (Project 844, 2016).

Data management, web comparison and credit scoring platforms are among the other areas that both Vietnamese and foreign-owned companies focus on.

6.5 Conclusion

This chapter has provided an overview of financial services in Vietnam, as well as of their legal governance and recent trends occasioned by technological developments.

Notes

1. Estimation of the total assets of the financial services is carried out by the author by using the different descriptions and statistics of the General Statistics Office of Vietnam (GSO) and the government agencies (MFV, SBV, SSC and ISA).
2. As defined in circular 02/2013/TT-NHNN dated 21/01/2013 and circular 09/2014/TT-NHNN dated 18/03/2014, since 01/01/2015 non-banking credit institutions (CI) have to reconcile reference of the

debt classification results for each customer from the CIC to redistribute the customer's debt group to the highest debt group if the customer is borrowing at multiple CI. Therefore, from May 3/2015, bad debt figures reflect more accurately on the credit quality of the CI, and there is no longer a lot difference between the reported CI figures and the monitoring figures of the SBV. For the above reason, the percentage of bad debt as reported by the CI in May 01/2015, 02/2015, 03/2015 has increased in turn to 3.49%; 3.59%; 3.81% and the highest increase at the end of the first quarter of 2015 (3.81%), since most of the CI had executed the debt reference under CIC, but in essence, bad debt is trending off when compared to the rate of bad debt under the supervision of the SBV (according to the results of the debt classification left from CIC's information) with the percentage of bad debt in turn 4.83% in 2/2014; 4.55% in 01/2015; 4.75% in 02/2015 and 3.81% in 3/2015.

References

Bureau Van Dijk. 2020. ORBIS, Access Account: Université Catholique de Lille. Retrieved January and February 2020, from https://orbis-bvdinfo-com.ezproxy.univ-catholille.fr/version-202036/orbis/1/Companies/Search.

GSO. 2018. General Statistics Office—Statistical Yearbook of Vietnam. Retrieved February 2, 2020, from http://www.gso.gov.vn/.

GSO. 2019. General Statistics Office—Main Statistical Indicators 2019. Retrieved February 2, 2020, from http://www.gso.gov.vn/.

Le, T. N. 2013. Banking Relationship and Bank Financing: The Case of Vietnamese Small and Medium-Sized Enterprises. *Journal of Economics and Development, 15*(1), 74–90.

Le., P. N. M., and Wang, X. 2005. Similarities and Differences of Credit Access by Vietnamese and Chinese Firms. *International Journal of Business and Social Research, 3*(5).

PCI. 2015. *The Provincial Competitiveness Index (PCI)*. Retrieved May 15, 2018, from http://eng.pcivietnam.org/publications/full-report-2015/.

Project 844. 2016. Government, *Supporting National Innovative Start-Up Ecosystem to 2025*. Retrieved February 2, 2020, from https://startup.gov.vn/noidung/csdl/Pages/QuyDauTu.aspx Accessed December 27, 2019.

SSC. 2019. State Securities Commission, Number of Investment Funds in the Stock Exchanges. Date of Access 20 February 2020, from http://www.ssc.gov.vn/ubck/faces/vi/vimenu/vipages_vicsdlcty/ctyquanlyquy?_adf.ctrl-state=tfo2hkc1f_4&_afrLoop=869160174190000.

VAFIE. 2019. *Update on Foreign Investment in Vietnam*. Vietnam Association of Foreign Investment Enterprises, dated 26 November 2019. Date of Access 20 February 2020, from http://www.vafie.org.vn/tinh-hinh-dtnn-tai-viet-nam.

VCCI. 2014. *Business Environment for Vietnam's Small and Medium-Sized Enterprises.* Retrieved January 12, 2019, from http://eng.pcivietnam.org/publications/business-environment-for-vietnams-small-and-medium-sided-enterprises/.

World Bank. 2014. *Vietnam—Financial Sector Assessment (English)*. Financial Sector Assessment Program (FSAP), World Bank Group. Retrieved January 15, 2019, from http://documents.worldbank.org/curated/en/216401468329363389/Vietnam-Financial-sector-assessment.

Index

R. Macdonald (ed.), *The Economy and Business Environment of Vietnam*, https://doi.org/10.1007/978-3-030-49974-7

Printed in the USA
CPSIA information can be obtained
at www.ICGtesting.com
LVHW010726271223
767526LV00006B/173

9 783030 499730